A proud mama and her baby daughter, my
sister photobombing (before it was cool) and
my brothers in the back.

Sometimes a peaceful family can be turned
upside down with the flick of a pen!

Praises for *Hillbilly Chess the Bastard Pawn*

"A powerful account of a life story that is at times so crushingly sad that I had to pause as I read it. And at the same time, I could not put it down. I highly recommend this book to those in the mental health profession. This is a memoir of not only survival but of creating a life that is the opposite of one's childhood experience. The author pulls the curtain back with grit and honesty."

— *Elle Ingalls, author of Pressure-Free Parenting*

"The author writes it as it is, without sugar-coating, filtering, or regard to how others may view her life or her memories because they are simply that—her memories of her upbringing."

— *Brittany Carpenter School Social Worker*

"Peggy's childhood is a nightmare. But unfortunately, a nightmare that many foster care children can identify with due to the depth of their pain. One bright light in her life experience is her foster family who embraced her in love and provided her with peace during her agony. This is an example of how foster care can and should work to bring joy and stability to a hurting child."

— *Sandy Schreur, Former foster parent*

"Hillbilly Chess the Bastard Pawn is an appropriate name for this terrible tale of childhood trauma. The author's raw, relentless honesty makes the reader both dread and need to know what is on the next page. I am so glad that Peggy Ann survived to share her journey of strength, freedom, and healing."

— *Carmen Moyer, Attorney, and Counselor*

"I could not put this book down. I loved it! My heart broke for what the author endured. Yet, she clawed her way out of the abuse and rose to fulfill her dreams. It emphasizes that your circumstances as a child do not determine your adult path."

—Jan Walters, Author of the Ghost, and A Cop series.

"A story of rising over the words, deeds, and secret sins of those who are supposed to protect you. A story of a person who finds healing, strength, and courage. A story of resilience and the grace of God. A testimony to others to never give up.... a story of HOPE!"

— James Hackworth, Minister

"A captivating memoir of the perseverance of the human soul. A heart-wrenching, traumatic account of one child's journey through hell on earth and her resounding determination to escape her demons and to live her best life ever. I shout, "Cheers!"

— Candie Armstrong, Nurse and aka, CC Mack, Author of, My Soul's Guardian.

"A gripping story of a child growing up in the middle of dysfunction. This book stays with you long after you turn the final page. It's about survival, resilience, perseverance, and the strength of prosperous adult woman today. It is about overcoming evil and learning to embrace life and welcome joy."

— Jen Collins, P.O. Master

Published by Word Journey Publishing in 2022

www.wordjourneypublishing.com

Some names and identifying details of some characters in this book have been changed.

For information about exclusive discounts for bulk purchases, please contact the publisher

Peggy@WordJourneyPublishing.com

ISBN:9-781732-765542

Library of Congress Cataloging-in-Publication Data

Grigowski, Peggy Ann

Hillbilly Chess the Bastard Pawn: a memoir/Peggy A. Watkins

Edited by Janelle James, janelle@transitionwell.net

Cover design by Darren Wheeler, www.BlackEgg.com

eBook & Print layouts by Jennifer Preciado, jen2preciado@gmail.com

CHESS

A game of strategic skill for two players in which each player moves and uses their pieces to capture opposing pieces according to precise rules.

HILLBILLY CHESS

A game of life and death that my family taught me well, especially the Queen on the opposing team. The pieces are family members, and I am their pawn!

TRUTH

My biological dad was my uncle for the first six months of my life, then he became my adopted dad. My siblings became my cousins, and my cousins became my siblings. My aunt became my mom, and my mom became my aunt.

DISCLAIMER

This work depicts actual events in the life of the author as truthfully as her recollections permit. While all persons within are actual individuals, the author has changed some names and identities to protect the innocent and changed other names and characteristics so she would not be sued.

Ann Lamont said it best, "You own everything that has happened to you. Tell your stories. If people wanted you to write warmly about them, they should have behaved better."

DEDICATION:

I dedicate this book to my biological mother,
Chelcie Watkins-Williams. We both knew and
understood the pain and heartache of having each
other within our reach but never being able to touch.

May we meet again in our next life
and have the mother-daughter relationship
we were robbed of in this one!

Mother, I love you more than you'll ever know.

HILLBILLY CHESS

THE BASTARD PAWN

a memoir

Peggy A. Watkins

FOREWORD

In writing this book, Peggy offers powerful and heartfelt advice that is woven across her own painful experiences. It is rare to find someone who not only understands the world of science behind parenting but can be vulnerable, authentic, and practical when sharing with and advising others. Peggy is resilient and filled with protective factors that were hidden or misinterpreted across some experiences. She is creative and informed, and approaches struggles as invitations to build skills so that she and others she supports and cares for can become stronger and more resilient on the other side.

What Peggy is offering here is essential. As a child development specialist with expertise in mental health, I have spent a lot of time considering how our earliest experiences influence overall development, brain development, resilience, and practices.

For example, the middle part of our brain allows us to do many important things that help regulate our body and emotions, feel empathy, communicate with understanding, bounce back after hardship, make thoughtful choices, and overcome fear. And the good news is that because it's one of the last areas to develop, it's the most open and available to influence ongoing experiences and relationships throughout childhood and even young adulthood.

Peggy offers a window into a part of the body we cannot see developing daily. Parenting and life experiences not only influence children's resilience and create a lens for how relationships are understood and viewed but also alter the structure of children's brains.

Experience changes the brain, especially when an incident is filled with emotion and challenge. Like a muscle, the brain grows and strengthens with use.

Peggy shares her wisdom through humor and challenging moments that can be used to make changes in relationships, home environments, and overall systems (such as the child welfare system) so that we can continue to focus on a felt sense of safety for children while helping them build skills at the same time. With each chapter, you can feel the power of relationships and see development unfold. She helps us remember that change, learning, and healing happens in the context of relationships.

The immediate need for connection has been wired into our brains since the earliest days. Our brain and nervous system are designed and primed to seek and find value and reward in our connections with others because, in essence, it increases our odds of survival.

Peggy's story shows the impact of distractions, hurt, trauma, and obstacles on this primitive need. We know from decades of research that the quality of our earliest relationships impacts our well-being, mental health, and ongoing relational experiences. We also know there are many factors outside of parents' influence–genetics, peers, life experiences, and many other variables. This book helps us remember that trauma isn't permanent. When we devote ourselves to understanding our stories, we can help ourselves heal, develop, change, and find joy.

We are all now gifted with these many gems from Peggy's courage to share her story about fostering the best outcomes. I am thrilled that *Hillbilly Chess, The Bastard Pawn,* shares a path of resilience to help adults nurture themselves and further a culture of connection. Inspired by such insight, may we all keep working together to help those we care for see their strengths know they are safe and lovable, and never have to question who they are in our eyes.

— *Kristin Tenney-Blackwell, M.A., LLP, IMH-E*

I

BREAKING

OUT OF HELL

My HEART IMMEDIATELY DETONATED, flip-flopping violently in my chest. I froze. And a feeling I knew too well was rushing over me like the pummeling of Niagara Falls. My hands instantly broke into a hot sweat. My knees shook with fear. It felt like her hand was again over my mouth, prohibiting my breath.

The hammering on the door was firm, even, loud, and demanding. The glass shook as an iron fist pounded on the front door. *She told. Aunt Marie told* was all I thought and knew because that whole family sticks together like spores in a goddamn shithouse.

Fuck! It's Virgie!

My victorious feeling was short-lived as the reality of what I saw sunk in. A man in a blue uniform stood on the porch. I could hear the radio on his side, announcing nothing but static and jumbled words from a dispatcher, all I wanted to do was cry. I just knew Virgie was behind this cop's visit.

Virgie is going to make me go back with her. Back to the hell from which I escaped.

One of the perils of a small town is that you inevitably run into someone you know when you least want to. And there she sat at the stop sign.

The previous night, a small group of us kids celebrated my and Alexander's (Alex) marriage. Mostly we were celebrating the fact that I was away from Virgie, safe, free, and allowed to be just a simple teen, something I had never experienced yet.

I saw her before she saw me, and when I spotted her, Aunt Marie— "Aunt Teabags"— was sitting in her car, her eyes squinting, searching her surroundings. My heart pounded, and I instantly had mixed feelings. I loved my Auntie.

She was a tall, skinny pretty woman with long brown hair and a smile that would melt your heart. Auntie cried at the sight of burnt cookies, loved her dog and kids more than life, and she loved me. I always knew that. Always in jeans and an old, tattered t-shirt carrying a teacup with two teabags resulted in her nickname "Aunt Teabags." She called me Lulu. She was an absolute gem, and I loved her.

Aunt Marie jumped out of her car and ran up to me, grabbing my arm like an enraged mama bear. "Lulu, you come with me! You are a runaway and belong at home!"

"NO!" I screamed as I yanked my arm away.

Alex and our group of friends stood there stunned. My friend, Teri, spoke up. "She's a married woman!" she shouted. "She ain't going anywhere, lady!"

It was indeed a moment made for a dramatic reality TV show. I shook loose from Aunt Marie's grasp and kept walking. She kept yelling.

"Help! Someone! She's a runaway! Help!"

We, of course, laughed and took off running—as she stood in the road, helpless and concerned for the well-being of a child whom she loved.

On the outside, I laughed and joked about how we got away. But, deep down, I knew, the shit show was coming.

My husband Alex and I headed downstairs the following morning to get breakfast. Alex, a tall, thin, acne-faced 15-year-old with shoulder-length blonde hair and no butt, was cute. He was continually running on a full tank at about 90 miles an hour on any project and was *always* busy. Alex was a smart guy and a great mechanic. Everyone brought their cars to him. He fixed anything which earned him the nickname "Kool."

I was a 15-year-old as well. Weighing in at about 85 pounds, with a 5-foot 3-inch thin frame barely filled out youth size 12 clothes, and I had boobs the size of mosquito bites (Praise Jesus, I have ta-ta's now), with long reddish-blonde hair that almost reached my butt, and framed freckles on my girlish face.

We were staying with his parents Stanley (Stan) and Nancy, in Albion, Michigan, in their small apartment. Nancy was a slender woman with black hair down to her shoulders, a big smile, and the kindest heart ever, she had always been good to me. Despite her nurturing personality, Nancy chain-smoked and could drink more wine than anyone I'd ever seen.

Stanley was a taller, thicker man who wore old, baggy polyester pants held up by a belt buckled but not tucked in his pants loop and stained-up t-shirts with the bottom of his belly always hanging out. He had a big heart, too, and always treated me well. Stan smoked as much as Nancy and drank more than his weight in beer each day. He was a balding man and wore a baseball cap to hide it. Stan once claimed that while fishing in his brother's boat, the top of his head was sunburned, which caused him to go bald. He could come up with creative excuses now and then.

Stan and Nancy had lived most of their lives in Albion, Michigan. With its small population of about nine thousand, Albion had an old-time red-brick road through downtown. The railroad tracks were at one end and a cemetery at the other. Downtown was booming with life and the bustle of a community with a purpose.

We had the Bohm Theater, where the infamous Purple Gang—a criminal mob of bootleggers and hijackers—would meet in the balcony to conduct business back in the '30s and '40s. We had a JCPenney store that was two stories tall and the only place downtown, which I knew of, that had an elevator. Ah, then there was Woolworth's Five-and-Dime, where I purchased my first 45 vinyl record, "Angie" by the Rolling Stones.

On a few corners, we had payphone booths, and with ten cents, you could call just about anywhere and talk all day if you wanted.

I frequented the Goodwill for anything I needed. We had a bakery, a music store, a hardware store, bars, restaurants, and a jewelry store. Albion was small but booming.

After running away, getting married, and returning, we first moved in with my birth mom, Chelcie, over in Sherwood, but that only lasted a few weeks. After that, we moved in with Stan and Nancy in their small apartment on Pine St. The apartment was two blocks from where I grew up, on Mulberry St., with my adopted mother, Virgie, whom I called Mommy, but she was anything but a mommy, at least to me.

Nancy and Stan's apartment was small, but it worked. They had an upstairs with two bedrooms and downstairs that they turned a utility room into their bedroom which also had no door for privacy but did have a door that led to a broken-down back porch. Off that porch was a cube of dirt in the alleyway where you could park.

And of course, the apartment had the basics, bath, kitchen, living room. Your first step inside the front door was an underwhelming sight, living room. The apartment had not been taken care of, the wallpaper was peeling off in spots, and the ceiling was stained a dirty yellow from years of cigarette smoke. The floors were linoleum with big pieces missing here and there and a different linoleum under each missing chunk and was rather slanted. You could put a marble on one end, and it would roll by itself to the other room, only stopping when it hit the ragged layers of old jagged pieces of floor or the other wall.

The kitchen was an ugly green. That magnificent color was the cheapest color a slumlord would pay for. Nonetheless, I loved the kitchen table and chairs. It was like a leap back into the 50s. Nan had an old checkerboard table, four tattered silver-based chairs with unbreakable plastic on the backs, but so cool! And the tattered stained curtain that hung in the small window next to the table I am sure had been a towel in a previous life.

The furniture itself was old and soiled. The couch was the old wagon-wheel brown with three cushions that looked as if they had been used as someone's dinner plate. When you sat on it, the middle caved in, creating a need for a shit ton of teamwork to get out of it. Next to the couch sat a rickety blue swiveling rocking chair with a creaking that was only a tad bit louder to the ear than the stains and rips were to the eyes. Nancy had taken old kitchen towels and laid them on each arm of the chair in a failed attempt to prevent stuffing from escaping. The coffee table was four cement bricks with a thin piece of warped plywood on top. Surprisingly, the big brown TV console with aluminum-foil rabbit ears sticking out of the back, which often needed jiggling while hitting the side of the TV, worked most of the time. Sometimes, Stanley would give it a swift bang on its side and a pep talk letting the TV know it was a "fucking piece of shit" and low-and-behold, it would straighten out after that.

Even though Alexander's parents were not the cleanest, both Stan and Nancy were up bright and early every morning like clockwork, Stan went to work, and Nancy started her daily routine. They were messy alcoholics, terrible decorators, and extremely poor but genuinely great people.

We woke up at about 8:30 AM, and I grabbed my jeans, a purple peace sign tee, and flip-flops. I pulled my hair back into a ponytail heading downstairs to make us some breakfast. We were enjoying our morning despite what had happened the night before, running into my Aunt Teabags.

Alexander was teasing me, causing a bout of laughter (quite common for us those days) that was interrupted by the loud pounding at the door. The urgency of the repeated thuds scared the shit out of me, and I froze. My body went stiff. My mind locked up, swirling with fear and worry. The all-too-familiar feelings I had experienced for many years growing up came rushing back 100 times worse.

Even though I wanted to hide from the cop, I felt I had to talk to him, or there would be hell to pay. I just knew in my heart and soul the cop's presence was Virgie's doing, I just knew it.

Once again, I would be her whipping post and a pawn so she could get money from my dad and scare my mom with threats of killing me or making me live with her.

Feeling defeated, I hung my head in despair. *I knew this life couldn't last forever. I just knew it.* My heart dropped out of my chest. I felt my knees go weak. And I knew that if I fell to the floor, I'd never get up. I felt like rolling into the fetal position and crying myself to a tearful death. I wanted to die. I wanted to fly away and never return this time. My world closed and went black. The beautiful smells of fall twisted into the old shithouses I would get whiffs of when we'd visit Mamaw's and Papaw's place down in the hollers of Kentucky.

Life will never be the same again if I go back. Not now. Not ever. God, if you are indeed up there, please help me!

As I tried to compose myself and clear my mind of what would happen, Alex and I moved towards the door. Remembering that my bio mom had told me Virgie threatened to put Alex in the juvenile home, I pulled at him and nodded for him to stay inside and out of sight. I wasn't going to let that happen.

As I stepped onto the front porch, my legs felt like Jell-O. The air was crisp with that fresh autumn smell. Fall leaves, fresh-cut grass, pumpkins. All the perfumes of fall that give hope of peace and happiness. But not that day.

Standing on that cement porch with short, shallow breathing, my body wanted to collapse on the spot, and I felt the previous night's pizza coming up. Although the sun felt warm on my face, I shook with chills as my mind screamed, *Get back inside!*

I wondered what the police officer wanted as my mind ran back to many painful memories. As I turned, glancing across the street, my heart fell from my chest to my feet as my worst fear was confirmed. Virgie's car was the first, Donny parked right behind her, and Denise was in her truck right behind him. There they sat, looking at me.

Staring. Glaring. The smirks on their faces said it all: We got you now! They had found me and come to take me back.

I broke in a cold sweat. Trembling. My heart beating hard. I lost my breath while grabbing at my chest. Looking intently back at them, gripping, and twisting my t-shirt. Mouth wide open and eyes as a deer in headlights while my kneecaps shivered as if the almighty God was coming down on judgment day, to send me to hell. Because if I had to go back to live with Virgie, it would be just that, **hell**.

It had been months since I'd run away and left home. I sure as heck didn't want to go back. *I can't believe this is happening.* Life as I knew it was over for me. No matter what, she always won. Virgie demanded what she wanted, and people did it. She got away with everything. I'd seen it for years. I lived it. I hated it, and I hated her.

I knew the officer well as he had frequented our house many times. Virgie would fight with her husband (whomever it was at the time) and then call the police to report abuse. Many of the cops in Albion knew us by our first names. She needed to be the victim. She was never innocent, nor were any of her husbands for that matter, but she did not care. She was too often all happy to try and get her husband thrown in jail or removed for the night. Which never happened. I'm not sure any domestic violence laws in the mid-1970s ruled for men or women to go to jail, but she sure tried. All. The. Time.

Almost every time the police were called to the house, Virgie would drag me out of bed and tell me what to say to them. I was the obedient child who told the cops exactly what I was instructed to say every time. Even though it bothered me to lie, I knew better than to say anything different, or I'd get it. I was the only innocent one in those situations, yet I remember wishing I could be taken to jail just to get away and not go through the turmoil.

They all sat in their cars, staring at me from across the street. Virgie, with her window down, started screaming with her trademark speech impediment, "You's better get in this car, little girl, before I's comes up there and beats you's ta deaf, do you's hears what I's said?" shaking her finger at me, squinting her eyes, curling her lips. I instantly felt her wrath.

This was the face I'd seen all my life and the look I'd come to know as pure hatred. I feared her. I was terrified of what she would do. I feared Denise and Donny. I was trained to be wary of them all, and I was. Virgie conditioned me with her constant threats. I was a scared child terrified of them all, and indeed I was.

By now, you may be picturing an ugly, sloppy woman with messy hair and dirty clothes. However, Mommy Virgie was rather a pretty woman. She was short, about 5 feet with red hair buffed up in a bouffant style, and an overbite that was stained with a slight yellow tint due to her tea drinking. She had a pleasant smile even with buck teeth and a kind heart at times, but never towards me.

Donny is about 5'5", a medium build with brown combed backed hair 1950s style and decayed teeth. His snickering and snorting were fiendish, while he would pump his shoulders up and down as he babbled, holding one hand over his mouth and the other at his side, all the while glaring at you giving one the creeps.

Donny sat in his car, window down, looking forward, avoiding any eye contact with me. Never even turning his head my way, he just sat there, waiting as if he was going to have a field day with me once I got home. I hated him. I am not sure which one I hated more, Virgie, or Donny. They both were callous to me, and I was so sick of them. The hate I felt for them spilled over inside of me like a river overflowing the banks after a long steady downpour. I wanted to puke. Scream. Shout *Fuck you all!*

Denise was third in line, her window down. She sat squinting her eyes, pursing her lips, and nodding her head up and down as if to tell me, hee-hee, you got caught, and now you're going to pay! Another look I knew well. Her nod made me cower.

My half-sister, to whom I referred as "mommy" until I was about four or five years old, was a thinner straight built woman with shoulder-length brownish hair, buckteeth and, hee—hee for a giggle, and a finicky smile when she wanted to give one, which was not often. Mostly she relished in sticking her middle finger up and giving dirty looks.

When I was a child, and even into my teens and adulthood, I was under the delusion that Denise was my only supporter. It took getting out of that environment and looking at things in a new hue to realize just how much my sister betrayed me, all my life. I can recall many times when Virgie would be scolding, hitting, or belittling me, and the one person I thought would protect me did nothing but laugh at what was happening. Her smirks, head tilting, and *hee-hee-hee* came right before the name-calling portion of my scolding. This was always more than I could bear.

My heart felt the pangs every time they called me names, but my heart broke when they called my birth mom, Chelcie, names and said horrible things about her, making death threats towards her and her other children, my other halfsiblings. I felt overpowered and worthless for not sticking up for my mom and siblings, but I also knew I had no choice. Had I spoken up, things would get worse, and there was no way of genuinely predicting what might happen. I was forced into agreeing with the hateful comments that made me throw up afterward.

There was hardly ever a scolding from Mommy, Donny, or Denise that didn't involve my birth mother for one reason or another, and I loathed all of them—and my dad, Ardy—for the same shit.

They all made threats like, "I'll kill her, and it'll be all your fault. I'll cut her head off and all their heads, and it'll be your fault. I'll shoot her right between the eyes and let you watch her die, and it'll be your fault. I'll kill every one of them bastards, and it'll be your fault. I'll cut them up and feed them to the hogs, and it'll be your fault." Hearing something repeatedly, you tend to believe it. Because it was four different adults telling me this kind of stuff, and I had already experienced their power. I understood them every time they made one of those intimidating threats.

That shit stuck in my young mind, and over the years, I learned it would always be my fault no matter the situation. They told me so often that what they said became gospel. I genuinely believed it. I did my best to protect my birth mother, her husband, Claude, and my siblings. I always worried about them, and I tried to save them all by being a good girl and staying silent permanently.

My silence turned into loathing. I kept it hidden inside of me. I was afraid to be myself. Afraid I would be ridiculed and made fun of, or worse, terrified Virgie and the other three horsemen of the apocalypses would find out that, I hated them all. Despite my efforts to be invisible, it happened anyway, the three of them ganging up on me.

And there the three of them sat. Waiting to pounce on me like a cat watching a mouse stuck in a trap, waiting to eat it up.

"Hello, Officer Lentz"

He was tall, a medium-built man with a deep voice. He was one of the most helpful police officers in Albion. He always waved at me and would stop if he saw me downtown and ask how I was, and how school was going for me.

"Hi, Peggy. How you been, kiddo?"

"Well, okay. You know that I ran away in March, and I just got back a few weeks ago. Am I in trouble? Do I have to go back home with her?"

"That depends. First, I heard you got married."

"Yes."

"I need to see the marriage license. Can you go get it and show it to me?"

"Yep. Hold on." As I rushed into the house with tear-filled eyes and my heart throbbing so hard the neighbors could hear it, Alex grabbed me, hugged me, and told me, "Don't worry. That the old bitch can't fuck with us now, we're married."

I wanted to believe him, but a part of me knew Virgie always got her way, and I had to buckle and do what she told me to do, or else. Or else my birth mother's life might be at stake as well as my own, again.

I grabbed the license and rushed back to the door. I was scared to keep Virgie waiting too long as that was never a good thing to do. When she said jump, the only response from me was, how high?

"Here. Here it is. Is it okay? Am I okay? I mean, everything is legal, so I don't have to go back to her house, do I? I am married legally, right? This is legal, right?" I spouted so fast and jumbled. I am sure my horror and panic were painfully obvious.

"Calm down, let me look at it. Give me a minute, kid. You know I'm on your side," Officer Lentz said as he stood looking it over and speaking to someone on a walkie-talkie reading off dates and numbers. I heard every word between them. They were checking with someone in Lima, Ohio, at the courthouse. I could tell the lady at the police station had the courthouse on the phone. Soon enough, I heard the words on the other side of that walkie-talkie that let me settle down a little. "All clear with that one, it's all legal. It's a-go. Good luck, Lentz, and I'm damn glad it's you and not me, buddy!" chuckled the other half of that walkie-talkie.

Lentz smiled at me and said, "Wait right here." He stepped off the porch with my marriage license in hand, looked back, smiled at me, and headed towards Virgie's car. I felt a flash of happiness and freedom before a gloom came over me. I just knew somehow, she would get her way, and I'd have to go back home to take whatever lashing was coming from all three of them—nothing I wasn't used to, just something I never wanted to deal with again.

Lentz stood at Virgie's car, talking for a few minutes, then he handed her my marriage license. I just knew she would destroy it, and then I would have nothing to prove I was married. *FUCK!* She was notorious for tearing things up. Destroying things was her specialty and then blaming someone else for doing so or claiming they made her do it, therefore, it was not her fault.

Once, she was so upset she grabbed the Holy Bible, threw it on the floor, then stood with both her bare feet on it yelling and screaming, "I's swear on the Bible, and I's stand on it! God strike me dead right now if I's a-lyin'!" I had secretly hoped God would reach down and strike her dead, more than once.

Virgie glared up at me standing on the porch waiting, and with a contemptuous half-cocked head, she held my marriage license up in the air and pretended to tear it up. Officer Lentz said something to her as he continued to shake his finger in her face while removing my marriage license out of her hands. Officer Lentz noted a few more things to her, still shaking that finger, and then returned to me. I couldn't hear what he said, but it must have been significant as she handed over my marriage license with her scowling facial expression. As she did, she gave me her death stare. Glaring at me with more anger than ever. It was apparent that if she could, she'd probably kill me. *Did she bring her baseball bat, belt, or a switch?*

"I need to ask you one more thing. Have you _consummated_ this marriage yet?"

Um, what the heck does 'consummate' mean? I was 15, not 30. I had dropped out of school to run away and get the hell out of that life. How was I supposed to know the meaning of that word? I'm quite sure by the idiotic look on my face, that he knew I had no clue what he meant, so he rephrased the question.

"Peggy, listen to me kiddo, this is a pivotal point that means you stay or go back. Have you had sex yet?"

I knew what it meant if Virgie found out the answer to that question. It wouldn't matter either way. I knew what she would do to get her way, anything she had to. And no answer I gave would matter, truth or lie. I knew what she'd do to us both, off to the juvenile home, just like she promised.

I WAS DROWNING. I couldn't move. I was about four years old in this earliest of memories. I was watching my mother's face while she covered my nose and mouth with one hand and held me under the bathwater with the other. I was a helpless little girl, frightened and confused, wondering, *what did I do this time?*

We were living in downtown Detroit, Michigan. It was the summer of 1967, and I'd turned four years old that April. My stepdad, Barry (Virgie's second husband), had some family living there, so off we went.

That was typical, moving from place to place. One day we would be at home, and the next we'd be living in a different house. It just was. It just happened — a lot.

I believe we lived on the ninth floor, in apartment number 6, which may have been number nine as the worn, metal number always swung back and forth on our door. I recall our apartment being big and empty, but then again, I was a small child, and many things looked magnified to me. I remember a small bed in the corner of the living room, by the windows, this was probably my sister, Denise's bed. It seems to me that Donny and I shared a bedroom as I recall being around him a lot. Or, perhaps, I was just a little stinker who bugged her big brother. The kitchen was tiny, a small table sat in the corner, and the old rounded top fridge beside it. The opposite side housed the sink and stove.

The bathroom had white walls, a clawfoot tub, a single white sink, and a commode. My mother had a small brown rug on the floor in front of the tub. There was a mirror over the sink, and the door which was a little tattered had a hook and loop lock on the inside door frame.

Denise, who aspired of becoming a hairdresser, decided that I needed the same pixie haircut as the trendy 1960s British teenage model, Twiggy. My long, curly strawberry blonde hair that bounced with Shirley Temple locks became nothing more than a very choppy bowl cut. I don't think it turned out like Twiggy's, but I loved it.

I remember sitting in the sink, letting her chop all my hair off. She told me I was beautiful, and I happily believed her. However, when I walked out of the bathroom to show my mother how beautiful my hair was, her reaction was not what I had anticipated. She started yelling at Denise for cutting off mine and Donny's hair.

Despite this incident, life still goes on and it was bath night for me. I usually got the last bath. Mommy would bathe first, then Donny then me. Tonight, I got the first bath and clean water which I do not recall happening a lot, but I was happy I got to go first.

As the blaring noise of Barry's show TV show competed with the sound of the water hitting the tub, my mother told me to get undressed, I obeyed and stood still and quiet while the water deepened. I needed help climbing into the bathtub, so my mother lifted me into it and told me to sit down and be still, sternly explaining that she didn't want me to splash water on her clean floor and ruin it. The warm and soothing water received me, and, despite my mother's agitation, I felt safe. Playing in the tub was not usually allowed, but I still enjoyed the gentle feel of the water, it made me feel happy and calm. I enjoyed taking a bath—until that day.

My mother bent down over me and began washing my hair. When she finished, she allowed me to play a little with the dead soap scum bubbles. Then, once again mommy reminded me shaking her finger in my face, giving me the look and barking out demands, "Yous better not splash water on my clean floor, little girl."

This was a look with which I knew, and I instinctively knew that each word was packed with a more profound implication. I sat still in the tub, waiting for directions on what I could or couldn't do next. Mommy kept dipping the washrag into the bathtub and pulling it back out, wringing it and lowering it again and again as I sat quietly watching her, waiting for guidance, waiting to breathe, waiting to move, waiting.

As I sat watching her, it was as if something inside her snapped. She tipped her head and told me to keep my mouth shut and lay down.

"Lay down under the water."

I tried to lay down without my head going under, but it was difficult. That's when she put her hand over my nose and mouth, holding me under the water while staring at me. I'd never seen someone through water but looking up at her as I lay in that tub, she had empty black eyes that I knew well, and I was terrified to splash. I lay there panicked and frozen in the bathwater that used to feel safe. Nothing made sense to me, and all I could think was, *why is Mommy holding me under the water?* I couldn't breathe. *What did I do so bad this time? Why do you hate me, Mommy? I love you, why don't you love me too?*

As I went under, some water went inside my nose, and I swallowed some too. It burned, and I began to choke, but I knew I'd better do as I was told, while she held my nose and mouth tighter and tighter.

It hurts. Why mommy? Why are you doing this to me? What did I do? I can't breathe, mommy! Let me get up, please! Help me! Stop mommy! Why? I'm so afraid. I won't get the floor wet. I promise. I won't talk. I won't ever take a bath again. Why mommy? Why are you doing this?

Breathing became increasingly more difficult. I began to wiggle, trying to get loose of her hold, but I was frightened to do too much. I started choking even more as I began moving my lips to get air, but all I got was water. I became increasingly panicked, and my plan to not move was taken over by flailing limbs and splashing water. As my mother yelled at me, I heard rattling at the door.

Barry had popped the lock and gotten into the bathroom. I recall him shoving her away, and then his hands grabbing me, pulling me out of the tub. He began pounding on my back to make me cough. I was scared, crying, and cold while the water was spewing out of my mouth and nose, it was horrifying.

My mother sat on the toilet, not saying anything to either of us. She stared into the labyrinth of her mind. It was terrifying, to say the least, and she scared me to my core that night.

Barry dried me off and sent me to my bed, where I laid and listened to them fight until I could no longer hold my tiny eyes open, watching and waiting for mommy to return and keep me under the water again.

I don't recall ever really feeling the love from Mommy. In return, I shouldn't have felt love *for* her, but I did. All I wanted was for her to love me like she loved the other two. For reasons unknown to me until later years, my mother would never love me as she loved them. She just couldn't.

SOMETIME AFTER THE TUB incident came the riots. This memory, although less traumatic than almost being drowned by my mother, was quite impressionable, forming an opinion I had to unlearn over the years.

That same year in July, the 1967 Detroit riot was lived right outside our apartment. This was also known as the 12th Street Riot, which is still ranked as the third worst in U.S. history. As historians report, this Detroit riot—which went on for about five days—began following a raid on an unlicensed bar known as a "blind pig."

A blind pig was an illegal, after-hours gathering place, like a speakeasy. These establishments were typical during the Prohibition era. Now, 1967 was far from the 1933 prohibition, but these places still existed, and many were for blacks as it was still hard for black folks to enter bars and enjoy a drink without getting shit from racists.

That day was sunny and warm outside. I loved looking out the windows. We were so high up that everyone looked shorter than me, and I recall giggling at how big I felt. Living downtown, our street was busy all the time with walkers and cars.

Donny and I were the only kids in the apartment, Denise was gone. I had no idea where my mother and Barry were going, but Donny and I were told to sit and watch TV until they got back. Usually, we did. However, that day we opened the windows and watched all the commotion. There we were both of us hanging out a ninth-floor window watching the streets that were full of people. I do mean hanging out the window as there were no screens, just the massive, tall windows that went from about two feet off the floor to almost the ceiling. We could have fallen out that damn window and plummeted to our deaths!

Jesus! I'd never seen so many people at once. Mostly black people with a white person sprinkled into the mix here and there. Everyone was yelling and screaming stuff, but I didn't even know what they were saying. Donny said there were a million people out there in the streets. As a four-year-old, I had no concept of what a million people looked like, but Donny said it, so it was. They were all over the streets, shouting, shaking their fists, holding signs that I couldn't read. I could hear glass breaking and saw people throwing bottles that were on fire. I had no idea it was a riot. All I knew was that there were angry people outside. I also knew the police were furious and arresting them. It was logical to me that they were getting into trouble because everyone knows you aren't supposed to walk in the middle of the road. I saw police officers and army men all over. I remember noticing they had these massive things that covered their bodies in one hand, and on the other hand, they had what looked like sticks. I remember thinking that maybe they were little baseball bats but smaller.

There were more angry people than the military and police and so much noise. It was a messy sight, and I was a little scared as we watched out the window, but I felt somewhat safe. They were outside, we were inside. And I had my brother there who sometimes protected me from the scary stuff, so we just watched as Detroit started to burn down.

When my mother and Barry returned it was scarier than what was happening outside as Barry flung hateful words with such revulsion. Barry and my mother's negative comments about "the blacks" sprinkled the room like confetti. Denise came in a few minutes after them, and then Barry packed us up and directed us to the car so we could get away. As he maneuvered his way out of the area, Barry cussed the blacks out and blamed them for everything happening that day, calling them "niggers, mother fuckers, sons of a bitching assholes," and lots of other names. He said they were trying to kill us all and take over. I wasn't sure what that meant, but it scared me, and I wanted to get away from the black people too. Barry said they were terrible, and so did Mommy, so they must have been horrible people, right?

It was a sad world I grew up in. Well, a terrific America for sure, but it was filled with unhappy people who were not open to everyone just living in harmony and being free as we all should be able to live. There shouldn't be division, but it exists today, and that's sad. I believe it's not color that divides us, it's ignorance and fear of the unknown.

I understand how racism works. If that's what you're taught, then that's what you believe is right. People teach their kids what they know. I was conditioned to fear black people because you learn what you live, and you live what you know.

Until you unlearn it.

AFTER THE RIOTS, WE MOVED into a big house with my Aunt Chelcie (my biological mother) and Uncle Claude, and I was so happy. I'm not sure why we moved, but we did again.

I thought my Aunt Chelcie was so beautiful. She stood about 5 foot 2 inches and had sexy legs, according to Uncle Claude. She had a smile that would outshine the sun and her laughter was pure happiness. She had the prettiest curly reddish hair and a beautiful heart that offered help to anyone.

Claude was a tall, medium-size man. His face was always scruffy as if he needed a shave but never shaved. His left arm was paralyzed. I'm not sure why or what happened, but it was stiff, and his hand stayed in the same position. He had a great laugh, a big smile, and the best hugs. The greatest thing about Uncle Claude was he could pick up bumblebees and rub their bellies, and they never stung him, ever. He could pick up snakes, wild raccoons, and anything untamed, and not one of them would hurt him. The skunks wouldn't even spray him. He was like a backwoods Doctor Dolittle in real life.

We lived outside the city in Homer, Michigan, a quaint little country town with about 1600 people. Our bluish-grey house sat on a dirt road, and it was huge. The home was a duplex. One side was big and had an upstairs. That's the side Aunt Chelcie and Uncle Claude lived in with their kids. Virgie, Barry, Denise, Donny, and I lived in the other part. Although the home was big enough that we could live on one side and Aunt Chelcie's family on the other, there was only one bathroom, and we *all* shared it. There were two doors, one on each side of the house for each family to use.

Upstairs, on Aunt Chelcie's side, the house had four simple, basic ole bedrooms. Once you walked up the stairs to the right, there were two small bedrooms, those were Aunt Chelcie's girls' rooms, Vickie Sue, Bonnie, and Addy Mae. The girls had a record player and records—vinyl 45s and albums. Sometimes they would let me come in and dance with them when they played the record player. I loved "Peggy Sue" by Buddy Holly, even though it was released in 1958, it was my favorite. I wasn't a Peggy Sue, but I was a Peggy, and that was good enough for me to claim it as my song.

When they allowed me into their room to listen to records, they thought it was funny to make me dance before I could leave, and they taught me how to do all the popular dances. I knew how to do the twist, the monkey, the mashed potato, and still do. They would laugh, and I'd cry as they held me hostage, until I did whatever dance they wanted me to do for them. I was mad at them then, but now I realize that was a fun time in my life, and I loved being in that room with them and dancing. Little did they know that someday in the future, all those dancing lessons would earn me a living. Ha! Ya, bitches.

There was one more door at the end of the hallway upstairs, but I never opened that door to see what was on the other side because Aunt Chelcie told me there was a crazy man who lived in there and he'd kill us all if we let him out. Well, enough said for me. If there was a crazy man in there, then I wasn't going to open the door and let his raging ass out. Fuck that! Why do adults tell kids that kind of shit? They're kids for God's sake! Still, to this day, I eyeball any door that even remotely looks freaky.

Each of the girls' bedrooms had a small window looking out to the backyard. You could see the big red barn on the left side and, in front of it, an old blue station wagon sitting in the weeds on bricks. A small red shed was on the right side, with a dirt path between, like something a tractor would use as a road. There were cows in the big barn, and behind it was a large area fenced in where they roamed. You could hear the noisy chickens in the mornings when they got their food and laid eggs.

I helped Aunt Chelcie feed the chickens sometimes. I never told her this because I wanted to be with her, but I hated them feathery fuckers.

They'd cluck and peck at my feet, I had shoes on, but still, that's scary! She'd let me have a handful of feed to sprinkle around on the ground for them. I would do it, but I loathed it. Furthermore, chickens stink. But fried chicken sure was yummy revenge!

Also, in the backyard was Claude's German Shepard, Big John. That big guy was chained up to a big ole tree and his doghouse sat under it. Not much grass around him but I recall Claude going out to visit him and his water bowl was a big old washtub. I was told to keep my distance, or he might bite but he never seemed mean to me no matter, I kept my space.

Chelcie and Claude didn't treat animals like Virgie and granny. I loved the animals—dogs, cats, cows, rabbits, and goats (not the chickens)—but they were not respected by most adults in my childhood. It was sad to see. They would call them names like "Old dog," "Stupid ole cat," no real names, no worth, no love, no life other than they made on their own. Granny would cuss out the dogs and cats while she kicked the shit out of them. Virgie, the same. To granny, Virgie and some others in the family, animals were to be eaten not loved. Dogs were no count and cats were well, bad luck! I suppose that was the way they were raised.

I am so glad I instinctively understand as an adult how to care for my fur babies the proper way — something this family never showed me how to do. Why are people like that allowed to own animals or, furthermore, breed? I don't get it. If you can't be kind to animals, the chances of successfully raising humans, in my opinion, is slim to jack shit. I'm proof.

The farm always smelled of baked biscuits and apples. Aunt Chelcie always baked, cooked, and canned. Many times, I went over to her side and baked homemade biscuits with her. I loved those times, they meant so much to me as I felt such a connection to her. She'd stand me up on a chair next to the table. Wrapping one of her old aprons around my middle, she'd brush my hair and put it up in a ponytail. Then she'd set a little pan of warm water in front of me and show me how to wash my hands, which we'd do together. We would laugh, and she'd sing songs to me and tell me I was her beautiful baby girl. It was okay if water got on the floor, she never cared or got mad at me for being messy.

Then she'd mix a batch of biscuits, pinching off a piece of dough for me to roll and place in the small, iron skillet. I got to roll them out on the table and then roll the dough ball in my hands, pat it a little flat, then set the round patties into the iron skillet. I did just like she showed me.

Every time I made biscuits, Uncle Claude would tell everyone those were "the best lip-smackin,' hot diggity, tastiest biscuits" he'd ever had, and I'd beam with pride. Aunt Chelcie would laugh and say, "Yes, they sure are tasty, Pooch," (her nick name for me), then snuggle me and pat my leg. My cousins (siblings) would all tell me they were the best too. Everyone made a fuss over my biscuits. Truthfully, they were probably right because Aunt Chelcie made the dough. All I knew was that everyone liked them, and I had a rare moment of happiness and pride. I loved her so much because she was the best person in the entire world. She loved me the most too, I instinctively knew it.

Not long after we moved in, Aunt Chelcie bought me a doll. When I received it, I felt exceptional. I don't recall having many toys, but *that* one, I remember.

One other doll I do remember well was when I was about two or three years old (yes, I recall many things from when I was young). Denise, Donny, and I were in the living room of the house we lived in at the time, playing near a silver Christmas tree with colored lights. Donny had his trucks and some big G.I. Joes, Denise had who-knows-what, and I had a soft cloth dolly with stiff plastic legs, arms, and head. They both wanted my doll to use for Godzilla or something, and they began fighting over it and pulling on it. Donny had one leg and one arm, and Denise had the limbs on the opposite side. They fought and pulled hard enough that my dolly ripped right in two, and all her gut stuffing came spilling out onto the floor.

I cried. They laughed. It was a sibling thing. It probably was kind of funny to see the doll rip and her bowels pour out on the floor, and

I'm sure the look on their faces and mine was priceless at the time. However, Mommy did not think it was funny. She yelled at me, "I's will never buy you's another doll again!" And she didn't.

So, you can imagine my heart singing happy songs when my Aunt Chelcie bought me a dolly. The doll, *my* doll, was old with hardened rubbery arms and legs that were movable but not bendable, and a hard-rubbery body too. Her head twisted both ways. She wore a yellow dress, and her brown hair felt like straw. This Goodwill doll looked as if some other little girl had chopped her hair up fairly good, but hey, I couldn't have cared less about all that stuff because I had a dolly of my own.

The day Auntie gave her to me, she called me over to her side of the house and said, "Be quiet and don't tell anyone I got this baby for you. If you do, Virgie will get mad and whoop you." Virgie, Auntie said, would never let me see her again, which was a worse consequence than getting a whoopin' so, shutting my mouth was the only option. I knew that keeping a secret from Mommy could also get my ass beat, but I wanted a dolly to love, so I risked it and stayed silent.

Every few days, I would get to rock my doll in Auntie's living room in her big, old, wooden rocking chair. She gave me one of her flowered dish towels to use for her blanket. When I was done rocking (usually only after a few minutes), I had to wrap her in the makeshift blanket and hide her inside the end table, one of those old, dark, plyboard octagon-shaped tables with a door in the front with the bottom fully enclosed.

Inside that end table, Aunt Chelcie also stored a Bible, so I knew my doll would be safe because it was with the Word of God. She was a churchgoer. She was so close to God that He told her things all the time. I would overhear her telling my aunts and uncles what God had shown or told her. Uncle Claude said so too, so it was true.

One day, I was rocking the doll, and I noticed a man outside the side door in her living room. He had a horse with him and was wearing blue overalls. He also had a squirrel tail hanging from his side pockets and a hankie out his back pocket. His horse was white. Next to him was a woman who looked like an Indian lady. She wore a brown dress with fringe on the bottom, and a blue necklace was as shiny as her lengthy, black, braided hair. I had never seen these people before, but they were right there looking at me. I wasn't scared at all, they smiled and just stood there watching me. After a few seconds of staring at each other, I went and got Auntie. I told her they were watching me and asked who they were. Looking concerned, she went to see, but they were gone. She sent Uncle Claude outside to look around, but he found no one.

The next day, I saw a picture in Auntie's house and told her that it was the old man I had seen with his horse. She looked at me and didn't say much for a few minutes. When she told Uncle Claude, he sat in the living room chair, looking stunned. He said God must have allowed grandpa to return and protect me from mommy Virgie.

At the time, I had no clue what the heck they were talking about, but I can tell you this; The man I saw was my half-Indian grandfather, Arlin, who died before I was born, and his horse was dead too. I have no clue who the woman was, nor have I ever seen her again. My grandfather often visited me throughout my childhood. I'm not claiming to be psychic; I'm just saying he was with me, and I have seen him.

I was told not to tell Virgie about seeing grandpa, or she'd get angry, so again, I kept another secret to save myself.

I am not sure what happened between Virgie and her sister Chelcie but, shortly after this incident, I was sleeping on the couch when suddenly, I was awakened by screaming and cursing coming from both outside and inside the house. Being jolted from a nice nap by screams and cursing wasn't strange for me. It happened a lot. Still, it scared me. I jumped up and ran to the door where I was quickly blocked by Aunt Chelcie and her daughter, Vickie Sue.

Vickie Sue kept pushing me back, but I could see outside between Chelcie and Vickie Sue. I watched Virgie and her then-husband, Barry, in an old pick-up truck screaming and yelling at Auntie and her boys who were outside on the porch. Barry got out of the vehicle with a shotgun screaming, "I'll kill all you mother fuckers! I'll blow your fucking heads off! You cock suckers, let her out!"

Barry was a tall thin man with black hair and nice looking. He drank beer, smoked cigarettes, watched football, and ate pork rinds. He'd share his pork rinds if I hooted for his team. I always liked Barry, but today, he was frightening.

Once again, the threat of death was thick in the air, and I just knew it'd be my fault if someone was killed, and I'd get a hard spanking if that happened. My heart began to race, as I tried to figure out what to do.

The drama was in the backyard of the house, where there was a long wood porch with cement blocks as steps. Peering between Aunt Chelcie and Vickie Sue, I could see the blue station wagon parked on blocks and Barry's truck. I saw Chelcie's three older boys out there, two of them had shotguns and were shouting at Virgie and Barry. Everyone with guns held them up and threatened to kill each other. Even though I was used to this kind of scene, I was shaking with fear because it was all my fault, somehow.

Virgie jumped out of the truck and started yelling, "Peggy Ann! You's better comes out little girl, or I's gonna beats you's ta deaf! Do you's hear me, little girl?"

That was all the threat I needed, my decision was made. I bolted through Vickie Sue's and Aunt Chelcie's legs and down the steps I went headfirst into the dirt. I skinned up my face, hands, and knees all without shedding a tear, I knew better than to cry. Virgie grabbed me by my hair, leading me to the truck then, shoved me in between her and Barry and he spun off down the driveway.

As we were speeding down the road, Virgie began screaming at me about not coming out, which "caused all this fighting." I wasn't sure what I had done, but I must have done something terrible. She told me this was all my fault because I was a bastard and not of God. She told me I was going to burn in the lake of fire with "them."

I began to cry and was slapped with an open hand in the face and told, "dry it up, little girly, or I's given you's something to cry about! Keep crying, and I's put my fist down you's throat and bloody you's legs and you's be sorry!"

Well, that worked. I shut it up, quick. Virgie grabbed a handful of my hair, pulling it hard while screaming at me that I was a bastard and ruined everything—her marriage and her relationship with her sister. She told me I was retarded, stupid, not right in the head, and ugly. When she had her moments like this, it was best not to say a word, just look at her and shake my head yes, so she would see me agreeing with her hateful comments towards me, I was four. Scared. I knew I was an ugly little girl. She told me so. I knew I was a bad kid because she said it was all my fault, whatever *it* was.

Barry began screaming at Virgie, then the fighting started full force. They fought a lot. They fought almost every day. Barry would tell her, "Give her back. She's not your child. You don't love her, you only want her for meanness." They fought the whole way to the new house, and the fighting continued all night. She threw glasses at him, plates, beer bottles, silverware, her knick-knacks, and whatever else she could grab and throw. He threw chairs, tipped over tables, and broke broom handles while jumping up and down, cursing and screaming. I have to say even though he would throw things, I don't ever recall him throwing anything at Virgie/Mommy. During many fights, windows would get damaged, and the neighbors called the cops, more than once.

It was morning before they were finished fighting this brawl. I got an ass whooping before breakfast because it was my mistake. If I had come out when Virgie called the first time, none of that fighting at Aunt Chelcie's would have happened. I "almost got people shot with a gun," and she blamed me because I was "too stupid" to do as I was told.

She jerked the covers off me, pulled me out of bed by my hair, whipped my pants and panties down, and spanked my ass in the hallway until I pissed myself. It hurt my legs when I peed on them. I cried and begged her to stop, saying, "Please, mommy, no, I'm sorry. I won't do it again, please, no mommy." It didn't matter. According to her, I deserved what I got.

It was a beautiful day, sunny and bright, with the familiar buzzing of a lawnmower in the distance and the faint smell of freshly cut grass.

We had Barry's kids for the weekend. It was a great day for a car ride in the country. Barry and Virgie loaded us kids—Theresa and Jeffery (Barry's youngest two children), and me—into the station wagon. They were always getting a different vehicle, trading car for car, or somehow swindling someone out of their things. That wasn't all either. Many times, they would cheat folks out of or outright steal assorted items. Virgie and Barry were always heading somewhere to get something they were owed or to set someone straight from doing something to them. Always something.

No wonder I hate watching Soap Operas on T.V. they are filled with drama, and I lived real-life bullshit drama, I guess I've just had enough. I don't care to watch it or live it anymore!

Us kids climbed into the back of the station wagon and were told to lay down and not look out the windows, and off we went. We did as we were told while looking out the window at an upward angle and played Watching the Clouds Run with Us. Maybe that's a game poor kids play, I don't know, but we enjoyed it. There was a small hole in the floorboard where the exhaust whiffed in, not a big gap but enough to smell it. Teresa and I kept teasing Jeffery that he was farting. We goaded him very quietly because they knew I'd get a spanking for saying the word fart or even thinking of a fart. We had fun when we could, and that day was a good day for a little while.

Barry stopped and filled a big red gas can and placed it in the backseat, which added to Jeffery's smelly farts. Soon, we pulled into someone's driveway, and Barry instructed us, not to look and to stay down while he grabbed the gas canister out of the backseat. Virgie told me specifically, "If you's look, little girl, I's will beat you's ta the blood runs down you's legs. Do you's hears me?"

I nodded my head. *Yes, mommy.*

Soon as the doors slammed shut, Teresa looked. I begged her not to, but she giggled and said they couldn't see us and told me to look because we were at Aunt Chelcie's house, the big old bluish-grey one in Homer, on the dirt road. Thinking I might get a chance to see Aunt Chelcie, I excitedly flipped over and crept up while gripping onto the backseat and hiding part of my face to not let anyone see me looking.

A couple of minutes later, we saw Virgie and Barry running from the back of the house with two big brown bags. We all gasped and laid down quickly. They opened the back-panel door and threw the bags in beside us. The bags were cold, and I saw lots of white packages in them. They shouted at us again to stay still and be quiet. We nodded our heads yes again until they were out of sight.

The second time we saw them, they were running out from the back, and large fiery flames were coming from the top of the house. We heard a loud pop-crack, and we were all three instantaneously worried. The house was on fire! I didn't know if Aunt Chelcie was inside or not, but I cried in silence for her. They threw two more brown bags full of white packages, and the empty red gas can in the back with us, and off we sped to our new home in Albion.

I cried all night thinking that Aunt Chelcie and Uncle Claude and the kids were all in the fire and died. The police came to our new house in Albion and asked Virgie if he could talk to me. She told him, "In a minute," and she took me to the kitchen and told me I had better not say anything or else she'd shoot Chelcie right between the eyes.

Virgie led me back into the living room where the cop was waiting. The officer asked me my name, and I shrugged my shoulders. I thought if I didn't say anything, it would be best. I didn't want to get Aunt Chelcie killed. I recall Virgie letting the officer know that I was stupid and slow, and I didn't know anything because I was retarded. He smiled at me and said I was a cute little girl. He patted me on the head, looked around the room with a big sigh, then left.

I was glad I didn't say anything to him. I didn't care if he thought I was stupid, slow, and retarded like mommy said I was. I had to protect Auntie from getting killed, so I saved her life once again. I had to. Only I knew all the horrible things Mommy was going to do to Aunt Chelcie and her kids if I didn't obey, so I had no choice. I needed to save her. I had to keep them all alive, so I did my best. And even though I rescued them over and over again by doing as I was told, I couldn't protect myself from Virgie, Ardy, and their spawns.

The funny thing about that house fire was that the old coffee table that held my dolly and Bible didn't burn at all. I recall this as we walked through the house after, and I saw it myself.

And ya know, I never named that doll. To this day, I have it, and to this day, she still doesn't have a name.

FIRST, LET ME SAY that both sides of the family had their versions of how I came to be. Not that I ever questioned it until both families continued to make my conception so important. I mean, I was a kid. When you are a kid do you really sit and think, "Hmm, how did I come to be?" Um, no.

A good handful of folks had a story, and often the people who continued to tell me these tales seemed to shift a lot. I wondered why their stories changed all the time, and then I grew up, and well...

One story was that Ardy and Chelcie got drunk, and she pushed herself on him. That story changed to they both got drunk, and Ardy did not know what he was doing. Then this same person changed that story again to, well, she wanted him to pull over, and she jumped in the backseat, and you know men will be men, right?

I was eight when this version came to life, and I had no clue what this person was even talking about, so I have no idea about men being men.

A different human told me that, He tried to resist her, but she forced herself on him, and he had no choice. Then that changed to something else and something else again. It was like this whenever someone was drinking on either side of the family and, the stories would start rolling off their drunken tongues with tons of other crap too.

Even Ardy had his few variations and would tell me in a way that always ended with him letting me know, "It was the worst thing I've ever done, and I wish to my god that I had never done it!"

There was only one person who never changed her story and not once offered it up to me until I asked. My biological mother. It was simple. She told me, "It's nothing for you to worry about, that's all."

Either way, the "story" goes, it was the summer of 1962, and my biological mother, Chelcie, had recently moved up from Kentucky to Michigan with her eight children (my siblings), five boys and three girls, all under 15 years old.

Welfare was popping for folks, and food stamps were the currency of choice. My biological mother told me that her first husband had left her and my siblings. The rest of her family was already in Michigan, and they convinced her to move because the state of Michigan "would give you free money and free food." Also, her husband had left her with eight little mouths to feed and no way to do so, so this was a way to feed her children rather than watch them starve. She moved.

My mother had shown me a scar from being shot by her ex. She told me while pregnant with my brother William her ex shot her in the pelvis with a shotgun trying to kill them both. She claimed he was in a drunken rage due to her being pregnant again, and he didn't want another child.

Because of that incident, my brother was born early, very tiny, and the most nervous child my mother would give birth to. Despite his unkind entrance into the world, he was a fine person and an amazing big brother, we became close later.

Even though my mother had been shot, she didn't leave her ex-Sam at that time. Nope, she stayed and got pregnant six more times during the next eleven years, birthing all my siblings right at home in the hills of the beautiful Bluegrass State, Kentucky. With a midwife and a chair, she would give birth, pick up the next day and get back to life and work.

Honestly, if you have never been to Kentucky, I think it is one of the most beautiful states. With rolling mountains, waterfalls, and caves, it is simply fantastic and, the folks there are wonderful, not to mention the cooking. Southern people can cook! I love Kentucky.

Nonetheless, years and six kids later she was a single mother, with no means to support herself and her kids. That is when she called and asked for help from her family, but no one had the money to come down and get them or to help financially.

Not surprising. Some of the adults I grew up knowing on my mom's side did nothing to help anyone but take, take, and take all that they could from everybody around them. If you asked a favor, you'd better pay or do something extra in a trade because they did nothing for free.

Contrary to the typical family response when someone needed help, one of my mom's younger sisters, and her husband made the trip down to Kentucky to get them and bring them back to Michigan to be with the rest of her family. By this time, almost all of my mom's family was in Michigan except one brother that remained living in Kentucky, despite being the closest in proximity, he didn't help her either.

My mom and my siblings moved to Marshall, Michigan, and into her mother's basement. Granny needed things to benefit her, or she would refuse to help you. She was like this with my mother as well.

So, my mom told me, and many others verified this as I did myself when I was older through granny herself. She told my mom, "If yuens were going to live in my home, eat my food with your "nasty ass little niggers," then you are going to clean, do laundry and cook." Plus, anything else granny bellowed about.

The cold, damp cement floor and walls, no beds, no carpet, with just quilts to lay on, was what they called their new home. They each got one plate, bowl, cup, and spoon to use. Yeah, that was Granny. She gave nothing to anyone yet took everything she could from people. She was greedy, and that gluttonous trait was passed on to some of her children.

My mother told me as soon as she moved into Granny's place, they took her to apply for Welfare, a medical card, and food stamps. Back in the early 1960s, they had the commodity food lines, which she also took advantage of. Hell, many people stood in those lines to get the free cereal, peanut butter, and cheese. I recall standing in line holding bags of food and waiting with Virgie. I must admit that the cheese was rather good.

My biological mom said she would get free clothing from churches and Red Cross, anything she could get, she took. Of course, Granny and some of her other adult children told her of these free things and took her around to collect. Then for their helping her, they would take their pick through what she got for taking her around and helping her out, so they claimed. As I said, if you ask a favor, you'd better be willing to give something in return. Many of them didn't do pleasant and compassion rather, they took.

My mom said when she'd get her welfare check and food stamps, Granny would demand it all, and my mom had no choice but to hand it over. She had nowhere else to go, and most of her siblings would not help her unless it benefited them. They all knew Granny was taking advantage of my mom, and they did nothing to help her.

Chelcie said that it didn't take long before she became the one everyone brought their laundry and kids to. She'd do her siblings' laundry and watch their kids—and hers—while they visited with Granny. My mom told me they sat in lawn chairs talking about people, and she stood at an old wringer washing machine pinning up clothes and corralling everyone's kids. No one paid her, and Granny demanded it because she lived in her basement with her "nasty ass little niggers."

Some of my siblings have beautiful olive skin rather than chalky white. My mother showed me pictures and told me her ex was a darker skinned man. Some said he was half-Indian and half-white, others said he was half-black and half-white. Who knows? Who should have cared? But they sure did ridicule my siblings for being a tad darker, having kinky hair, and not looking the pearly cracker white like the other grandkids. (I prefer croutons. They have flavor!)

Many were racist and used the "n" word freely with disgust in their voices. I hated it when I heard anyone call them names, it made me sad and hurt my feelings as a little girl. Even so, I could never tell anyone I didn't like it, especially when Virgie would say it. I could never tell her as I was afraid of what she might do to me for speaking out. Silently I held it inside as the bricks began stacking, and my hate mortared them into a wall, blocking my heart from the daily life I was living.

Virgie and Chelcie were close when they were kids. As I was told, when Virgie was little, she had been struck with rheumatic fever, and my mother, her big sister Chelcie, took care of her through it. My mother had to drop out of school to care for Virgie, so she never learned to read or write over a third-grade level. Both Chelcie and Virgie were deprived of schooling. Chelcie had to quit in third grade and Virgie in first. I wonder, had they been adequately schooled, would they have been the way they were? I think not. Educate people. Educate!

During the fever sickness, Virgie lost either all or most of her hearing in both ears. I do not know the level of what she could or couldn't hear, but she did wear hearing aids in both ears all the time. While I was growing up, even though Virgie complained about not being able to hear, if someone let a fart in the room down the hallway, she heard it. There were mirrors set up in the house so she could see in the living room and watch people trying to read their lips, often accusing them of talking about her because she couldn't hear. Virgie trusted no one. She claimed she was disabled and couldn't work due to her hearing loss, and she got free money, Welfare all her life because of it. What a crock of shit! Although uneducated, she figured out how to get free money, food, and medical care. It was a top priority. This was life, and the mentality was, the government owes me, and goddammit, I'm going to get mine!

No wonder the disability benefits for our veterans and people who have paid all their lives are horrible! Because of people like her. Virgie never worked a real job, nor did many of her siblings. A few worked in the traveling carnival my uncle Buck owned for cash, but it was always cash and, the wife collected welfare too. A couple of aunts had actual jobs for a portion of time.

It was no wonder so many folks moved to Michigan in the 50s they got free welfare, food stamps, and medical care. I blame the damn government for making it too easy for people to sit on their ass and get free shit. Don't get me wrong, when a person needs some extra help, they should get it without the caseworkers, making them feel like losers. I'm talking about the people who use welfare as a lifestyle, not a temporary resource, which is entirely different. I do not begrudge anyone who needs a little help here and there, I needed help more than once.

Anyway, the conception stories were rampant throughout the family. In addition to the family expecting my mom to accommodate them at Granny's house, my mom began visiting Virgie and helping her with her household chores. Virgie was married to Ardy then, and they had three children, Denise, Donny, and Patricia, who died at three days old. When my mother was done working at their house, Ardy would give my biological mom a ride home to grannies.

As told to me by my Aunt Opal, my dad did have his way with my mother, but the family turned a blind eye and went against my mother even though she was taken advantage of. It's something that "just happens in the '60s," and men will be men," she said.

I've no idea what happened (obviously, I was just a little squirt then) but I have my suspicions. No matter how it transpired, sex took place, and nine months later, I showed up. That is when all hell broke loose.

Aunt Opal said their side of the family turned against my biological mom after I was born. They were upset because Virgie was distraught. The family always petted Virgie and let her have her way due to her hearing loss, which resulted in Virgie becoming a very mean and overruling angry person. Whenever she went somewhere it was always a drama mess. She brought tragedy all the time.

Aunt Opal also confirmed that Chelcie (bio mom) was forced to give me up to Virgie and Ardy. Apparently, the family pressured my mom so much, that she felt she had no other choice than to give me up. I was told there were threats made against my mom and siblings. Others I've talked to about this claim the family made threats of calling the welfare people and having her kids taken away because she was still married to Sam and that she was unfit to have an illegitimate child. It wasn't what women did back in 1963, they proclaimed she disgraced the family by having me.

Aunt Opal claimed that Granny threatened to literally burn my mom, her own daughter, and kids if she didn't make this right and "give that baby to Virgie and Ardy to raise." Virgie admitted to Aunt Opal that she didn't want me, but she didn't want her sister to have me either because she felt it would make her "too happy."

There were many stories from different family members. During one of those conversations when I was older, my mom disclosed that, when the news was out that she was pregnant, Ardy came to her and told her he knew of a doctor in Detroit that could help get rid of the baby. She said he explained that if she went to him, everyone's lives would be back to normal, and no one would need to know. Then there would be nothing to worry about. She "aborted" that "advice."

I am not sure all this is 100% accurate, but there is an exceedingly high probability it is. During Aunt Opal's long talk with me before she passed, she told me many things about this time, all of which I believe because I have no reason to think otherwise. Aunt Opal was not like most of her family. Even though she was around the family, she was different in an honest good-hearted way. Auntie said it like it was. She broke the mold she was born into and moved on. So, when she told me the family pushed my mother to an ungodly limit about giving me up and, those threats were made, I believed her.

At six months old, I was legally adopted by my then-aunt, Virgie, and biological father/then-uncle, Ardy. At that point, my birth mother legally became my aunt. My biological aunt became my adopted mother, and my biological father/uncle legally became my adopted dad. My siblings became my cousins, and my cousins became my siblings. Do you think you're confused? Try being me and explaining that shit storm to your kids!

In the legal system, I now have two siblings and eight cousins. With the flick of a pen, my family just flipped, and my life spun out of normalcy.

WHEN I WAS ABOUT four or five, my sister Denise, about 14 or 15 years old, got married to a man named Johnny from Kentucky.

Johnny played the guitar and sang to me as he bounced me on his knee. He called me his little darling or his little girlfriend, and I enjoyed the attention. He was cute, and I suppose I had a little-girl crush. I thought I loved him.

We were in Kentucky at Barry's parents' house up the mountain and down in the holler. They lived between two huge mountains, you could see mountains everywhere you looked, which was scary back then to a little girl. I used to look at the massive mounds of trees as if they were giant monsters who could come to life at any given moment, snatch me up, and crunch me like a chocolate bar. The mountains were just so big and overwhelming to me at that age.

The house was a small, white, wood-sided home that sat upon a hilltop. They had a big front porch with chairs and a churn to one side. The inside of their home was tiny, with a small living room, kitchen, and a couple of bedrooms. They had a back door in the kitchen and no bathroom inside.

The outhouse sat down from the house next to the creek that flowed in front. You had to go over a cement bridge to get to their home. At night if we had to go wee-wee or doo-dee, we took someone else with us and a flashlight so we could see. Barry's dad, who I called Papaw, used to tell me there was a big bear down there that'd eat me if I messed around, so I better hurry right back. I hated going to that outhouse to potty no matter when.

The latrine itself was an old brown shack made of wood. When you opened the creaky door, you'd see all the spiders in the corners and dirt on the bench-like seats. It had two open holes in a long sort of wooden stool with a strong smell of piss mixed with rose-smelling turds, and then there was the toilet paper, a big thick catalog sitting between the two holes. I was told to pee or poop in the pits and use the pages to wipe. It was disgusting!

I always looked down the shitholes, watching the creek running under it, looking for snakes. I was told a snake might crawl up and come out the poop hole and bite my ass, so I'd get on top of the wooden seat, stand up above my hole of choice, and squat down to do my thing. I wanted to make sure I could see if something was coming up to bite my booty. Then I figured I could run and get away. I'm not sure how that would have worked out, but my intentions were good.

And, as I think about my tiny little self squatting down in that old smelly, intimidating outhouse, I must laugh at the picture in my head. No wonder I need therapy!

Nonetheless, I recall being down at Mamaw and Papaw's house when my sister got married. Then we all went back to Michigan.

ONCE, I WAS GIVEN A PUPPY, and it was so cute. That little furball was white with brown spots and a pink spot on her nose, so, I called her "Pink Nose." I had to keep her tied up inside an old shed out back. I was given a bowl of water and a slice of bread to give her each day.

I only had her for about four or five days, and I am sure she was starving. She was starving for not just food but some love too. Unfortunately, I was never allowed to play with her, clean the shed, or anything. I had to leave her tied up and give her the food (if that is what you call it), then shut the shed in the hot heat of the summer and be done. Mommy said, "that's a no-count old dog!"

One day I got home from school, and my puppy was gone. Of course, I cried, I was five. I asked Granny where my puppy was. She was a well-built woman, not fat but solidly framed, with short curly red hair, big knobby knees, and flabby upper arms. She always wore dresses, no panties, and chain-smoked. She stood there, puffing her cigarette, smirking, and said, "It ran off down the road, and a car hit and killed it." Then smiled at me as if she enjoyed my horrified look.

I asked where Pink Nose was and if she was still on the road. Granny looked gave me her smart-ass bitch smirk and told me, "Barry threw it in the trash and took it to the dump." Then she laughed and back to her house, puffing her cancer stick all the way. I cried my eyes out over my puppy that was dead and thrown away in the trash. I hated Granny for telling me that. I hated Barry for throwing my puppy in the trash.

Not too long after this incident, Granny, Virgie, Barry, Donny, and I went over to some relative's house in Burlington, and as usual we stayed outside and play with all the little half-dressed dirty hillbilly kids running around with no shoes on. Sort of like us. Hell, exactly like us.

That's when I noticed a dog chained to a tree and barking like crazy. I went over to it, and it was Pink Nose! I couldn't believe my eyes. *Is it really my puppy?* I yelled at Donny, and he ran over seen her too, then he told me, that granny, and mommy had given it away because I didn't take care of it.

I ran inside shouting even though I knew I'd get it. *"Mommy! Mommy! My dog Pink Nose is out there chained on a tree, and I'm taking her home!"*

Despite going in with a brass attitude about my puppy, I wasn't taking her home.

Virgie yelled at me, "I told you's ta stay out-side little girl! Now, you's better gets out that door before I's gives you's something ta run you's mouth about. Do you's hears me?"

Granny looked at me with her shitty smirking half-grin/half-laugh and said, "You don't need that ole dog. You ain't smart enough to take care of it, anyway, now get on outta here!"

Donny grabbed my arm and tugged, and out we went. There I stood, letting the silent tears roll off my dirty little face, down onto my grimy t-shirt, and Donny telling me to *shhh*. We went to the little patch of dirt by my dog and sat petting her until we had to leave. Donny held my hand to the car. We climbed into the backseat, looked out the window at Pink Nose, and we said nothing more about it ever again. We knew better than to speak of that, "old no count dog."

Shortly after that, we moved to Albion, and I was in Kindergarten at Crowell Elementary. We lived on Maple Street in a big blue house. I met a neighbor girl, we became friends until I stole her coloring book and colored all the Barbies in it, then gave it back. I had never had a coloring book or crayons, and she did so I wanted it. I had watched Barry and Virgie take other people's things and then sell them to different people, so I figured I could take the coloring book. You learn what you live, you do indeed!

I am glad I stole that coloring book. Life lessons come in a variety of ways and from a mix of many people. If we just pay attention to them as they come, we'll learn a lot. I learned. Thank God that I did.

When I went to return the book, her mom answered. I handed her the coloring book and told her I took it and colored all the Barbies but was giving it back now. I didn't want it anymore, the crayons too.

I recall my friend's mom standing there, glaring at me. Then, she opened the door and said, "Where did you learn to steal from, young lady?"

So, I shared with her that day that "my stepdad Barry and my mommy do it to other people, and so do I." She stood at her door, listening with a look of unbelief on her face. I'll never forget the kindest yet harshest words I will hold forever in my heart and mind.

She laid into me. She bawled me out. She told me how mean and wrong it was to take things that do not belong to you. She explained that other people work hard for the things they have, and thieves rob and take belongings that people worked hard to earn. She said my parents were common thieves, and so was I. The truth was, she was right. She shamed me and made me feel so bad that I never wanted to steal again.

She said she wouldn't snitch to my parents if I promised never to steal again. I promised, and we shook hands. She also told me her daughter could never play with me anymore. So, my friendship with my neighbor seemed to be a short one, but on the bright side, I got a life lesson I needed. My thievery days were behind me, at least for a while.

Losing her as a friend was okay because we moved again, and I had to switch to the kindergarten at Harrington Elementary. Alex (yes, my, Alex) was in my room. Our teacher, Mrs. Davis, played the piano and sang pretty. And she let us sit in the alphabet circle on the letter that began with our name. Funny how life goes. I had no idea that I was sitting in that circle with my future husband singing the Farmer and the Dell.

DURING THE SUMMER, when I was about five years old, Donny and I were sent to Barry's relatives in Detroit. That was a good summer.

Often in the summertime, Virgie and Barry would work with my Uncle Buck on the road with his carnival. Uncle Buck was Virgie's— and Chelcie's— younger brother who owned a small traveling fair. Uncle Buck was a tall, thin, black-haired, clean-shaven man who drank a fifth of Black Velvet every day and called his workers "worthless SOB's, fucking pricks, and scuzzy pukes." He had a not-so-good way with his words, but he was always kind to me growing up until I turned 10, then he turned into a dick.

It was great having an uncle who had his own carnival. Me and a few cousins would run wild down the midway when Uncle Buck was in town. We all got to ride the rides for free, eat junk food, and play tent games. We were a wild bunch of hillbilly kids running free like we were jacked up on catnip. Great times!

Almost every summer, both Virgie and Barry would travel to work the carnival. Sometimes it was a few weeks and other times like this summer, they both went for a long carnival gig, so they sent us to Detroit to stay with Barry's sister, Jinan, and her husband, Troy, they had three kids, Shannon, Troy Jr, and Katie Lynn, she was one year younger than me.

Every afternoon, The Monkey's T.V. show would come on. Katie Lynn and I would rush to the T.V., and whoever got there first got to be married to Davie Jones for the duration of the show. The other had to pick Mike, Mickey, or Peter to wed. I never got to marry Davie all summer long because Katie Lynn would cry and act out if she didn't get her way, so I'd give in because I felt sorry for her. And I thought if I didn't, I might get the belt or switch when Virgie returned. Even though it was just kid stuff, which was how I viewed everything. But, on the bright side, I got to marry all three of the other Monkeys all summer long.

I liked staying with them until about the second week of being there, at which time I discovered that Jinan had an issue where she'd get mad and start throwing things while yelling and screaming. The first time this happened, Shannon rushed over to Donny, and I and all of us kids went into her room and sat quietly in a circle on the floor. She told us that her mom did this sometimes, and we all must stay out of her way and be very quiet until she calms down.

Shannon was accurate. Jinan would calm down after a little while. But it happened often, and when it did, we would all run into Shannon's room and sit whispering and listening to her throw her fits. Most of the time, she'd break things and throw stuff at Troy like Virgie did to Barry. There was a lot of cussing and yelling, mostly from Jinan, and we would hear Troy trying to calm her down with sweet talk.

Once during our stay, we were playing yard darts in the backyard. I threw one, and it hit Donny in the ear and made him bleed. I giggled, and the only thing that happened to me was I couldn't play with the darts anymore. I didn't get spanked, smacked, thrown in a closet, nothing. I was shocked that they didn't punish me at all for making Donny's ear bleed. I did tell him I was sorry and that I didn't mean to. Jinan told me it was okay, accidents happen, and to be more careful with things, that's all.

It was nice not having to worry about getting in trouble, being called names, and hit, choked, or something worse, over an accident. I felt like I could live with them forever, even with Auntie Jinan freaking out sometimes. It was better than what was at my house.

Heading back home after a long summer of fun and relaxation, I was sad to go and wished I could stay and go to school with Shannon, but Barry and mommy came and took us home.

I'M NOT EXACTLY SURE when this happened, but mommy, and Ardy, my biological dad/uncle, divorced when I was about two years old, after which my mother married Barry. Some years later (not many), my dad, Ardy married Barry's ex-wife, Ilene. *They switched spouses.* How messed up is that? Yeah, that's all I got to say about that.

I don't recall visiting their house much, but once when I was visiting my dad and Ilene, Teresa (Barry and Ilene's youngest daughter) and I were playing with her dolls, and we overheard my dad and Ilene having sex. We had no clue what was going on. We just heard Ilene moaning and calling out my dad's name, so we snuck down the hall and peeked in their door and saw my dad on top of Ilene with her legs up in the air.

We giggled while running back to our room, got under our sheet tent, and took our dollies, and played out what we had just witnessed. I was giggling and saying, "Oh, Ardy! Oh, Ardy!" and Teresa was grunting. We thought it was the funniest thing ever to mock them. Isn't that what kids do? Hell yes!

Well, my dad heard us and rushed into the bedroom. He pulled me out from under the tent, yanked my pants down, and spanked my ass. Teresa didn't get anything. Ilene told my dad not to touch Teresa, so he didn't. It was like that a lot when Teresa and Jeffrey visited us at Virgie's house too. They never got yelled at or in trouble, but I'd get a spanking for all of us. If there was a spanking to get, I took one for the team, always. It happened with them, and it happened with Donny.

Speaking of Donny, he was a decent big brother when we were little. Many times, when our mother, Virgie, and Barry would begin fighting, he would come and find me, and we'd go hide in a closet together. We'd just sit in the closet, and he would say, "Shhh, they will stop soon, then we can go out." When we lived next door to Granny, we hid under the trailer a couple of times. They had some aluminum around the bottom, but many pieces were missing so, we had a way to slip under and disappear, and we did—plenty of times. We also had a little shed out back (the one I kept Pink Nose in) and sometimes we'd hide inside that too. Sometimes he'd have crackers for us to eat while we waited as it was often an awfully long time until they stopped fighting. A couple times we fell asleep in our hiding spot.

He didn't really pick on me much when I was little. He was more of a protector to me. Until we got older or until he lived what he learned.

School had started, and I was so excited because it became my escape from the real world. It was great. But, as soon as I walked through the door at home, all hell broke loose. I can't begin to count the days I'd walk into yelling, screaming, and fighting between Virgie and Barry. Once, I got in the line of fire and caught a broken beer bottle across my face. I still sport the scar, just with makeup nowadays. Thank God, it's not deep or very noticeable, but I know how it got there, and I am reminded every time I look into the mirror.

Donny picked me up every day in my classroom. We walked home together from school each day and back again the next. One day as we were starting to walk home, I told him I had to pee and begged him to let me use the bathroom before we left. He was so worried we'd be late, that he told me to hold it because we had to hurry and get home before we got in trouble.

Donny never got in trouble like I did, so he wouldn't have been risking much if he had let me pee. He had his misfortunes, but it was different for him. He was Virgie's kid. I was the one who ruined her life, the bastard. He knew it too, and he would snicker and giggle many times when I'd get a lashing. Sometimes he would point at me, mocking and chuckling as I'd sit down and cry. I hated him for that. Donny was mean like that, but, when we were alone, he was nice to me. It was confusing for me. I bet it was somewhat confusing to him as well. I've often wondered if he was mean because he felt he had to be to keep his mom's love. Kids sometimes think that way.

We walked to and from school about six or seven blocks, and one day, and I had to pee so bad that I ended up wetting my panties. Down my legs, it went. I stopped and cried, on the sidewalk as I knew what I was facing for peeing in my panties. This behavior wasn't allowed. I knew I was in trouble when mommy finds out.

Donny told me to run upstairs, hide my dirty, wet panties under the bathtub, and mom would never know. I honestly think Donny was trying to help me from getting a spanking, as I said, he was nice when we were alone. It was when he was with our mother, that he was cruel and did and said callous things to me.

Well, she found the wet panties, and I got whipped with a switch, a punishment often consisting of picking a branch from a tree outback.

A few days after the pee incident, Donny and I were outside playing in the yard late into the evening. He went inside, then came out with a chocolate bar. Well, I wanted some, of course, so I begged him for half. Finally, he gave me the entire candy bar. It had tiny little bits I could break off and eat one at a time. It was a giant candy bar, and I gobbled it up like a kid who'd never had chocolate before.

Donny laughed and laughed the whole time I ate that chocolate bar. I didn't care. I was happy to get a candy bar and pleased as pie that he gave it all to me. He never did that before, but he did today, and I was so excited.

The following day, I woke up to intense pain, soiled sheets, and our mother washing the wall beside my bed. It smelled awful, and my legs and butt were hot. My stomach hurt so bad I began crying and holding it. Then suddenly, I couldn't help it, and I just started shitting, right there in the bed. It was uncontrollable. The pain was almost worse than the switch spankings. All I knew was that I was hurting, and the poop wouldn't stop coming out of my butt. Then it turned to blood, it ached something awful.

Donny and Denise were both laughing while this was going on. I was a sobbing, scared, nervous little five-year-old child. That fucknut could have killed me with as much Ex-Lax as he gave me. I shit uncontrollably for two days. I think I shit enough for twenty people that day, and my abdomen hurt so bad that I never wanted to eat another chocolate bar again. No wonder I have bowel issues today, that dick!

Donny never got in trouble for giving me an entire bar of ex-lax, but after I felt better, I got the switch for shitting in the bed and smearing it on the walls. A story they still laugh about today and try to embarrass me with.

ALBION HAD FIVE ELEMENTARY SCHOOLS, one middle school, and one high school. Because we moved so much in my younger years, I attended three out of five elementary schools, Crowell, Dalrymple, and Harrington Elementary. Mostly it was short-lived, like a few weeks or a couple of months at a time, which was a lot of change. While we lived on Mechanic Street, I went to Dalrymple elementary. I met a new friend, Teresa. She lived up the street, and we became good friends for a short while. I liked playing at her house because that got me away from all the bickering and feuding at mine. I'm sure her parents knew about my home life, as the cops often came. Eventually, she couldn't come down to my house anymore to play. I could, however, still go to her home, so I did when I could. Nonetheless, we walked to school every morning for as long as I lived there, which again wasn't long.

The school was big and scary to me. The reason it scared me was that it was a predominantly black school. Barry and Virgie had made it very clear to me that black people were "niggers and can't be trusted." They "killed white people and took white kids." Barry told me—of course, when he was drunk—the "nigger men would take little white girls, kill them, and eat them." Well, I didn't want to be killed and eaten, and this "knowledge" frightened me to play with black children in my classroom or on the playgrounds. I feared their dad's killing and eating me.

Who tells their kids shit like this? What a fucking nut job!

Once, Teresa asked me why I didn't want to teeter-totter with her and another little girl who happened to be black. I was scared to say it, but eventually, I told her. She said that wasn't true, and no one ever hurt her. Then Teresa explained it all to the little black girl. She also told me that it wasn't right. She told me how nice her daddy and mommy were and that her older siblings went to this school, and they would protect me if I needed it. We all met after school on the playground, and they walked Teresa, and me, home. They were not scary at all, and they were so sympathetic to me. I liked them, even if they were black. Quickly, their color meant nothing to me anymore, and we were just friends.

Well, one beautiful sunny afternoon as we walked home from school, laughing and teasing each other, Virgie caught us walking together.

Oh shit.

She rushed off the porch to the sidewalk, grabbed me by the hair of my head, and led me inside while yelling and screaming profanities at my new friends. Virgie called them niggers, told them to get away from her house, and never come back. Then, she whooped my ass! My ass, my legs, and my back, she lit me the fuck up! I hurt for days after that walk home.

I was never allowed to walk with them again because they were black. The next day, I saw my friends on the playground, and the two girls came up to me and asked me how I was and told me they were sorry that I got in trouble. The oldest girl looked at my back and said she would tell the principal, Mrs. BeeBee, and let her know what my mother did to me. I begged her not to. I told her if anyone found out, I'd get it again. My back must have had marks from the tree switch. I don't know if she ever told anyone, but she hugged me and said sorry.

I loved my new friends. They were so good to me. There was nothing scary about their color because color was unimportant to me. I began seeing black people differently and I'm glad I did. I learned right then that the "n" word was terrible, and it wasn't called for at all.

Even though I couldn't have my black friends come over and play, I had many colored friends that year and in the years after. I never talked about my new friends or invited them over. I knew better.

IT SEEMED TO ME that mommy was always mad about something. She often ranted, raved, screamed, and acted out about how someone did *something* to her. "Someone" seemed to be mean to her regularly, say something to her, or do something in some way that set her off. No matter if the sun shone or the rain fell, someone did something to her, and they did it on purpose.

I think she misinterpreted almost everything. Someone could smile at her, and she would say something like, "Hmmm, did you's see the way she smirked at me? What's she's thinkin'? Did you's see her glaring at me? I'll bet she knows Barry and wants him." It often boiled down to her being jealous of Barry and accusing him of being with other women when he was out getting drunk and stealing shit with some of Virgie's brothers or his buddies whenever he was not home.

During their marriage, I witnessed many nights of Barry and his friends and Virgie's brothers bringing stolen items into the house to hide what they had pilfered. It happened all the time, not unusual. I knew it was a bad thing to do, and I was always told I had better not say anything, or else I'd get her fist down my throat. So, I kept silent.

One day, they had stolen a complete set of exquisite dishes, white with red roses. The collection consisted of plates, bowls, cups, and serving bowls. My biological mom, Aunt Chelcie, came over, looked at them, and tried to buy them, but Barry wanted more money than she was willing to pay. That started an argument which led to Aunt Chelcie threatening to turn him into the police.

Virgie blamed me for the entire incident. She was upset because I began to cry while Aunt Chelcie and Barry fought loudly. He threatened to shoot her, which is when I started crying because I didn't want him to kill her. I was a six-year-old child listening to two adults fighting, and it scared the fuck out of me. Nonetheless, I should have known better than to make a spectacle of Virgie, which is what she said I did. I made her look bad because I cried. Once again, I endured name-calling and a bare ass spanking with a switch, ending with hot and hurting body parts.

Aunt Chelcie did end up calling the police. Before the cops got to our house, Barry had moved the dishes to another person's home. The guy he called—a tall, darker-skinned man with a five o'clock shadow, curly black hair, greasy, dirty jeans who smelled like whiskey—came, they talked, loaded up the set, and he left.

I was pulled into the back room and instructed to tell the cops that Chelcie had come to our house with a gun, screaming she was going to kill us all. My mother explained that if I didn't say it, she'd kill every one of them that was at Aunt Chelcie's house, "the whole black bunch of them mud-der fuk-ner-ing niggers."

Once again, to save Chelcie and her family, I told the cops what I was supposed to say. It made me feel sick.

Even though we moved around a lot, our primary home was on Mulberry Street, and my central school was Harrington. I loved school. I treasured it for many reasons, library time, art, recess, lunch, gym, math, social studies.... normal people. In addition to being an escape from home, I loved school because I appreciated the lessons, I have learned which helped shape who I am today.

My second-grade teacher, Miss. Martin, who was tall, and always wore cool clothes and was so beautiful, taught me a valuable lesson. Although I didn't do anything wrong, I'm glad it happened and that I learned from it.

Once during a spelling test, she thought she caught me cheating, but it wasn't me, although I was trying to help my friend Tina cheat. The teacher always gave us the words but also gave us the test in the same order, so all one had to do was study the direction the words were in, and the spelling of the words and one could get 100% or, preferably, a smiley face or a big star.

Tina was having trouble with the one word spelled three ways, to, too, and two. She wrote them on a small piece of paper and had it tucked under her leg. When she moved during the spelling test, the cheat sheet fell on the floor right next to my desk. Being a good friend, I picked it up, and as I started handing it back to her, the teacher looked up and saw me with the cheat sheet in my hand. She thought (and by all rights) it was mine.

Miss. Martin was thoroughly pissed off. She tore up my spelling test and lectured me on cheating, stealing, lying, and doing the right thing right in front of the entire classroom, which embarrassed me even more. You see, I was learning from Barry and Virgie to lie, cheat, and steal at a young age. Even though I wasn't cheating at that moment

I was learning to be like them. I was going to give that little piece of paper back to her so she could continue to cheat because I thought it was okay.

Nonetheless, with the harsh life lesson through her humiliating and scolding, I realized that regular people do not lie, cheat, and steal. In that incident, she taught me not to do those things and to be a decent and honest person. I love her for that and her cool clothes.

I also loved my third-grade teacher, Mrs. Fierke. She was another beautiful person in the world, and she truly cared.

She hugged us in the mornings and would give a goodbye hug to any child that wanted one. I always took one. And she could play the piano and sing. I can still hear her singing and pounding that old piano, she taught us in French and in English.

Frère Jacques, Frère Jacques,

Dormez vous? Dormez vous?

Sonnez les matines, Sonnez les matines,

Din, din, don! Din, din, don!

And in English, we'd sing,

Are you sleeping, are you sleeping?

Brother John? Brother John?

Morning bells are ringing, Morning bells are ringing,

Ding ding dong, Ding ding dong

Once, around Christmas time, she gave the class an assignment, we had to write a Christmas poem and submit it to our school newspaper. They were picking a first, second, and third-place winner out of the entire school, and the winner would get their poem published in the school newspaper.

I wasn't about to do this ridiculous assignment, and I had no trouble letting her know I wasn't going to do it. So, after I finished drafting that poem in the hallway (she sent me out there so I could have a moment to gather my thoughts), I went back to the classroom and sheepishly rejoined the rest of my class.

In the mornings, everyone sat listening to the PA announcements for the day. Our principal would mention birthdays and what we were having for lunch and other important things. About a week later—I had completely forgotten about the stupid poem—he announced the winners, third place, second, and then he said very slowly, "...and now, the first-place winner of the Christmas poetry contest is... (drum roll) ...Peggy in Mrs. Fierke's room!"

Wow, I won something! I was important! Mrs. Fierke called me up to the front of the classroom and asked me, "What would you like to be when you grow up, Peggy?"

"I think I'd like to be an Author-or and write books."

She laughed, corrected my language, then commenced, "Peggy, I believe in you, and I believe you can do anything you set your mind to do, young lady."

With the help of people such as my second and third-grade teachers who loved me with daily hugs and smiles and life lessons on honesty, I sit here writing my memoir. I love you both! You'll never know how much those hugs and your smiles and kind words meant to this little girl. I still hold your hugs, laughter, and kindness close to my heart. You brightened my world, if only for a few hours a day.

SOMEWHERE IN THIS ERA, Denise was still married to Johnny, and they lived in a trailer close to, or in, Albion or Homer, I'm not sure which. I recall that Denise and I were riding around in her GTO (the coolest car ever) listening to music, making me feel way older than eight. When we had stopped at a red light, Denise spotted Johnny, who was running up to the car. She yelled for me to lock the door, but I couldn't do it fast enough, and he jumped in on my side.

He demanded that Denise drive back to their trailer in a crazed state. When we got there, we all went inside, where he sat down in a chair, grabbed me, and stuck a loaded gun to my head. I recall him telling Denise to sit down, and she began to cry and beg him not to kill me.

I can still picture the look of horror on her face. She was pregnant and being tortured. Johnny held me with one hand around my throat and the other hand on his pistol pressed against my head. He screamed at Denise, telling her that he was going to blow my "fucking brains all over the place."

I was a little girl in the wrong place at the wrong time. Johnny was drunk. Angry. In a rage. Out of control. He used what he had at hand to get to my sister, and I was at hand. Easy to grab. Easy to control. Easy to maneuver.

I sat very still, not speaking, breathing, or anything. I was terrified. Freaked out. And worried I was going to be shot. I didn't budge.

Still pressing his pistol against my head, he held me by a fistful of hair and laughed while yelling at my sister. It seemed like an eternity while he shouted, and my sister cried and begged him to let me go.

Eventually, they came to a truce, and he moved the gun from my head while shoving me to the floor, telling me to sit still. I did as I was told.

Soon enough he fell asleep, and Denise and I slipped out the door and drove to mommy's house in silence.

Some days after this happened, my dad was picking me up for the weekend. Right when I got in the backseat, he began criticizing me. "What are you, slow or somethin'? You need to listen to what people say and do as you're told, you hear me? Stop playin' around," he scolded. "Grow up and pay attention!"

He made sure I knew this was all my fault. He repeated how worried he was for Denise and his unborn grandchild, but not once did he show concern for me. Not once did he ask me if I was okay. Not once did he ask about me. Nope, not once. I was a little girl being held captive by a drunk who had a loaded gun to my head, and my own dad showed no concern for how I was, not a drop of concern, nothing!

AFTER SECOND GRADE was over, we had company one summer afternoon. I remember the day like it was yesterday. It was sunny and beautiful, and I was in the front yard. My cousins were gone, and it was just me, hanging out when a man came to visit our house. My mother said he was my cousin and to say hello, so I did. He had brought a dog with him and asked me if I would watch him while he went inside and visited with my mother. Of course, I said yes. Watching his dog was the most exciting, good thing that had happened to me in a while.

She was a mini collie. So beautiful. She looked like the real Lassie on T.V., but smaller. I loved her immediately, and I think she loved me. Not long after he began his visit, he came out and asked me if I'd like to keep the dog. Of course, I said yes. Mommy was standing there, and I looked as cute as I could manage to look and asked if I could have her.

She nodded yes then said, "Yous better take care of it, or I's will gives it aways."

I was beyond thrilled and told her I promised to take the best care of her and announced I would be calling her Lassie like the one on T.V. The man laughed and drove away.

After playing with Lassie for about an hour in the front yard, mommy came out and told me to get in the car and bring the dog. I did. I also knew something was up. It was never just simple living with her. There was always something about to go down.

As we drove out of town towards Granny's, I figured we were going to visit. I was wrong. As we rounded a corner, there was a big white farmhouse with a white picket fence and a substantial red barn. She stopped and screamed at me, "Throw that dog out the window!"

I sat there blank-faced, dumbfounded, doing nothing. I felt sick to my stomach. Mommy shouted it again, and this time she added her

71

common threats. "I's stick my fist down you's throat if you's don't, little girl! Do you's hears me?"

The worst feeling in the world was rolling down that fucking window and picking up my new dog only to throw her out the window, but that is precisely what I did. *I threw my dog out the window.*

She drove away, screaming and yelling at me about being too stupid to know how to take care of a dog. She made sure I knew it was my fault that she had to make me get rid of that ole dog. She told me to dry up my face, or she'd pull over and put her fist down my throat.

I stopped crying, dried up my face, and never said another word about it to anyone. Inside I felt dead and wished I could have jumped out that window and gone to the big farmhouse with my Lassie. Maybe the people who lived there would have taken both of us in and cared for us forever? Mommy said they were rich and could afford a dog, so perhaps they could provide for a kid too...I wished.

All the way to Granny's, I wanted to throw up but knew better. So, I tucked that incident inside and filed it under the folder in my head labeled, "Fucked Up Shit."

IN THIRD GRADE, I got my first-ever birthday party. I was so excited. Having a birthday party was the icing on the chocolate cake for me (pun intended)!

Barry's son, Jeffery, had a birthday six days before mine. Jeff was a few years younger than me, but we were close because we saw each other a lot growing up. In addition to my cousins who were coming, my mother gave me permission to invite one friend from school. She told me I'd have a big cake and games and people would bring me gifts. I was *so* excited.

Things were starting to turn around. I just knew it.

I told my best friend, Sarah, about my party. Sarah was my height and size with long brownish hair and big brown eyes. Her smile was so huge you could see it all the way across the classroom, she was the nicest girl in my grade. Her contagious giggle was like a chipmunk laugh, we laughed a lot at school. When I asked her if she could come, she told me I needed to give her an invitation. So, I crafted one out of a piece of paper at school. I drew a flower on it with a happy sunshine face. I folded it up and everything.

Sarah's mother went to my house one afternoon to see if the invitation was real or made up by little girls. It was a legitimate thing to do. However, when Sarah told me her mom was going to my house that day to talk to my mom, I instantly became worried that my mother would be angry about her visit, and it would be my fault. I was always expecting to get in trouble the second I stepped through the door, no matter what was going on, but this was a new level of concern.

When I arrived home after school that day, my suspicions were correct. My mother called me into the kitchen, sat me down in a chair, and asked why "that little girl's mom" thought I was a liar. She shook her finger in my face, and her voice began to escalate. She scolded me for a couple of hours, all because a mom checked about a party. Nice. Instead of getting the switch, I was sent to my room with no supper. She told me I had "made that woman come all the way across town" because she thought I was lying about the party and had to check if it was real or not. It was all my fault.

The following day, I was instructed to tell "that little girl" she couldn't come to my party. When I asked why I was smacked across the face and told to stop being stupid and stop asking questions. It wasn't my business, and I just needed to do as I was told. And, furthermore, if I didn't do as I was told, I could go out back and get a switch so she could teach me a lesson.

When I got to school, I was so sad and worried that Sarah wouldn't want to be friends with me. I threw up as soon as I entered the classroom and was sent back to the office, where my mother was quickly called to come and get me. This was a Friday, and my party was scheduled for the next day at noon.

I never had the chance to tell my friend she couldn't come.

I remember that beautiful, sunny day so well. The streets were quiet, and the neighbor to our right was mowing his lawn. Virgie invited Aunt Chelcie and Uncle Claude since it was, after all, my first party *ever*. What an exciting day! What a perfect day! It was really happening. I allowed myself to be swept away for a minute with the excitement.

Aunt Chelcie had purchased a big cake and ice cream. There were gifts on a table with balloons taped to the plastic tablecloth. I was wearing my best shorts, a tee-shirt, and flip-flops. I'm sure I looked good for a welfare kid who was often dirty and usually wore hand-me-downs and second-hand clothing.

Let me clarify that I am grateful that I had clothing and a house to sleep in. And there is nothing wrong with resale stores and hand-me-downs. I still shop at many consignment stores and always will. But as a child, my typical wardrobe was not from the type of resale shopping I do now. I was usually dirty and in soiled clothes—but that day, I was clean and felt like a princess.

Sarah and her mom showed up promptly at noon. I knew she wasn't supposed to be there, which made me nervous, but I tried to act normal. As she handed me a neatly wrapped gift, Sarah stated that her mom would be back in an hour and a half to get her. My heart pounded harder. The gift was in hot pink wrapping paper, a large, shiny deep-purple bow in the middle, and a name tag that read, *To Peggy, From Sarah.* I had never received a gift this wonderful before. I was in awe. It was mine, and it was the coolest thing ever, except that I was about to be in some serious trouble.

As I took the gift from Sarah, my mother glared at me with a dirty look, the look I knew all too well. She then pointed and told me to "set the gift over there with the others and get outside." We scampered out the door, and I felt slightly relieved, like I had dodged a bullet. I also felt a sinking feeling in my stomach. Although I was glad that the typical yelling, cussing, and fighting hadn't followed my mother's dirty look, I wondered when it would happen because it always did, without fail.

I quickly dismissed what had just transpired. Sarah and I walked around the block and talked like we knew something at age eight. I loved that day, being with my friend and having things go well. I was so excited, and Sarah was excited for me too. I told her this was my first-ever party, she said she has one every year for her birthday. I privately wondered what that would be like.

After our short walk, we were called inside to have cake. Sarah, Jeffery, Teresa, my cousins, and I rushed through the door, ready for our sugar buzz.

As we stood behind the coffee table waiting for the cake, Aunt Chelcie and Uncle Claude began singing, *Happy Birthday to you...*

My mother brought the cake in and sat it on the coffee table in front of Jeffery and me. However, as I looked down at the cake to blow out the candles, it read, "Happy Birthday, Jeffery!"

My name wasn't there.

I am sure my happy face immediately changed to the saddest face a kid could have. Mommy scowled at me, telling me to stand back and let Jeffery blow out his candles. Then she instructed us, kids, to sing happy birthday to Jeffery. I stood stunned as everyone else sang.

I felt like crying. *This is* my *party! Where is* my *name?!*

That day, I learned what a broken heart feels like. Even though I had experienced my mother's mean-heartedness consistently for my entire short life, at that moment, I felt it in the depths of my little being. Maybe it was the public humiliation, and perhaps it was the confusion and disappointment in Sarah's face, possibly the lack of anyone speaking up for me, I don't know. I know that day brought a new level of loneliness that I will never forget. I felt so alone and sad. All I wanted was my name on the fucking cake and one happy, goddamn day!

I managed to hold back the tears and silence my emotion. After Jeffery blew out the candles, the cake and ice cream were served, and it was time to open gifts. Thinking that I might have one more present in addition to Sarah's, I managed to have a glimmer of hope that the day wasn't lost. This, too, was short-lived and a blow to the heart.

I was very excited to see which gifts mine were and which were his and especially excited to see what my friend had gotten me. As I stood and clapped my hands together in excitement, waiting for Mommy to hand out gifts, I was told to calm down, or Sarah had to go, and I'd get a whooping. My friend seemed worried and suggested we just sit down. So, we sat and watched Jeffery open every one of the gifts except the one from Sarah.

We both sat quietly on the couch while Jeffery was loud and got to act like a kid. He jumped up and down while clapping his hands and snapping his fingers (I had just taught him how to finger snap). He giggled and threw wrapping paper all over the living room, grabbed his new toys, and out the door he ran with the other kids following, except for Sarah and me, we were still sitting on the couch. I could feel the tears welling up, tingling in my eyes.

Mommy looked over at me and told me to straighten my face out. Aunt Chelcie and Uncle Claude said nothing in my defense, nor did I. She told me I was acting like a baby and to grow up and stop it, or I'd get her fist down my throat.

Sarah was terrified as I am sure in her household words and threats like that were non-existent. She stood up and told me she was going outside to wait for her mom. She had tears in her eyes, and my mother told her to sit down for a minute and stay inside. Then, the taunting with the gift began. My mother scoffed and threatened that I wouldn't get to open it, or even have it if I didn't act right. Confusion consumed me once again as I wasn't sure what I had done. I fear that she'd make Sarah leave and spank me or, worse yet, spank me in front of my best friend.

After she goaded me, she then gave me the gift and told me, in front of Sarah, how stupid and spoiled I was and how I didn't need anything. I had to wait for permission to open the gift. She took her time, making sure Sarah knew I was unworthy of anything, including being her friend and that she shouldn't even play with me.

Sarah sat quietly, looking at me with a sad face. I've no idea what was going on in her mind, but I am betting she was horrified.

When I was finally allowed to open it after all that bullshit, I gleaned. It was a game! Alley-Up. It was mine. I'd never had my own board game or any game for that matter. I didn't have to share it or give it to Jeffery. Sarah and I were ordered to get outside, so we dashed. Sitting on the grass in my front yard, we played, and we managed to get about halfway up the alley when her mom came. She told me thanks, hugged me, and off they went. She seemed excited to see her mom and in a big hurry to leave. Hell, do you blame her? I would have been running for my life, had I been her.

Sarah and I played together at school, but her mom never allowed her to come back to my house again, and I never invited her back. I was embarrassed. My home life made me feel so ashamed of my life. I felt less than my classmates. I became jealous but not in a vindictive way, just wishing I could have a family like them rather than what I had.

Hate began stockpiling inside my heart for a "Mommy," who was never my, "Mommy." With every breath I took, the walls of revulsion grew thicker and taller each day. I hated the life I had. I hated the family I was in, and I hated being alive. Things were becoming more and more clear to me every day. Things such as Mommy hates me and is ashamed of me, but why? What is her reason? What did I do to her? As a kid, it never occurred to me that the reason she hated me was that I'm the child of her sister and her first husband.

What I knew was she was supposed to be my Mommy and love me like she loved Donny and Denise, but she didn't and never would. Recognizing that truth was the beginning of a lifelong battle in trying to just be enough.

WHEN I WAS FIVE, one of my older cousins and brother Donny, both told me that Aunt Chelcie was my real mom, and Virgie was not. On the outside, she was my aunt, but inside my mind and heart, I always knew she was my real mother, so their "confession" confirmed my suspicion. They explained that Virgie was mean and had stolen me from Aunt Chelcie. They said I shouldn't ever tell mommy that I knew, or she'd kill Aunt Chelcie. Thus, at the age, I learned Aunt Chelcie was my mom, and Virgie was my aunt. Talk about one confused little girl. I understood that they switched places but didn't know why. And once again, two more older people told me, "Virgie will **KILL** Aunt Chelcie" if I do the wrong thing.

Ironically, the subject of who my real father was, was never brought up, and I never asked. It was as if I always knew Ardy was my real dad, or maybe I just didn't care enough to question it. He wasn't someone I was close to, and he never seemed to try to show me any compassion. To me he was simply the guy who picked me up when he had to. Since I wasn't receiving the proper nurturing, a child should, I had no clue how any adult should have treated me. It was what it was, and I did my best to roll with whatever came my way. *SURVIVAL!*

Every day, there was a constant worry about whether I would be allowed to see Chelcie, or not. I always wanted to see Aunt Chelcie but knew it was something I had better not ask to do, or I would regret it. Seeing my biological mother was something Mommy had to want, not me. And when I did get to see her, I could never be happy about it, or else she would cut the visit short or not let me go at all. However, sometimes in the summer, I would get to spend a week with her, and I loved every minute of it.

Shortly after I found out the truth, I got to go there for an overnight. Aunt Chelcie was rocking me in her rocker before bed (which she did every time she got the chance, and it was terrific). I looked up at her and, rubbing her beautiful face with my tiny hand, asked, "Are you, my real mommy?"

She began to cry. Squeezing me tight, she said, "Yes, I am your real mother, and I love you with all my heart." She tried to explain to a five-year-old how important it is to keep this secret from Mommy, or else Mommy Virgie would hurt Aunt Chelcie. Once again, more mention of Virgie harming Chelcie. And, once again, I was left with the burden of protecting her, Uncle Claude, and my other siblings. I had to save them all! That was *my* truth.

WHEN I WAS ABOUT seven or eight, mommy Virgie took one of her cousin's little girl, Tabby, and me over to visit Granny. It was a beautiful day. Full sun shining, not too hot, and just right for shorts and flip flops and two dirty-faced little girls to play and have fun.

When we arrived at Granny's, we went inside to say hi, and then we were told to get outside with our nasty little selves and not bother the adults. Off we went, out to the front yard to the big old oak tree. We were playing freeze face tag, where you make a goofy face trying to make the other person laugh, and when they laugh, it's their turn to make you giggle. We made up a lot of games. That's what underprivileged kids did, and it was great for our creativeness.

Tabby always cracked up at me and me at her. We were two little redheads about the same size, but she had much longer hair than I. Her hair went down past her butt, mine went to the top of my butt, but both red-headed, freckled-faced, snot-nosed sweet little hillbilly kids.

Soon enough, Aunt Chelcie and Uncle Claude pulled in. As they got out, we both ran up to them to give hugs and kisses. And right behind them, another of my mother's siblings was pulling into the drive as well. Everyone always went to Granny's house.

Tabby and I continued playing, and soon enough, we heard yelling, screaming, cussing, and threats to kill coming from the house. There were loud crashing noises and lots of roaring going on inside. We held each other's hands and ran to the tree where the bickering was muffled in the wind. The breeze must have been still that day as their voices carried all the way to us. We sat waiting as we always knew what was coming, well, I knew. After a few minutes, mommy came running out the door with two purses in her hand, screaming, "You's get in the car right now, Peggy Ann! Get in the car Taaaaaabby!"

We jumped up and ran for the car as we knew it was most important to do as we were told ASAP. Virgie jumped into the car and threw both purses on the floor beside my feet in the front passenger's seat. She sped off down the road and turned down a dirt road shortly down from Granny's place. She pulled off to the side, took Aunt Chelcie's purse, and rummaged through it, screaming, "She's a fuk lie-ner! She's a fuk lie-ner!"

Meaning to say, she's a fucking liar.

She pulled out a bunch of food stamps and some twenties. I knew what money was. We'd learned this in school. I always thought it was something only rich people had since I only had ever seen food stamps. After she went through Aunt Chelcie's purse, she shoved the food stamps and twenties into her own pocketbook. After she finished, she looked at me—only me—and told me I better not tell anyone what just happened or else I'd get it. Then she sped home.

Once we arrived home, I asked if I could play with Tabby, who lived nearby. She had a Big Wheel, and I felt like I was something special when I got to ride it. We'd take it to the top of the sidewalk, and we'd push each other down the little slant in the walkway so we would go faster. We'd roll down to the pavement, careful not to get too close to the road. It was a thrill!

While we were playing, a police officer showed up, followed by Aunt Chelcie and Uncle Claude, who pulled up behind the cop in their car across the street from my house. Aunt Chelcie pointed over towards Tabby and me. I am not sure what she was telling the officer, but I knew trouble was coming. I pretended not to see them and kept riding the big wheel.

The police walked over to Tabby and talked to her for a minute. As soon as she pointed at my house and Mommy's car, I knew what was going on. Aunt Chelcie wanted her purse back and had told the police that her sister had stolen it. Well, she did, and she also took Aunt Chelcie's food stamps and her money and put them in her own purse.

Aunt Beulah (Mommy's cousin) came outside and made Tabby and I go inside their home and play upstairs in Tabby's room. We did, but we watched out the window to see what was going on. We were nosey little girls!

The police officer, Aunt Beulah, Aunt Chelcie, and Uncle Claude all stood there in Aunt Beulah's driveway, talking and pointing at my house. Then the officer pointed back at Aunt Chelcie and Uncle Claude's car, and they walked back to the old jalopy, got in and waited. Aunt Beulah stood in her driveway for a few more minutes, then came inside. We couldn't see to my house, but we knew he was going over there.

I have no idea what he said when he spoke to my mother but, I soon found out. What happened next was something even I didn't expect.

Mommy came bursting into Aunt Beulah's front door, yelling and screaming, "Where is she? Where is that little bitch? She turned-ed me in. I's kill her for doing me's this way!" And up the stairs, she stomped. I froze. I think Tabby ran into the next room as I don't recall seeing her after that moment.

I stood there knowing what was coming, but I never imagined she'd do what she did this time. I guess she was really pissed. Aunt Beulah came running up the stairs telling her to calm down, and it wasn't right what she did by taking her sister's purse. Aunt Beulah kept telling her I was just a little girl. Nothing helped. No words Auntie said were helping. Mommy stomped and screamed that she was going to kill me, because I knew better than to lie on her.

I didn't lie. I didn't tell the truth either because I certainly didn't say a word. *Mommy, you were the one who stole your sister's purse and took stuff out of it, and I lied? Are you fucking nuts? I wasn't the one who turned you in, Tabby did! You were squealed on by an innocent little child.* But I stayed quiet, frozen in panic.

When she entered Tabby's bedroom, all I saw was one hand grabbing my face and the other grabbed a big handful of my hair. She got a good grip on my hair, and down the stairs, we both went. I was dragged while she threatened me, jerking my head every which way. I thought she was going to kill me as my body was being drug down those stairs. She never gave me a chance to get up and walk. Aunt Beulah tried to stop her, but she kept yanking me. She held tight to my hair with both hands now and her nails digging into my scalp. She pulled me through the living room, out the front door, down the porch steps, and halfway down the sidewalk, before she finally let go and only when, Aunt Beulah yelled, "Virgie, you'll go to jail if you kill her, let her go!"

When she let go, she gave me a swift kick in my stomach as I lay on the cold cement driveway. She also had a handful of my unattached hair still in her hand. I got up and ran as fast as I could, even though everything hurt—especially my head. (I never *really* knew the feeling of being sore until the next day.) I ran to my bedroom and hid in the tin closet, my special place.

It was a metal closet with two doors and a latch that kept it closed. It sat in the far corner of my room. I would often hide in there thinking no one knew, but they knew. Minutes later, Mommy came into my room, screaming, "Why did you's tell the cops on me's? I told you's to keep you's mouth shut, little girl. You's did this. You's made me upset. You's are going to pay little girl. No one lies on me's."

I came out as I knew I had to, or it'd be worse if that were even possible. I crawled out of the tin can with a face full of tears and a scalp full of blood. Shaking, I looked up at my mother, and I riskily said, "I didn't tell on you."

What I wanted to say but would have never spoken to her is that it wasn't a lie! That was the truth. No one lied. This statement was one that became her go-to when she would do things that she knew were wrong, she'd say "someone lied on her."

About that time, Aunt Beulah came boldly through our front door, yelling, "Virgie, it was Tabby Sue. She told not Lulu. Virgie, she didn't tell!"

Mommy stood looking at me and, with no remorse at all, and told me, "Well, you deserved it for letting Tabby tell on me." Then she waved her hand at me and said, "Now, go sit down in the living room so I's can keeps an eye on you's!"

My head hurt. My scalp was bleeding, and I had open scrapes and cuts all over my legs, knees, arms, face, back, and abdomen. My entire body hurt. I turned red, dark purple, blue, green and then yellow in various spots, and I was told not to say anything, so I never did. Good thing it was summer and there was no school. I had to hide out until the bruising and swelling was gone.

That was the real lie.

Nevertheless, Aunt Beulah knew what happened that day, she saw it. She watched the rage Virgie had for me, the bastard child. She saw the hate, the bitterness, the longing to physically hurt me, which happened often, but more so, she mentally broke me.

I didn't get to see Aunt Chelcie for about a year after that.

IT WAS ALWAYS MY SUSPICIONS that the majority of Virgie's siblings knew what was going on in our house yet turned a blind eye to everything—except for Aunt Marie and Aunt Opal. Others never said a word. I never noticed or knew of them trying to help. It is my thoughts that they just accepted that Virgie was the boss, and it was okay for her to do the things she did to me. I believed—and still do—that they knew, but this is only my theory. Should I be angry with them? Or should I just accept that they might have known and did nothing? They all fought and threatened each other, it was just the way it was. But no one really fought *for me*.

Even though I sound pissed here and there as I tell my story, I can honestly say that I am no longer angry for not having any family support or help when I was little. For many years, I was livid with Virgie until I started really dissecting the whole big picture. Then I realized I needed to let this shit go because if I hold it inside, they win. And well, fuck them!

They had taken enough already, and to allow me to live in the prison of unforgiveness was just inflicting misery on myself. Why allow that bunch to ruin me completely? This led to studying psychology and earning my degree in counseling so I could figure myself out and really begin to let go, and I did!

I say Aunt Opal knew because, during one of her visits, she witnessed how I was treated. I was in middle school, and I had no money to eat lunch and did not want free lunches any longer. So, I came home to fix a pizza patty. I took one, baked it, and then started to get another but was yelled at for eating up all Donny's pizza patties. One, I didn't know they specifically belonged to King Donny, and two, there was an entire box-like, 20 in the box—and I was hungry because I didn't have breakfast.

Aunt Opal told Virgie it was wrong of her to scold me that way just because I was hungry. They had words, and Aunt Opal left, but before she did, I heard her tell Virgie, "Virgie, you have never treated Peggy Ann right. It's not her fault she was born. You wanted her as a baby, and you should love her like you love your own kids because that's what's right!"

Auntie left slamming door on her way out. That is the only time I ever recall anyone sticking up for me from that family. I wasn't allowed to have the second pizza patty and I also wasn't allowed to go back to school. I had to stay home and clean since I made her and her sister argue, that was my fault, I started it.

WHEN I WAS a youngin', my dad would pick us kids up for his weekend. He often would take us to his sister, Alieen's house. I loved my Auntie Alieen. She lived on a lake in Indiana and had three kids as well. She always had yummy things to eat, and she had the best lap to sit on. She'd rock me and sing to me and tell me she loved me. She told me when I was little, I'd push her daughter away when she tried to climb up in her lap, and I'd cry out, "Don't let her sit on your lap!" I was starved for that positive attention and wanted it all to myself.

I recall the clock on her kitchen wall—a black cat with a tail and eyes that moved back and forth as it tick-tock. It was sort of creepy when I think of it now, but, at three and four years old, I thought it was the cat's meow (pun intended). Even though I thought it was cool, I was a little afraid of it because Auntie Alieen would tell me it would get me when I was acting up. I'd stop dead in my tantrum moment and watch that damn thing, waiting for it to jump off the wall and chase me. She never scared me with threats of violence, just the cat and only in a fun-loving way.

Other times, we'd visit Grandma and Grandpa, my dad's parents. Oh, how I loved-loved-loved visiting Grams. She had a piano and would play a little song for me, and it was so fun. Many times, dad would leave me. Seems when he left me with Aunt Alieen or Grams, he would take Denise and Donny with him for the weekend. I never thought much about this as a little kid.

The older I became, the more I began noticing the difference. I started looking at pictures taken with my dad. Most of the images with him were where he'd be looking down at the ground as if he was ashamed. He didn't put his arm around me like he did his other two kids in pictures, not all but many that I see. I'm assuming he felt so much shame he couldn't even hide it in pictures. The opposite was true as well, when posing with the other kids, he would be smiling and looking up. He still does to this day. Truthfully, it hurts. Nonetheless, it's time to tell them all to piss off and move forward.

However, when I was with my 'Christian' Grandma (or the Godly one, as I've referred to her before), she taught me to pray and say or think beautiful things about people. She taught me that Jesus loves me and forgives me. I never knew what I needed forgiveness for, but it was good to know he would absolve me if I ever needed it. Pretty sure throughout the years, I've needed a whole hell of a lot of forgiveness. She was a fantastic Grams.

Grams was an old-school Christian, and some of her theology may have been a bit…off. She taught me to ask forgiveness for what my mother did. That was the problem with *both* sides of the family, my conception and birth seemed to be **ALL** my mother's fault. Apparently, they believed that my dad was coerced and forced to have sex with my mom, and it was *her* fault she got pregnant. *Her* mistake she gave birth to a bastard. And then *her* fault, she gave me up for adoption. I never realized at the time, but Grams specifically instructed me to pray for my birth mother's pardon, again placing the burden of saving her on me. Despite this theological error, I'd like to believe Grandma Dorothy loved me. She treated me very well and fussed over me, just like all the other grandkids she had. I felt loved by her, and grams gave the best and lengthiest hugs. She would say she was gonna squeeze me till I fart, which probably happened a time or three. She offered me some normalcy, great hugs, kisses, and genuine love.

Grams had Snookie, a black and white Boston Terrier. She painted Snookie's nails red all the time, and she would sit there and let her do it. She only kept red polish to paint her baby's nails, never painting her own nails that I can remember.

Anytime, Grandma Dorothy was cold, she'd stand in front of her wood stove, pull up her dress in the back, and stick her butt up to the wood burner to warm her buns. She stood about 4'8" and was about 90 pounds soaking wet. She had six kids and many grandchildren. I can't even begin to count how many grandkids, great-grandkids, and great-greats there are today. She lived until she was 98 years old, and in the last ten years of her life, she didn't know any of us. She was diagnosed with Alzheimer's disease, it was so sad to watch her decline and pass through the dark hole of nothingness.

Grandma Dorothy was a good influence in my life, and I will always remember her lovingly even though she accepted me as the "adopted one" and not her "real" grandchild. Grams said that although my dad claimed me, she wanted more proof, but I think deep inside her heart, she knew the truth, I was her son's bastard child. I think Grandma Dorothy found the whole situation hard to accept. Nonetheless, she loved me, and her love was real.

WITH DENISE MARRIED and living on her own with her husband, it was just Donny (a teen) and I (a munchkin) that would get pick up and take for the weekend by dad (Ardy). He lived in Jackson with his new girlfriend, a.k.a. Soon-to-be wife. I liked going over there as it was much more peaceful, and I didn't get hit, screamed at, called nasty names, or made fun of by Donny. He left me alone while we were there.

We'd have an easy-going weekend and watch TV a lot. I played outside in the front yard, and there were plenty of kids in that neighborhood to hang out with. It was fun.

Their home was tiny. They had one bedroom, a small front room, the kitchen, and one bathroom that had only a shower, sink, and toilet. Donny and I slept on the couch in the living room, one at each end. Many times, he spent the night down the street at his friend's house, so I got the sofa to myself.

Even though the house was small, they had a great neighborhood. I made lots of friends. One of my best girlfriends, Susan, lived only two houses down on the same side of the street as us. Her parents had owned and lived in our home before we did, my dad bought the house from them. They housed four kids, two adults, and two extra kids every other weekend. I am not sure how they all fit in their tiny square foot home at one time, but they made it work.

When the weekend with dad was over, he would give me a buck or two when he dropped us off. He always gave Donny more, but he was older, so I understood. I was so happy to get a dollar or two because it meant I could walk to the Snack Shop. The Snack Shop was only a few blocks from my mother's house, so my cousin and I would walk down there and buy nickel candies and whatever else we could afford. My favorite was Reese's cups and root beer or an orange soda. And, when pop rocks came out, I would get a little bag of those and put the whole bag in my mouth, waiting for the fizzy crackling and popping to commence.

It was a huge deal to walk to the Snack Shop. We felt entirely independent because we had to cross over busy Michigan Ave. We were also told to watch out for "the niggers." By this time, my cousin and I both knew that *that* word was not acceptable to use, no matter the situation. We also learned that black people were just like us in every way other than the shade of skin. She and I never really talked about it much, but we would say hi and talk to everyone on the way there and back, and in the store too, no matter their color. We did not care! We loved the chance to get out of our normal everyday life and get some candy and mingle with everyone. Black, white, or purple, we didn't care what color anyone was. We just liked people.

The Snack Shop was the most significant pit stop in Albion at the time I was growing up. Anyone who was anyone went to the Snack Shop. The guys who owned it were the best, always chatting with us. They knew our names, and when it was our birthdays, they'd give us a free bottle of pop, our choice, which saved us 0.35 cents, and that meant two more candy bars or a bunch of nickel candies.

The joy of going to the Snack Shop with my own money diminished quickly. After every weekend with dad, our mother was upset when he'd drop us back home. In all actuality, no matter where she was, or where I was, she was just pissed off.

However, one particular weekend's return from dad's was a doozy. As soon as I walked through the door (and of course, I was in a great mood having just had a pleasant and quiet weekend), she began yelling at me about all the money he owed her and asking why I got money and not her. Mind you, my dad always paid his child support, and he was never late, but she felt he should give her extra money whenever she said so.

She made me stand in the living room and empty my pockets and my brown grocery bag of clothes and hand over any money I had.

I then had to pull off my shoes so she could make sure I wasn't holding out on her and hiding cash in them. This became the routine after each visit with our dad because Donny was the genius that told her I hide things in my shoes, which he'd seen me sometimes do. Rat fuck fink! After each interrogation, I had to go to my room and stay there.

Eventually, giving her whatever I got from my dad wasn't enough, so she told me to ask for more money and tell him I needed it for school lunches, which I got for free. He gave me three dollars a couple of times then asked why I didn't get free lunches since Virgie was on welfare. I couldn't lie to him, so I just shrugged my shoulders, implying I didn't know.

Speaking of free lunches … once in second grade, I brought home the application to get the parent signature, which was needed to get the free lunch program at school. When I gave it to my mother and asked her to sign it, she got upset with me, yelling that she needed me to read it so she could sign it. Well, I didn't know all the more critical words, as I said, I was in second grade. She was so angry she tore up the papers and threw them in the garbage.

No signed paper meant no free lunch for me, which meant I went hungry all day at school. So, I told the teacher, Miss. Martin, that I lost the paper and needed another to take home. She gave me another one, and I hid it from my mother, signed her name myself, and then turned it in to my teacher the next day. I did this in the third and fourth grades as well. A girl's gotta eat!

Mommy, always being mad at my dad for something (often after my weekend with him and his new wife), would make me sit in a chair in the living room and tell her how ugly his new wife was, how long her nose was, and how much I hated her. Even though I didn't feel this way, I had too. So, I did.

Virgie would laugh and call my dad's wife, "Bugle Nose." She said she had a long nose, and that's why my dad liked her, which made no sense, but I knew better than to argue. Her rantings never made any sense to me. I never understood why it was a good thing to make fun of other people and call them names. It hurt my heart to take part in that. However, I had no choice other than to make her happy and do it.

Then she would tell people how much I hated my dad's new wife and that I said terrible things about her. That felt even worse since she was the one making me say those things. I felt powerless. I knew that if I didn't say what she wanted to hear, I'd get it, A.K.A. an ass-kicking for not doing what she wanted me to do, state, or how she wanted me to act.

My dad's new wife wasn't the only one I had to trash talk. Whomever she was pissed at was on the docket for bashing, belittling, and running in the dirt. The bashing became worse the older I got. Maybe that was because I noticed it more, paid more attention to what others were saying. Or perhaps it was because as time went on, Virgie became more and more bitter. Then again, many of her family also trash-talked to, and about, others they knew and those they didn't, so it was just the culture, I guess. They never seemed to have any pleasant things to say about *anyone* unless you were doing something for them or giving them what they wanted at that time.

After they got what they wanted, that person became a Son of a Bitch again. Someone was always an SOB for something. And without fail, the family usually made threats about cutting someone's head off or shooting them between the eyes the next time they saw them. I was little, and they were the adults, so I figured they could. Back then, I knew my mother could kill people because she said she would. And she always did whatever she wanted to do.

In my dad's house, it wasn't as violent, and at first the trash talk was nonexistent but then eventually he began trashing my biological mother, her husband Claude, and my Grandma Ally. He called my bio mom, Chelcie, a "filthy rotten bitch" or a "no good for nothing worthless bitch." These rants were fewer than at my mother's house, but I still had to endure them. Hearing the hate-spewing from their hearts was enough for me to know that if I disagreed with them, it was going to be my ass or maybe Aunt Chelcie and Uncle Claude's asses. So, I tried to hate Chelcie and Claude, but my heart could never do it. And my mind would never allow me to betray my heart.

I loved and longed for my real mother so much it hurt, and my night prayers always ended in tears. I felt I had to ask forgiveness for faking hatred towards my mother due to both my adopted parents ridiculing her and making me feel as if she was nothing. It was so messed up.

BY THE SPRING, when I turned about eight, Virgie had divorced Barry and had started dating Richard. She and Barry had been married since I was about two years old, so that was a little weird for me.

Richard had four kids, one with whom I went to school and didn't like, Doris. We called her Dory, and she was fucking crazy, even for a fourth grader. She would give me dirty looks with one rotten tooth sticking out of lips pursed on a scrunched face, and shaking her doubled-up fists at me, saying, "You want me to beat you up?!" I was told by Mommy to leave her alone and not bother her. I knew if I kicked that little bitch's ass, I'd get it, so I left her alone.

Although I have to say, after taking her shit for one full weekend, Friday after school until Sunday afternoon, I'd clearly had enough. So, Sunday, about an hour before they had to leave, I went to my hiding spot in the backyard to get away from her stupid ass. There was a row of lilac trees next to the neighbor's garage—the friendly neighbors with the cute son and lady with fancy hairdos. On the other side of our house were my Aunt Marie and Uncle Mickey's house.

The lilacs were big enough to cover the entire side of their garage with a small opening and a place for me to curl up and sit, which I did a lot. It was my thinking spot. A place I'd go to hide and wish for things I felt I was never going to get, like a new family or to go live with my real mom. The bushes were so big that they blocked the sun, so no grass grew back there, it was a dirt floor hiding spot, but it was mine. Besides, I loved the smell. It was so fragrant, and the colors were a light purple. Maybe that's the reason I love the color purple so much. I was never allowed to pick them, but I sure did go out back and smell them whenever I had a chance.

I was pretty sure the squirrels lived there as well. And some fairies. I would always find nutshells and pretty little rocks. I used to make tiny pixie houses back in the bushes for the fairies to live in, and I figured they liked it because the next time I'd go out there, I'd find more tiny colored rocks waiting for me. I would gather them up and keep them in a tin box I found and tuck them into the bushes. The secret tin box also had some coins in it that I had managed to keep hidden from Mommy. My personal stash of goodies.

I knew Dory was following me, so I let her see only my hiding place. Nothing else inside it, just the magic doorway to get inside. As she came in, she began informing me that she was going to tell on me and get me in trouble and blah blah blah…

So, I grabbed her pointer finger as she was wiggling it in my face, and I bent that fucker back so far, she cried. I told her if she said anything to anyone, I'd beat her ass at school on the playground and say to the teacher that she fell off the swing.

I gave her the same shitty look she had been giving me since her daft dad started dating my angry mother. I was so sick of that little bitch's shit. However, being now older and wiser, I have to wonder if she also had a hard life at her mom's house. Usually, bullies are beaten down at home and poorly treated, not always, but many times they are. Nonetheless, she never bullied me again after that. You gotta stick up for yourself against bullies! Let them turds know whose boss, and they will change their attitudes...hopefully.

OFTEN, WHEN SHE WAS PISSED at me, which was pretty much all the time, Virgie would tell Donny I did something to upset her. She'd say, "Peggy Ann's upsets me's!" with her whiney voice and pouty lips. That was all it took for Donny to get his redneck on and use his trailer park attitude to snatch me up by the throat, slam me against the wall, and threaten to beat me, while choking me and blowing out his threats of killing Chelcie.

On many occasions, my feet dangled off the floor, and I'd gasp for air while he would hold me by my throat, squeezing and spitting in my face as he spewed these threats and much more. I was sick of them both. I never knew when I'd piss Virgie off or how, but I knew it was inevitable to have daily confrontations with her and Donny. I hated them with a passion and wanted them both to just fucking die or fall off the planet into the dark vortex of nothingness and forever be gone. Either way would have worked for me at that time.

It seemed almost daily, I heard how much of a whore Chelcie was (whom I still wasn't supposed to know was my birth mom) and listened to them continuously threaten her life and her other kids' lives. Even though I was beginning to move from being primarily fearful of being mostly angry, the fear was still there, and I always believed them. I thought I had to do as they wanted or else they would do as they said. My conditioned response kicked in. I went into protection mode like a dog, and I never figured out how to come out of it, until recently. That's some fucked up, prolonged shit right there!

Things over the next couple of years went from bad to worse, if that's even possible. When my mother began dating Richard, she also started leaving me with Donny more often. He was older, so he was in charge and the "Boss!"

During this time, Denise divorced Johnny after they had one more child. She was around us but not there for me much. I'm not sure she knew all the shit that was truly going on, and if she did, would she have made a difference in my life? I'm not convinced.

My dad and his then-wife were doing great, and I still visited, but the visits became every couple of weeks rather than every other weekend, which was fine with me too. I was pulling away, but they never saw it. I felt it, and I wished I could run away from all of them and live by myself. I hated everyone that hurt me. I really wanted to get away from that family and never come back. I wished I could live in a home with just me and my real mom, Claude, and my siblings, but that wasn't an option, nor was running away at this time.

I was the child whose only fault started at conception. I was wanted by one. Not liked by others. Tormented by the four horsemen of the apocalypses and thrown away by the rest who should have protected me but didn't.

By this time in my life, I had stopped praying and asking Jesus to take me to live with him in heaven. I think I was about six when I began to pray that prayer. I would justify to Jesus when I prayed that if he'd let me live with him, I wouldn't have to get hit so much and yelled at all the time. I tried my best to reason with the Big Man upstairs but, I don't think he heard me. At some point, I realized that was a pipe dream, and I began to question if he existed at all. He left me with these people who were hurting me, and I was angry about that. I felt he could have done something but choose not to and I couldn't understand why.

I hadn't realized it at the time, but I was transitioning from loathing to pure hatred. The family let me down when I was a little kid, and that I will not forget. Forgiving is necessary—I do that for my sanity—but I shall never forget. I wish people would understand the difference between forgiving and forgetting. We're human beings with memory banks and a nervous system that stores data, so we will always remember, but we can forgive someone for doing us wrong. It doesn't mean we have to be buddy—buddy with the people who hurt and abused us. Still, instead, we are aware they fucked us over and accept that it happened--*okay, it's done with*--but we do not have to put ourselves in the position of allowing them a second chance to mess us over again, because they probably will. Absolutely no additional opportunities!

This spring break was different from any I'd ever had. My dad had plans, so he wasn't taking me for the week, and truthfully, I was glad. By this time in my life, I wanted to spend more time with my real mom than anyone else. I was sick of the arguing, fighting, and the abuse I was getting from Mommy and Donny. Although life was not good while living at home, but it was momentarily decent when I got to visit for a day, overnight, or longer with Aunt Opal or Aunt Chelcie.

Because my dad had plans during this particular spring break, I got to go to Chelcie's for a week. I was picked up by Claude, Chelcie, and Glenn. I loved riding in cars with them anywhere. It was always a fun time. Claude would sing hymnals, and mom would always yell at him, telling him, "Look out, ole man, your gonna hit a tree. Wake up, old man, your gonna kill us all. Watch the road, Claude! Look out for that other car, you're over too far, you're gonna hit it!" In her defense, Claude really was a dreadful driver. He always fell asleep, stopped paying attention to what he was doing, or would joke around with Glenn and me and forget he was driving. There was usually something that made him forget he oversaw the wheel. The drive was amusing, to say the least.

As soon as we got to their home, Glenn and I headed for the field beside the house. The open land had two apple trees and lots of tall green grasses. We loved the green apple trees. They were easy to climb, and the little fruit was sour, but oh so yummy! Mom did remind us not to eat more than a couple apples each, or we'd get the squirts, which we also learned from experience. We ate a couple each, and then we'd throw them at each other while in the tree since they were so close. It was fun kid stuff and the kind of memories I enjoy keeping.

I had spent two nights with my mom, Aunt Chelcie when Mommy decided to come by for a surprise visit. And as usual, she roared up with an attitude about something and someone who had pissed her off. This time it was me. Shocking, huh?

All my siblings from my real mom were visiting. They would typically gather at her house on the weekends. My half-sister Vickie Sue (Chelcie's oldest daughter) was cutting hair, but she had no clue what the fuck she was doing. However, everyone thought she did a great job at cutting hair, and I did too. So, with having very long hair past the middle of my back and it being hot out, I thought it'd be great if she could give me a new look too. That was always my problem, thinking. I shouldn't have even thought about it.

Virgie used to say, "You's think too much. You's brain ain't thinkin' right. You's think you's know something, and you's don't." Ya know, when you grind shit like that into a kid's head, they begin to believe it's the truth. Eventually, it breaks the child's spirit, confidence, and self-worth, leaving them with unresolved sadness and hate, mostly towards herself.

When I excitedly asked if Vickie Sue could cut my hair, I was shot down quickly. Virgie grabbed me by the hair of my head and led me to the car, cruising and screaming, "I's is you's boss, little girl! You's do what I's says! You's get you's haircuts when I's say so not Vickie Sue!" I was puzzled because Vickie Sue never asked, I did.

I was shoved into the backseat by the head of my hair and told to dry my eyes and shut my mouth, or I'd get her fist down my throat, so I sat quietly, saying nothing and faced the back of the seats. Afraid to look out the window, I listened to her and Chelcie by the side of the car arguing. Virgie claimed I made her look like a fool, and she wasn't going to let me get away with this. She was going to tell Donny and Denise and let them deal with me. Chelcie cried and begged as usual, and Virgie snickered, got into the car, bitched at her husband Richard, who was in the front seat, and we drove off in the typical fashion of squealing tires and excessive speed.

After that altercation, we drove into town to a bait shop, they needed worms for their afternoon fishing trip. Virgie went in to get the fishing worms while Richard stayed in the car to lecture me. He told me I messed up his plans, and he didn't like it. He then said to me, if I kept my mouth shut and didn't piss her off again, he'd try to talk her into taking me back to finish out my week. I was trying not to even breathe loudly so I could go back to my mom's.

It worked! As we pulled into Aunt Chelcie's drive, I noticed everyone had cleared out and was gone. No one was there. They told me to get out and wait on the porch as "Chelcie and Claude had better get back soon," Virgie threateningly predicted. They took off and left me there, which didn't bother me one bit because it meant I wasn't with her, and I could finish my week at my real mom's.

As I waited patiently sitting on cold cement steps in shorts, a halter top, and no shoes, it became country-dark, pitch black with nothing but moonlight. I was cold, hungry, and scared. I was pretty sure werewolves were howling out in the woods next to their house. The evil hooting owls could have swooped down at any given minute and snatched me up, just like on Creature Feature T.V. shows. Cats were shrieking so loudly nearby I was confident they would jump out and claw my face up. I thought I could feel the bushes vibrate, which I was convinced was a snake or a bear. Or both at the same time! I was a very spooked little girl.

By the time Chelcie and Claude pulled in, I was crouched down and hiding at the front of the house behind the bush (after I decided no wild cats, snakes, or bears were in there). As Chelcie and Claude stepped out of their car, I jumped out, scaring the shit out of them. Cold, hungry, and scared, my mom took me inside, ran a bath, and made me some hot cocoa and a warm biscuit with her homemade fresh strawberry jelly. After the warm bath and my food, I fell asleep in her arms on the couch, exhausted from the day's dilemmas.

That next morning, she fixed a big breakfast of biscuits, gravy, pork chops, eggs, fried apples, and fresh milk from the old goat. My mom always cooked big meals, and they were delicious. One thing was for sure, my mama could out-cook anyone—and I do mean *anyone*— especially when it came to Southern Soul Food cooking.

After breakfast, she called me into her bedroom, and we sat on the bed together. She began by telling me the Lord showed her things and told her stuff, which she knew was the truth because the Lord told her. *Well, okay, it must be true if God told her, and she wouldn't lie to me because that's my mom, and she loves me.*

"What did he tell you?" I asked, ignorant of what was coming.

She asked me if Donny had ever put his fingers inside of my privates. I said no. Because well, something happened but he made me do it, he didn't.

She asked me again, and this time told me that the Lord showed her that he had done this.

I was dumbfounded. I had no idea that God could do that kind of stuff, but, then again, I was a nine-year-old (almost ten). I told her I didn't think Donny stuck his fingers inside of my privates. Too afraid to say what really happened. Lost as a scared little girl in a world of threats and violence and duty to keep my birth mother safe.

After a short time of this debate, she told me that if I would tell the Social Services people that he did this and let them know that Virgie beats me, I could come and live with her and Claude, and we could be a family.

Well now, that sparked my interest, but I didn't want to tell other people what really was happening.

I know the night she's talking about, and I didn't want to talk about it. Ever.

ON THE NIGHT she was speaking of, my cousin Bobbie Jo and I were babysitting my nephew Dee in the apartment attached to the house I grew up in. We loved babysitting together on those weekends because after Dee would go to sleep, we'd play records, dance, drink Pepsi, and watch Creature Feature while sitting on the couch under a blanket holding hands because Creature Feature was scary. We were inseparable for a couple years growing up next door to each other. I loved Bobbie Jo as a sister. She was my BFCF (Best Friend Cousin Forever) growing up.

One night while babysitting, we got a visit from two of our male cousins, and we all danced and played truth or dare. We dared each other to sing or cackle like a chicken or make a monkey face, kid stuff, stupid things but funny, at least we thought it was funny. I had to walk like a chicken and cluck and move my head all at the same time. It was so fun, and everyone laughed at me. We dared Glenn (my sibling from my bio mother) to sing using the broom handle as a microphone and act like he was playing the guitar all at once, he was funny too. The silly, stupid things you do and laugh at when you are young. Young at heart and free to laugh, well, for a minute, I was.

As we all laughed and played, Donny came over to let me know Mommy left on a date with Richard, and he was watching me. He also told me she wanted me home by 10:00 and in bed, which was never the case before. I was usually allowed to stay the night since it was my sister's (Denise's) apartment. We lived in a house that had three different residences, one upstairs and two down.

He then left but was peering in the window outside watching us. I noticed him first and screamed. For some reason, he got pissed off, burst through the door, demanded me to get my ass home and in bed right then, or he was telling Mommy, and I'd get an ass beating.

My older cousin spoke up and told him to calm down and go home. He was acting strange, and he him to shut the fuck up, or he'd kick them out too.

I went home and crawled in bed. I figured it was best to do as he said, or I'd get it when mommy got home. Shortly after I was in bed, Donny came into my room. He asked questions about Bobbie Jo's privates.

"Does Bobbie Jo have hair on her pussy?"

"I don't know," I replied crossly.

"Now, Peggy Ann, you know, and if you don't tell me I'm telling mommy, you guys were playing nasty. You know she'll beat your ass if I tell her to."

I knew he'd tell a lie, he usually did, and if the prick wanted to impose misfortune upon me, he would. The thing about Donny was, he was a mama's boy. Always has been. He'd wake in the mornings and sit in the living room and demand mommy to go fix him some eggs, biscuits, and gravy, and she'd jump to it as if he was the king of her palace. He did this whenever he was hungry or wanted anything, she'd jump and get it, or cook it, or go buy it, or give him money, whatever it was, he got it. All he had to do was bellow and he got his way. Even when it came to him telling her to whoop me for anything he felt I should have a beating for, then the hitting game would begin. Either she'd do it, or he'd do it.

So, when he would threaten me with telling Mommy, I always knew he would follow through, and I would meet their wrath, whatever storm they felt like giving. Sometimes Virgie would tell Donny she was worn out so he could take care of me, so he'd snatch me up and mentally and or physically torture me for a while. Many times, by the throat up against the wall until I couldn't breathe then he'd let go and I'd fall to the floor gasping for air.

Therefore, I thought it out and responded to his nasty questions as necessary.

"Yes," I replied.

"How much pussy hair does she have? Is it way up here?" as he pointed to his covered private area while asking.

I shrugged.

He repeated the question and reminded me what would happen unless I told him.

He turned and walked out of my room, then stopped and stood in the doorway. I heard the rattling of his belt and thought for sure he going to beat my ass. I lay there, glancing into the hall at the brown fridge next to my door. All reflections could be seen in that fridge. It was how I could always tell what was coming.

I lay there, gripping my covers tight, gritting my teeth, waiting for the belt and watching. Then Donny pulled his pants and underwear down and began to stroke and shake his erect penis while asking me if I knew what it was.

I started crying and told him to leave me alone. My body began trembling and shivering so fiercely that my teeth chattered uncontrollably. I felt sweat on my forehead and sick to my stomach. My kneecaps were jittering back and forth hard I could barely move my legs. I felt a little puke come up in my mouth, and in fear, I swallowed it back down. I knew I couldn't get out of bed. It was too dangerous. I feared seeing what I thought was his privates. I wasn't supposed to see a grown man's privates or even talk of them, I was a little girl for God sake!

Why is he doing this?

He stood there stroking his privates. Then returned to my bedside with his pants undone and penis erect inside his underwear. He instructed me to pull the covers down and remove my panties so he could see my pussy.

I began crying more and telling him to get out of my room. He reminded me what would happen when mommy gets home and finds out I was playing nasty with my cousins. (Lies). I knew, it didn't matter what I felt, if I didn't do as he instructed, he was going to tell mommy a lie and if I did do what he wanted, I felt violated, sick, terrified, freaked the fuck out!

Again, he ordered me to remove my panties and the covers so he could look at my privates. What does a nine year old do in this case? If I don't, I'm getting the shit kicked out of me and if I do, he's going to do nasty things that he shouldn't! HORRIFIED and in absolute fear, I did as instructed.

Tears falling from my eyes, my throat knotted and hard to speak but still begging him to leave me alone, he didn't.

He shouted, "stick your fingers in your pussy and let me smell them!" as he stroked his self-hard while his breathing was loud and forceful, mean and angry.

I have never been more ashamed, afraid, and confused in my life as I was that moment. Knowing if I didn't do what I was told, all hell would break loose. I was sick of being a whipping bag and sick of being scared, but I did what he told me to do because I knew he meant what he said. And God only knows what else he might tell mommy this time to get my ass beat.

Again, he barked his demands, "pull the covers back, spread your legs, let me look," all while masturbating at the side of my bed. When he finished, he told me, if I ever spoke a word to anyone, no one would believe me. He said, everyone would believe him because, our family knows I lie "just like that whore mom of mine, Chelcie."

He polished his threat by telling me that if I did say anything, he'd make sure that—that fucking bitch Chelcie got what she deserved for breaking up his family, he continued, I'll blow her fucking head off, and I'll do it if you open your bitch little mouth, do you hear me?"

I lay there, staring at him in disbelief, hurt, anger and I wished I was older so I could defeat him for what he just did to me. I responded, "yes, I hear you." Then in my mind silently I screamed, I hear you—you worthless mother fucker and I hope someone blows your fucking head off you cock sucker! Words that I had only heard, now I was screaming them in my mind holding back tears and anger towards him, but that's all they were, silent words and a defeated little nine year old who had just gotten molested by her half brother who should have protected her but instead had his way with her.

I'm not sure how long this incident took but this was not a night I'd ever forget and one that I would never talk about to anyone, ever!

After he walked out of my room carrying his threats and pride with him, I started becoming disconnected and like I was in a fog. Eventually, that fog cleared, and hate settled in its place.

After that night, I hated my room. I hated Donny. I hated mommy. I hated everyone. I wished I was never born. I wanted to die. I just hated myself for doing what he made me do, but I was powerless. I knew what would have happened if I didn't do "the thing." I had to.

I felt dirty. Gross. Broken. My life revolved around making two people, Donny and Virgie, "happy." They always knew what would make me bend over backwards, jump, and or do whatever they wanted, they knew I was too young to know any other truth.

I was Peggy Ann, the pawn. I was always the pawn. I was the little front-line chess piece that felt she had to protect her Queen. The puppet used to fight the battles of the two queens who were against each other. The pawn who Queen Virgie hated, snickered at, shoved around, and used as a tool to make her sister, Chelcie does whatever she wanted. I was, The Bastard Pawn of my world as I knew it, Hillbilly Chess.

Your move next, Queen Chelcie.

MY MOM, AUNT CHELCIE, was determined to make me believe Donny was the one who stuck his fingers inside me, but I knew different. I knew what happened, and I wasn't about to tell anyone, ever. I had managed to keep it quiet for a year until she talked with Jesus, and he told her things. So, she claimed.

Why would Jesus tell her? Did it happen the way she said? Did Jesus really clear my mind of it? Well, if mom said so, and Jesus told her, maybe it's real. I was so confused.

Aunt Chelcie had me believing God told her differently than what I was recalling, Donny had me scared for Chelcie's life, Virgie kept me living in fear of what she'd do to me next, and all I knew was that I had to protect my real mom from being killed by Donny or Virgie. I would do anything she said to do, but I couldn't do *this*. It was telling a lie, and I already learned that lies are wrong, and people shouldn't lie about anything. And I wasn't totally convinced that God told her what Donny did when I knew what really happened, that one night.

Let me be clear, my brother, Glenn witnessed Donny molesting me one night while I was sleeping, and he was spending the night. Glenn testified in court that, Donny came into my room and molested me while I slept. He told the court that Donny told him to watch what he does to Peggy while she sleeps and Donny laughed telling him, she usually sleeps through it. Glenn said he was in shock and disbelief to see what Donny was doing and he told our mom so she could save me. Therefore, in this case, Glenn was God to my mother. I didn't know Donny was doing this, and I am not sure how long this had been going on. I do

remember the one night that he advanced his plans
and, in my mind, now that I am older, I am wondering
what move would have been next?

She convinced me to go with her to Social Services and talk to the
man she'd already phoned. As we walked into his office, I anxiously
scanned the room and saw a desk with two chairs in front of it. We sat
down across from him, and he asked simple questions such as, what
is your name? Where do you live? Then he went right to the more
significant, more pressing problems.

"When did Donny stick his fingers inside your privates?"

My head drooped, and my eyes were glued to the floor as I sat
quietly. He asked the same question again. I continued looking down,
saying nothing. He asked me for the third time. I shrugged. After a
couple of dead-silent minutes, my bio mom speaks up and tells him,
"She is scared of Virgie, my sister because she beats her."

The man then turns the question and asks me, "Are you afraid of
Virgie beating you?"

I never looked up and never spoke a word but nodded my head a
couple times at him.

It seemed like the only way to not have to look at this strange man
but to just respond non-verbally as I could by shrugging my shoulders
or nodding, so that is precisely all I did. I never spoke a word. I never
even looked at him other than when I walked into his office. And I only
nodded to that one question about being afraid of Virgie because I was
fucking afraid of her and Donny and what they would do to my mom,
Chelcie!

The man wrote furiously as my mom told her version of what
Donny did to me that night. After all his questions and writing, the man
told me to go out to the waiting room and wait for Chelcie. Off I went.
I was glad to be out of that man's smelly room. I was happy to be rid of
his endless questions about fingers in my privates and getting beaten.

I hated him too. I didn't like all the questions. However, the happiness I felt about leaving that room quickly faded. My heart began racing as I thought about what could happen now. I knew somehow Virgie and Donny would find out, and then all holy hell would break loose. If they knew this time, they might really kill Chelcie, Claude, and all my siblings. This time, it was terrible.

Mom stayed in the room with the Social Services guy and shortly after I left his office Glenn was called in for a few minutes.

After Glenn came back, we sat in the waiting room playing I Spy games. Soon enough, my mom came out with a big yellow envelope in her hand and told Claude, "We got to take Pooch to a foster home over here in the country." I didn't give that statement much thought, and off we went.

All I knew was that we were done, and maybe that yellow envelope was permission for me to move in with her, and we could all be a family. I was glad. I sat in the backseat and thought about how maybe this wasn't so bad, after all. *I didn't say a word, so I never lied, and I can go live with my real mom, Claude, my brother Glenn, and see my other siblings whenever I want. Life is good.*

After a short drive to the country, we pulled into the driveway of a strange home. My mom got out of the car clutching the yellow envelope, opened my door, and told me, "Come on, get out," looking at me with teary eyes. I looked up at her, smiling, not even thinking anything. Not knowing or understanding what was happening.

I got out and told Glenn to come on, but mom spoke up and said, "No, you are going alone." Then, she took my hand and led me up to the front door without saying a word to me. She knocked. The door opened, and a lady stepped out and said, "Can I help you?"

Mom said nothing to her, handed her the envelope and my hand, looked down at me, kissed my head, and said, "Be a good girl, mommy loves you," then turned and walked away.

I stood there, lost. My mom just handed me and the envelope over to a stranger. *Why? What is going on? Why is she leaving?* I stood watching her rush back to the car and get in, and then they sped off. My mom just rushed away without me. I was confused, to say the least. *I thought we were going to be a family.*

II

CPS

CHILD PROTECTIVE
SERVICES

TURNS OUT MY MOM HAD DROPPED ME off at a group home. The lady to whom I was handed off was a tall, skinny, flat-chested woman with very short brown and grey hair. She wore jeans and a t-shirt, and was plain, wearing no makeup, with a rough voice and a stern look. She wasn't exactly warm and fuzzy.

The house was a large white farmhouse with two red barns and a big garden. The inside was pretty, and everything looked clean. *Maybe this is, like, a rich person's house.* The lady explained that the dining room was where they did schoolwork and ate. The kitchen was big, with two cooking stoves and a huge sink. They had two refrigerators, both had locks on them, and as I looked around, I noticed the cupboards had locks too. I thought that was strange. *Don't they want anyone to eat?*

I was led into the front room where I saw a TV, a giant window, and lots of flowers in the yard. I've loved flowers ever since I was a little turd, so my eye was drawn to that garden instantly. Looking left, I saw a staircase, and on the opposite side, a door that led to the biggest bathhouse I'd ever seen. The lady with my envelope told me to follow her.

The bathroom had cement walls and light green shower curtains separating the five stalls. I was told to strip my clothes off and bend over and spread my cheeks so she could see that I had nothing up my butt.

Are you kidding me? After what Donny made me do, and now this strange lady wants to look at my bare butt and up my butthole, really? I started crying and told her no.

She looked at me, sighed aloud, and said without blinking an eye, "We can do this the easy way or the hard way. Either you do what I said, or I call in the aids, and they hold you down while I remove your clothes and insert my finger into your anus and vagina. Either way, it's going to be done, like it or not!"

So, in a cold, wet, cement room with no privacy, I cried, removed my clothing, and grabbed my butt cheeks while bending over and spreading them apart so this woman could look up my ass. The foster care lady stepped close, and I felt the poke in my vagina first, then my butt. Again, I had just turned 10 years old.

I didn't even know people would put things in their buttholes or crotches. On a better note, if there is one, this experience taught me that my coochie is called a vagina, and my butthole an anus. *Hey, wait a minute, isn't there a planet in our solar system called 'your anus? Um, who named that planet, and why?* That thought was an ever so slight distraction from the trauma that was happening at that moment.

After she found nothing, she told me to take a shower and put my clothes back on. "Oh, and make sure you wash your hair," which she also checked for head lice.

As soon as I finished, a young girl was waiting for me in the front room. It was quiet, and no one else was around. She said her name was Vickie, and she took me to my room. I had nothing with me, no clothes other than what I wore and no toothbrush, no clean under panties, nothing but me and the clothes on my back. She took me to a room with two beds, two dressers, and two nightstands by each bed. It was a first-rate room. She said, "This is your bed, and here is mine. Are you hungry?"

My mother left me at the group home after dinner had already been served, so I had to wait until breakfast for anything to eat, no matter if I was hungry or not, that was the rule. All I had that day was breakfast, and it's a good thing, it was a big one.

"Yes," I replied, and the tears began falling.

She sat down beside me, reached over, pulled me in for a hug, and handed me some cheesy crackers and a glass of water. She rubbed my back, telling me it'll be okay, and I wept.

I felt safe for a minute in her arms. She was 15, pregnant, and doing time for running away from home. She told me she was sorry that the old bitch made me bend over and said, "That bitch makes everyone do it because she's a lesbian cunt."

Well, I wasn't sure what a lesbian cunt was, but I knew what a bitch was. It was her job to do intake on us, but she could have done a whole lot better than making us girls do a striptease and then bend over so she could finger us. I do hope she got caught and fired, cunt!

The next morning, we all had to rise at 6:30, Shower, breakfast, clean up, and then school work. We did homeschool until lunch then broke for a quick bite, after which I was told to gather my things—which I had nothing—, and they took me to the next town over where they had a juvenile center. I had to stay there for the weekend since my pending foster parents were out of town and couldn't take me until Monday. Here I go again, off to another new place in less than 24 hours.

Juvie also made me strip down. However, this time the lady checking me in was more understanding and a lot easier on me. She even brushed my hair out when I finished in the shower. There were no inappropriate mishaps here, she was just pleasant. She never made me bend over and spread 'em, nor did she stick her fingers up my stuff. She told me she knew I was a good girl and wouldn't do ugly things, so it wasn't necessary. God bless her!

On Monday morning, which could not have come soon enough for me, I was once again carted off, and this time it was by a social worker named Martha. Martha was tall and thin with brown hair and spoke in a soft voice. She wore pretty shoes, and her purse was brown with fringe, it was cool. She never asked me much other than how I was and how I enjoyed my stay at the Juvie.

Oh, yeah, I so enjoy Juvie, please let me visit again, and while you're at it, take me back to the country group home so that the lesbian can finger my vagina and asshole too, please! Really, what a stupid question. "I'm fine, it was fine," I replied.

As an adult, I have replayed that scene a little differently. *How the fuck do you think I liked it, Martha? I loved it, just like the Ritz. How about you take me back and call the masseuse to give me a hot stone treatment to release some of this fucking tension. Please have the bartender mix me a double martini with four goat-cheese stuffed olives and have the cook fix me a complimentary cheese and cracker dish with purple and green grapes. Hold the salt since I'm salty enough right now.*

I was a kid! Scared shitless, how did she think I was? I know, I know, she was just being a friendly professional and doing her job. I do realize that now, but then I wasn't so sure what she even meant asking me those questions. I didn't like it at all, Martha.

And Mother Mary in heaven, where the fuck was my mom? Why did she just drop me off like a sack of old potatoes on someone's porch?

When we arrived at my new foster parents' house, I was a little freaked and figured I'd have to strip and show her my butthole too. I wasn't at all happy about this and wondered why I was being tossed around from home to home. Not one person took the time to sit me down and explain about living in a foster home or why I had to. Not one person. Not even Martha, who really should have made sure I understood what was going on, rather than just delivering me to my next cell.

In all fairness, I didn't ask either. I didn't say much of anything to any of the adults on this journey. I wasn't sure I could trust them or where they might stick me next, literally and figuratively. Why would I trust an adult? My own real mother just left me at some strange house with no explanation. I felt like a prisoner who was being transported from facility to facility with no legal representation at all.

My new foster home, owned by Marylou and Jim, was reddish-brown brick with a stone porch and a big front window. The yard was big and completely fenced in. The garage was detached, but it looked the same as the house did with the same brick and stone.

As we stepped inside, there was a small foyer, and to the right side was a staircase and to the left, the front room. Straight ahead, the dining room was open to the living room. The dining room table and chairs were elevated, and the rest was level with all the other areas of the house. Through the dining room was the kitchen, which housed a small half bath, and the backdoor to the yard.

Upstairs there were four bedrooms and a full bath. They had two sets of bunk beds in there with four small dressers and one closet. Next to the boy's room was Marylou and Jim's bedroom, and on the other side of theirs was an empty chamber, which became my room. Brian, one of their adopted sons, had the small room next to the bathroom across the hall, and Chad, their other adopted son, had the room with all the bunks.

When I first meet Marylou, I thought she was pretty, she seemed nice, but I was still worried about the vagina and butt checking issue. I couldn't help but worry about it happening again. Because the lady at the Juvie didn't do it, I had concluded it must be a foster home "rule," and I knew my tears were on their way.

After Martha dropped me off there with nothing but the clothes on my back, Marylou asked me if I was tired and if I wanted to lie down. She took me upstairs to Chad's room, and told me to rest on the bottom bunk, handed me a blanket, and smiled. I couldn't hold back my tears any longer. All I could think at that moment was the 100 things going off in my head, and I began crying. Everything was coming at me like a nightmare with no warning signs, right there in my face. I felt as if I could collapse on the bed and never get up again, ever.

Here I am, alone in my third home in three days. Please, someone, talk to me. Tell me what is going on, please help me understand.

Nothing was making sense to me. My mom told me I could live with her, and now I'm being sent to all these unusual places. My mind was reeling thinking about my mom and if she was coming back and how she'd find me if she did come back.

Why is this happening to me? Why am I here, and who are you, Marylou?

She asked if I was okay, and that's when I asked her if she wanted me to strip so she could look in my butt. I'll never forget the look on her face. She was shocked, to say the least. Her mouth dropped, almost hitting the floor, and her eyebrows raised to high heaven. She stood there in the moment, not knowing what to think or say to me, I'm sure.

She told me, "Oh, dear. You poor thing. What have they done to you? No, honey, never. And you'll be okay while you are here with Jim and me." She pulled me in for a hug then gave me a little peck on the forehead while patting my back. Vickie, and now Marylou, were the only people who made me feel like a human during this time.

The first night was simple. We had pizza and played a board game. Marylou gave me one of her oversized t-shirts to sleep in, and I slept on the bottom bunk in Chad's room. He slept in his brother's room.

Breakfast came early but not too soon, and it was cold cereal, which was great. Marylou had some little pieces of paper with a bunch of colors on them at the breakfast table. She asked me what my favorite color was. I wasn't sure, so I kind of shrugged, looking at the colored tabs. Then I saw a dark purple and pointed to that one. Marylou fumbled around with the clips and found a few colors like the one I chose and showed them to me. After a little bit, she had somehow convinced me to get lavender, and it was a pretty color like the lilacs at my old hiding place.

Jim left for the store that same day, returning with some paint and began painting the room next to theirs. It only took two days for him to get my room all finished. I watched as they had brought a modest single bed up from their basement and a small dresser and staged the room. It looked wonderful!

After Jim finished painting and setting up, Marylou and Jim led me into the room, excitedly explaining that this was going to be my very own bedroom while I lived with them. They showed me the closet and told me that was mine, too, even though I had nothing to hang in that closet. Marylou bought me a Holly Hobby poster for my room and told me I reminded her of a pretty Holly Hobby girl. When she gave it to me, it was rolled up and tied with a purple bow, which kind of matched my room and reminded me of the present from my best friend, Sarah. I loved it!

Marylou took me shopping, and we got everything. New shoes, dresses, shorts, tops, under panties, flip flops, a hairbrush, and a toothbrush. She even let me get a new sweater, "in case it gets chilly out." I felt like a princess for the first time. I knew they were rich too because we went to K-Mart. I was used to Goodwill and garage sales or hand-me-downs, which are all fine, but to get to go where the rich go was excellent.

I had never gone shopping like this before. I was overwhelmed and very happy. I began to think maybe this foster home living is okay if I can stay with these people and not have to go back to the other places ever again. And maybe Vickie could come here and live too, we could share a room like before. Pleasant thoughts were all had, and I enjoyed life.

For the next eight months of my life, I had the best childhood I had ever experienced, and I wanted to stay forever.

During my stay with Marylou and Jim, I learned how a regular family acts towards one another, a family who loves each other and wants the best for each other. Moreover, I learned how they *don't* behave. They don't yell, scream, and throw things, and they do not make the kids lie to police officers (they don't even regularly interact with police). I began to understand what a real family was like. We ate together at least once a day. The man of the house works a real job and earns his pay. There was no waiting for food stamps and a welfare check. I learned that standing in welfare commodity lines to get free cheese and peanut butter isn't earning what you eat, it's a handout. They taught me that hard work pays off, and you should live by working for all the things you need or want. Oh, and if you can't buy it with your own money, you don't need it. Either save for it or don't get it.

I learned that God does love us all, and he doesn't hurt us when he's pissed off. I was thrilled to learn that God wasn't the beast Virgie made me think he was. For many years Virgie told me that if I didn't do what she said, God would punish me for not obeying her because she was the adult and my boss. She once told me that God was going to make me get into a car accident, and he would cut off my leg because I didn't want to carry something so heavy it hurt my back. So, I did it even though my back hurt for a long time after, I'd rather have back pain than my leg cut off.

She told me another time that someday, when I have a baby, God will kill it if I didn't listen and do exactly what she told me to do. I was horrified, and from the age of seven, I never wanted kids. I was afraid Virgie would tell God I didn't do something, and then he'd kill my baby or cut off a leg, an arm, or something. She told me all kinds of shit, and I believed her. It took most of the eight months for me to realize that God was a good guy and wouldn't kill or dismember me for not being a good kid.

Marylou taught me to be a team player in a family setting. She taught me that family sticks together, and they don't hurt each other. They took me to church every Sunday and one evening a week for a Bible study. I gained so many friends at church, and not one of them looked at me differently because I was a foster kid. They treated me just like one of the gang. They burped in my face and laughed about it. They farted and waved it my way. They did the armpit farts, and we all laughed. One boy always picked his nose and wiped it on the wall behind one of us, and because he did that to me too, I felt a part of the group. The kids treating me the same as everyone else was key to making me feel something I had never felt before, a part of something greater than myself, a team of friends.

We did a newspaper drive, a pop can drive, and sold candy bars to get enough money to go to Cedar Point for the day. Marylou had to get special permission to take me out of state, she made that happen. My first roller coaster ride was the Blue Streak, and I rode it four times, the last time holding up my hands and screaming. We ate cotton candy and peanuts, and the church brought a picnic, we met up and had lunch and dinner together at the pavilion.

I had the best day of my life. And I loved my foster family. I never wanted to leave. I had a family, and I was able to just be a kid—no more worrying about Virgie and Donny abusing me. I never worried about giving any chore money I earned to Virgie anymore. She wasn't there. I didn't even miss anyone, but I did think about my mom, Chelcie, more so than anyone else, often wishing I could see her.

When I first arrived, I was worried about playing outside because I had overheard the social worker say to Marylou that Virgie was very upset and claimed she would find me and take me back home. It was a couple of months before they got me to go outside and play with the other kids. I was scared she'd come rolling up in her old car and start yelling, screaming, and hitting me, or worse, have Donny with her who would grab me up and then kill Chelcie. I felt it wise to stay out of her sight, so I did my best to stay invisible and keep Chelcie safe in this process.

Poor Marylou. She talked to me all the time about how it was safe, that Virgie was two towns over, and that she'd never find me. But I knew how dangerous Virgie was. I knew what she could do, she told me, so I didn't want to put Marylou and her family in any danger with Virgie or Donny. In addition to protecting Chelcie, I now felt responsible for keeping Marylou, Jim, and the boys safe

THE ENTIRE TIME I was in foster care, my dad and stepmom only came to see me once. He claims it was more, but I know it was only once. The day I was taken to Social Services to visit with him, Martha picked me up, and we went into a small room. The room was all white with two big windows. There was a big, long, square table and chairs for us to sit and talk. I sat, Maudie Jo sat, but my dad stood at the head of the table. We had zero minutes of small talk, and right away, first thing, he asked me why I accused my brother of "this"? Why would I do something like "this"? What made me so angry to blame my brother of "this"?

Neither offered a hello hug, or peck on the cheek, or a pat on the head. They just came in and spewed their hate on me like projectile vomit. It was nothing like I had played out in my mind. In my mind, I thought my dad would be so happy to see me, he will hug me and kiss my cheeks and tell me how much he missed me. I thought the day would be a great one since it'd been six months since I'd seen him. I hoped for happiness and love, but all I got was yelled at about someone who enjoyed threatening me, threatening to kill my biological mother and siblings, hitting me, and making me finger fuck myself.

I sat, looking at him with no words. He got loud, and I could tell by the tone of his voice he was upset because I wasn't answering quick enough for him. I shrugged my shoulders, and that infuriated him even more so. He told me that if he found out that Chelcie was behind this lie, he was going to blow her head off and that dumb son of a bitch Claude too.

His wife told him, "Watch yourself, she might lie on you next."

He looked at her and said, "I don't give a damn. Look what she did to her brother."

It was about 2 seconds later when Martha burst into the room, telling them they had to cut the visit, and she took me out. No hugs goodbye, no kisses, no wish-I-could-see-you-longer, just a scowl and a head-shaking from my dad while his wife turned her head to look away.

What a great visit! I don't see him for about six months, and when I do, I get this? Fine!

I cried on the way back to Marylou's house, so Martha stopped at the Dairy Queen down the street and got me ice cream before she returned me. We sat talking. She told me that everything would be okay, and she asked me if I wanted to see my dad again. I shrugged (my thing to do). She told me it was okay if I didn't want to, so I told her no. I didn't want to see them again. I figured if I did see him, it was going to be the same, and honestly, I sincerely hoped for Marylou and Jim to adopt me. I thought, *why did he want to see me anyway? Why tell them anything? They will just believe what they want rather than what really happened. Why would I bother to tell anyone anything?*

I visited with my mom, Claude, and Glenn once. Their visit was a little better than the one with my dad. I thought they were all going to squeeze the breath out of me for the first five minutes. And, kisses, enough to last me a while. I loved it. I loved them. We talked about the farm animals, the dogs, and all the kitties. She told me that all my brothers and sisters said to tell me hi and they missed me. She told me about a baby deer they found by the house and how they doctored it back to health. Then she told me to be careful about going outside because Virgie was looking for me, and that scared the shit out of me, again.

She explained that if Virgie found me playing in the streets, she'd make me go with her, and no one could do anything, so I should stay inside and away from the windows. "And make sure you cover your head when you walk outside so she can't see you," she said.

It was about that time Martha came into the room and ended the visit.

On the way home, Martha took me to Dairy Queen again, and I asked her if Virgie was looking for me because Chelcie said she was. Martha told me Virgie wasn't, and I was okay to keep playing outside in the backyard. I felt better. I figured Martha was telling me the truth. She wasn't like my family. She was kind.

The two visits with both my bio parents and the actions and attitudes they continued to display only made me want to be adopted by Marylou and Jim even more. I felt as if my family never loved me, and I was only a burden to them, which was why they were always in an uproar and mad about something. Not my mom, but trust me, she had her moments too. I guess I figured if I had a new beginning, things might be better. Obviously, I didn't do any favors to my older brother other than supposedly tell a lie on him. A lie that I never spoke out of my mouth yet took the blame for all these years.

I never got to visit with Chelcie or my dad again while in foster care, and Virgie wasn't allowed to come near me. For months, I lived free of that family, taunting me with their hate and bullying about who I was, the bastard, the pawn.

My time in the foster home was undoubtedly the best of my life at that point, and I didn't want to leave. For eight months, I was happy with people who weren't my blood, but they were my family. I wanted more than anything for Marylou and Jim to adopt me, then I would be their real daughter. And no more fighting. No more hitting. No more screaming and name-calling and threats of killing people, just no more of them!

I had moved into their home in May. I had just turned ten years old. I finished fourth grade while in their home, had the best summer of my life, and began the fifth grade. I left foster care in late October, a few days before Halloween.

THE DAY I LEFT, it was a bright, beautiful sunny day, and yet one of the saddest days of my childhood. Marylou told me to wear my favorite dress, wipe the dirt off my church shoes, and take my sweater. She told me I'd be back as I'd have to get all my things. She told me she'd wait for the call, and when Martha called, she'd pack things up for me and have them ready when I stopped by with whoever I would be living with. Jim stayed home that day to see me off. He hugged me and told me to be a good kid and study hard in school. Brian and I said our goodbyes early since he was off to school. It was sweet. He told me I was his favorite sister. I was the only foster sister he had, so of course, I was his favorite.

During our long embrace, Marylou told me to be brave and strong and not to forget she loves me. Chad was about three, and he was still sleeping, but I hugged Marylou twice, once for her and once for Chad. I was sad that I was going to court even though I wasn't sure what court was, I was scared and anxious all at the same time.

Martha came to get me. She told me Virgie would be there, but she said not to worry as we were going to use the backdoor, and I never had to see or be around Virgie if I didn't want to. I was freaked out. Seeing Virgie after all this time meant she was still in control and I would have to do as she said, my heart broke. I lost my faith in humanity. I was told I would never have to deal with Virgie again, and now I was going to see her. Nonetheless, Martha said she wouldn't leave me, so gripping tight to her hand by her side, I stayed.

Martha and I went into the side of the building and to the second-floor Juvenile division. The judge was waiting, so as soon as we got out of the elevator, we went into his chambers. His room was terrific, he had books from the floor to the ceiling. They were in excellent

126

condition, not like the school library. They were in wood bookcases, and his desk was the same color of wood with big diplomas on the wall behind his big chair. He told me to come in and have a seat.

We talked about how I liked my foster home, and if I'd miss them. I told him I'd like to stay living there, but I know I can't. He laughed and told me he was glad I enjoyed the people I was staying with and that I enjoyed my time there. *Why is that funny?* I wondered.

Then he asked me where I'd like to live for the rest of my life, "Well, until you turn 18, that is."

I sat there and thought about it for a few seconds, and then I told him I didn't want to ever go back to Virgie's house as Donny always comes around, and he and his mom were both mean to me. He asked me to explain, so I told him they say mean things and do mean things like hit me and pull my hair, and sometimes Donny chokes me and holds me up against the wall. I also told him they both threaten to kill Chelcie all the time. I wanted him to know so he could make them stop. I thought he could because he was the judge and in charge.

He asked about my dad. I told him he worked and had a job, and his wife stayed at home. I continued, "I think it would be best if I lived with my dad because he works and earns his own money. Even though I really want to live with my mom."

I continued to explain that "I love her the most and I'd like to live with her, but I don't think she can afford another kid because she has Glenn and having me would make her spend more money than she gets from the welfare people."

I asked him if he would please have my dad and stepmom not say mean things about my mom Chelcie. I told him, "They do that, and it hurts my feelings, and when they threaten to kill her, it scares me because I know they will."

He listened, nodded yes, sighed loudly, then smiled and told me he had to go and talk to all the adults in his courtroom and for me to wait in his office. He handed me a book to look at while I waited. I told him I loved books and wanted to write them one day. He laughed and told me to study hard, and I could when I got older.

Soon enough, the Judge returned to his room, and Martha was by his side. They told me I would be living with my dad and stepmom, and they were waiting in the hallway for me. The all-white hallway smelled like a medical office. I noticed the pictures on the walls, but nothing I cared to stop and view. The sun was shining through the all-glass windows, but there wasn't anything pretty about the courtroom hallway. I instinctively knew it was the stage of a pivotal heartbreaking scene in my life.

There they were, my dad and his wife—and so was Claude, Glenn, my brothers—Robert and William—my mom, and Virgie. Chelcie grabbed me first and held me to her side, patting my butt then she said, "Be a good girl, and I love ya." She then turned and walked towards everyone else sitting and waiting for her.

It was as if I could feel the pain butchering her heart. Once again, Ardy won the little girl she carried and gave birth to. Once again, she was beaten down and losing to Virgie and Ardy. The look on her face was so aching and lonely. I wanted to cry, but the tears were already rolling down her cheeks. She was a lost woman, and I felt terrible, it was my fault. I told the judge I wanted to live with my dad because he had a job. Her agony this time was all my fault. I did this. I hurt her when I tried to make it better for her, but I was wrong.

Virgie saw me and rushed to my side. She grabbed me and sort of hugged me with tears in her eyes and told me, "I can't believe you'd do this to Donny."

After Chelcie and Virgie said their goodbyes to me, my dad and his wife came up to me. Dad told me, "Well, you're going home with me, come on." They both started walking towards the elevator, I followed in silence. As we stepped inside, dad reached over and pushed the 1st-floor button, looked at me, and shook his head. His wife stood by his side with a mean-looking scowl, and her head turned towards the wall, away from me as if she couldn't bear to look my way.

I asked if we could get my things from Marylou's. I mentioned my Holly Hobby poster, and I was excited for him to see it since it was my first. He immediately started his whining and bitching. "Oh, Peggy! You don't need a poster. What clothes do you have there? Why didn't you bring them? You should have known better than this."

Yes, dad, you are correct. I should have known better than this. Why in the fuck did I say I'd be better off with you? That's my current lesson. Why didn't I just ask to go live with who my heart wanted me to live with?

Martha met us as the elevator door opened. She grabbed me and hugged me and asked my dad if he'd like to follow her to my foster parent's house so I could get my things. He told her he didn't have time and needed to get home to Jackson. Maudie Jo stood there, speechless with her lips pursed, a look that I quickly got used to seeing. Not sure what my dad's reasoning was other than a bullshit excuse for nothing. All I wanted was my fucking clothes and my Goddamn Holly Hobby poster! I was sad that I wasn't allowed to go and get my things and say a proper goodbye. However, in my dad's defense (now that I am older), the court was in Marshall and my foster home in Battle Creek. It was about 17 minutes in the opposite direction we needed to go, which would have added 34 minutes extra to our day. The gas in 1974 was around 0.40 cents a gallon, and we might have used an extra gallon.

What-the-fuck-ever! He should have let me say goodbye, and he should have let me get my goddamn Holly Hobby poster.

Martha let me know that it would be okay, she'd mail them to our house in Jackson, and I should get them in a few days, including my poster. I hugged her again, telling her thanks and that I'd miss our ice cream dates and talks. I asked her if she would tell Marylou that I couldn't come back but let her know that I will miss her very much and Jim and the boys.

Had I not had to make a choice to live with family again, I would have hands down lived with Jim and Marylou for the rest of my days. I loved them very much and had the best life as a child with them.

The courts were fucked up. They should have left me in foster care. And, I am not sure if my stuff was mailed or not but, I never received anything.

THE RIDE TO MY NEW HOME in Jackson was long and seemed as if it took forever. We stopped to get something at McDonald's because they were cheap. We went inside and ate, and neither one of them spoke a word to me. As I unhappily ate my happy meal in silence, they talked between themselves and made many comments about poor Donny and how they were going to deal with him visiting while I lived there. These poor people. What were they going to do?

Hmm, I guess it would have been too much to ask that someone talk to me and try and find out what happened that night. You'd think they would want to know the truth, and you'd think they would sit me down and talk about it. But they were not a healthy family. Can you say dysfunctional?

I felt lost, lonely, and unwanted. I had no clue it was going to be so hard to have me move in with them. I wondered, why did they even come to court? Why would they take me to live with them? Why not just tell the judge, they didn't want me but were just trying to make themselves look good? Let Chelcie have her. I would have gone with my mom eagerly, but again, I made my decision based on ten-year-old logic.

Thanks for making me feel so loved you fuckers!

As we rounded the corner one block away from dad's house, we saw Donny standing at the end of a welding building where he worked. My dad pulled over while rolling his window down so they could talk for a few minutes. As we pulled away, I figured I had better be good, so I told Donny goodbye.

Well, that wasn't the thing to do. I was yelled at, cussed out, then lectured on why I should never speak to my brother again, all the way home (even though it was one block, it seemed like forever). He asked me, "Why would you talk to your brother after you lied and accused him of doing what you said he did? Why would you think he'd want to speak to you?" I began to cry, which made him even more upset because I had no reason to since I was the liar. His wife piped in, telling me to "dry up those tears, young lady and own what you've done. You lied on your brother, and now nobody trusts you, and they never will because you're a liar!"

As we pulled into the drive, he shut off the truck, I got out slowly and walked into yet another new home. Dad wasn't happy, he told me to go to my room and think about what I had done to my brother. As I hung my head down in shame I didn't earn, I crawled up onto the bed and allowed the tears to fall.

I sat there reflecting on the whole day starting out with saying— what I didn't know would be—a final goodbye to people who actually showed me they care about me for the past eight months. Then I thought about the court hearing, visiting with the Judge, dealing with the trauma of Virgie and Chelcie both in the hallway at the same time, ending with the unbelievable blame coming from my dad and Maudie Jo. I was not asking for, nor did I think I deserved, someone to roll out the red carpet for me, but a little compassion goes a long way, especially to a ten-year-old kid who just went through hell and back. Nonetheless, I was used to the family treating me like I didn't matter.

Dad came into my room and spouted off about Chelcie, reminding me once again that, if he finds out that she had anything to do with all this, he will blow her head off "and that SOB Claude's too." Sarcasm began settling in as I glared at him from the bed. *I'm so happy you remind me of this often. I had forgotten how much you hate them. Will you do us all a favor and just shoot me too?*

As I sat on the bed, listening to my dad threaten my mom's life, I realized what a terrible mistake I made when I told the judge Chelcie couldn't afford me. I honestly thought for a quick minute, life might be best with my dad. At least the drama wouldn't be there, and maybe I could have a chance at some peace and a somewhat normal childhood. There I went, thinking again.

I cried myself to sleep that night.

The next day I was enrolled in school and, because he had to take me, my dad missed a half-day of work, and that was all my fault too. He'd already lost the day before because he had to go to court over me. That was a day and a half of pay he "doesn't need to be docked for." I prayed I would never need him to go to my school again. *Goddamn, that'd be too much if he needed to miss any more work and money over me. How would I make that up to him?*

I was enrolled at East Jackson Middle School, a newer school that had a pleasant smell. I was in fifth grade. I had a room in which three teachers opened folding doors and integrated us all together for part of the day. We all enjoyed such a large classroom. It was fun. I made many friends, and school was still my escape to get away from the reality of the monsters I was living with and all the harshness of daily life.

I liked the bus ride. I learned how to cuss, spit far, and drop a loogie, I learned boys stink and fart (which I already knew, but this just reassured my thoughts about them), and I also learned that they don't always brush their teeth at that age. Riding the bus was a big part of my school day, and I always looked forward to walking to the bus stop with my BFF at that time, Lori, and another friend and neighbor, Penny. Lori and I hung out all the time for the entire summer before this school year. My first summer living with my dad and Maudie Jo wasn't the great summer I hoped for, but Lori made it fun.

I also hung out with Samantha down the street when Lori was busy watching her siblings. I was 11, and Lori was 13, so she was old enough to babysit, which she did all the time. She had four younger siblings, Katie, Raymond, Candy, and Sammy. Sammy was a baby in diapers, and he ran around cussing all the time. His vocabulary consisted of, fuck, fuck you, mother fucker, bitch, and pussy. Really. His dad had a horrible mouth, and well, so did his mother. Lori cussed all the time, too, when we were together hanging out. I used to swear and say the F-word when I was with her, and she would laugh, which encouraged it, I thought it was fun to speak, not to mention cussing was something I was already accustomed to from my younger years of living with Mommy.

Raymond Sr. was Lori and Katie's stepdad, he was a tall, bigger-built man with brown hair that was thinning and went crazy in the wind. He always had very rosy cheeks, and they were puffy too. His belly protruded over his pants, which hung down enough to see his butt crack. Raymond Sr. worked on cars in his backyard and pounded his tools while cursing at them. He had a job away from his house, but after work and on weekends, he was in his driveway or backyard working on his or someone else's vehicle.

Despite his wild nature, he was always kind to me, he always called me squirt and would acknowledge me every time he saw me. He'd say, "Hey, squirt, what the hell ya doing?" I'd smile and say, "Hi, Raymond, nothing, is Lori home?" He'd reply, "In the house sitting on her fat ass like her mother." I think that was about the extent of our conversations. As I said, he was good to me. I was never afraid of him even though he was a big guy and looked as if he could really kick some ass if he needed or wanted to, yet Raymond was like a big teddy bear to the other kids and me even though he yelled and cussed all the time.

One time my dad and Raymond Sr. had words about his constant cussing, and he stopped for a long time. Not sure what was said, but I know my dad wasn't happy about his loud, dirty mouth. Pot meet kettle. In my dad's defense, Raymond *was* very loud, his voice carried from his backyard to both sides of neighbor's yards, and we were one of his neighbors.

Once around Easter, the local dime store was selling baby ducks. Well, I was fortunate enough to earn an allowance if I did all my chores each week. I always did. I worked hard for that $1.00, and sometimes I'd get an extra 0.25 cents. (Yes, dammit, that was a lot of money back then. Stop laughing!) Lori and I would walk down to the dime store and get trinkets. I was frugal, though, and I counted every nickel, dime, and penny and would also save a little every week. I was saving for my retirement. I had a small tin box I kept under my bed that had a piece of masking tape on the top I labeled, "Retirement Cash."

We saw the ducks, and I just had to have one. Without asking or thinking, I spent $.50 on one baby duckie and took her home. I figured she could sleep in my room, and I'd take care of her myself. I also thought it was a female duck, so I called her Darlene. My older brother William had a girlfriend named Darlene, and she was so sweet I just loved her, so I named my duck after her.

Lori bought one too. Then her mom went back and bought all the other kids a duck for Easter. My dad, Maudie Jo, and Becky (Lori's mom) explained to me that since my duck was alone without her siblings, it would be a good thing to keep Darlene with the other ducks so she wouldn't get lonely, so I did.

I would go over every day and visit the ducks. The adults said it wasn't right to handle the ducks too much, but I did anyway. I mean, she was my Darlene, I had to. Until one late fall, Becky was plucking feathers off a dead duck. Becky explained they were actually chickens. I didn't believe her until I realized my Darlene was gone. The other kids laughed at me, calling me a stupid bitch.

It all sank in. *Becky and Raymond had taken my duck, Darlene, raised her, fed her, killed her, and now they are going to eat her. Them assholes!*

I was pissed at Lori as she knew the whole time, and of course, my dad and Maudie Jo knew too. I told Becky and Raymond they had to pay me my 0.50 cents back, and my dad said that was a good lesson for me to learn that next time, I better make sure I have the means to care for a "duck" before I go and buy one. I disagreed that watching my Darlene get her feathers plucked off and then stuffed in a bag and put in a freezer was a good lesson. I have never even tried duck in my life, and I am sure I never will. Therefore, this is why I shall never touch dead duckie to my lips, right here.

It was summertime and no more school! Lori and I got to hang out together every day, and one of our favorite pastimes was listening in on our parents' talks. Maudie Jo went over to Lori's house to visit with Becky, almost every single day. Off she'd go with coffee in one hand and her cigarettes in the other. One day Lori said we were going to listen like 007 and get information, then go on a hunt to solve the mystery. I was okay with it, I didn't know what the hell she was talking about anyway. Lori sometimes would carry on a conversation, and I would be so lost, but because we were friends, I'd always agree with her and tell her, "That is so cool."

It was a hot summer, and Becky had no cooling system other than fans, so she kept her kitchen window opened. Lori and I crouched down under the window, plopping quietly, and listening to Becky and Maudie Jo talk. They talked about soap operas, some Hollywood people, and about recipes and cooking, Maudie Jo always liked to cook and bake.

Then Becky asked how is Peggy doing living in the new house? That's when I heard Maudie Jo tell how she really felt. I was used to hearing mean shit about me, and I would ignore it when it came from Virgie and Donny, which is where it came from most of the time. I just never thought Maudie Jo felt that way towards me, but she did.

Through eavesdropping, I learned that my stepmom hated my mom, Chelcie, and thought she was a whore. I also realized that she never wanted me to come live with them, especially after I "lied on Donny."

I cried. Lori told her mom that we overheard her and Maudie Jo talking and that my feelings were hurt. Well, that wasn't received positively. I was scolded for listening in on the two ladies talking privately, and then I was promptly grounded. I had a week to stay inside and do nothing, no TV, no Lori, no outside, no nothing but sit in my room and think about what I did wrong.

Her giving me this jail sentence and taking away everything for a full week—and being such a bitch about it—made me hate her even more than hearing her call my mom a whore or say she didn't want me because I was a liar. It was at that time that my hate began building in my heart for Maudie Jo. I stopped loving her. I stopped thinking she was the smartest woman I'd ever met. I stopped thinking that her cooking was the best I'd ever eaten. And, I simply stopped wanting to even be around her.

I made it through the week like a fucking champ. And I was grateful that at least I wasn't hit and called terrible names. I only got grounded for eavesdropping and hearing the truth.

Virgie got visiting rights back, I was with her on the weekend, and we went to Granny's to see everyone. All her siblings were there. Everyone was in the trailer next to Granny's laughing and talking, having a grand ole time—at the moment, anyway. I mean, they hadn't started threatening to kill each other yet or blow a hole in each other's head, shit like that which would start fights and name-calling and all the typical festivities.

All of us kids were running around in the front yard playing tag and doing kid things when I decided I needed a drink. I had to go into the trailer to get a drink, so, inside, I went. I said a cheery Hi! to all my aunts and uncles, and when I said hi to Uncle Buck, he shouted at me, "Get the fuck out of my trailer, you little lying bitch before I blow your head off!" Shocked, sort of, I stood there and asked, "What did I do?" Uncle Buck looked at me and said, "You lied on your brother, and I don't want you around me. I'm afraid you might lie on me too. Now get out and don't come back or I'll kill you!"

Not one adult said anything to him. Virgie snickered, shrugging her shoulders, and told me to get out and go to the car and sit until she was ready to go. One of her siblings spoke up and said, "Well, when you lie, this is what happens. You should have thought about it before you lied on poor Donny."

I stood there dumbfounded and glanced over at Chelcie and Claude, hoping she would speak up and tell everyone that she was the one who told, not me. She didn't. She looked away and left me standing there, getting screamed at by a drunk uncle who might have pulled his gun and took me out. No one ever knew what crazy will do when they are drunk and pissed off, such as they always were.

Here again, thrown under the bus by the adults who were supposed to love and care for me, I stood alone to fend for myself. I turned, went to the car as I was told to do, and waited.

I never looked at my Uncle Buck the same again. From that day on, I felt that I saw his true colors come out towards me, and I also knew that my own birth mother was going to let me take the fall for the lie, which I did. Repeatedly. But I did it to save her life and to save my other siblings, so I thought.

LORI AND I HUNG TOGETHER from sunup till sundown all summer. I was eleven, and she, thirteen, and we were inseparable. She got a job babysitting a young couple's newborn baby. The couple lived next door to me. His name was Joe, and hers, Katie. My dad didn't like them because they would have parties and invite their friends over who had long hair, drank beer, smoked pot, and played loud rock-n-roll music. They didn't bother me since drinking and loud people were things, I had been around all my life except while in the foster home, but my dad certainly wasn't a partier. I don't recall seeing my dad even drink a beer, ever!

Nonetheless, Joe was a good-looking guy who liked to mow his lawn shirtless. Lori would stalk them since she had a big crush on Joe, and when he cut his lawn, she'd sit in my front yard and watch him while making up little stories of her and Joe running away and kissing, which actually grossed me out, but, I listened, laughed, and chimed in here and there as girls do.

His wife, Katie was skinny, short, had long brown hair, and wore the coolest clothes, hippie stuff, which makes me smile still to this day. She was pretty and had a big smile. They were friendly people, but Joe made me mad back then because I knew he went frog hunting and ate frog legs. I thought killing frogs so you could eat their body parts was awful. Now, I still think it's *gross* and disgusting. Funny, I'm not sure there is much difference than eating a burger or a piece of chicken, but what did I know, I was a kid, thinking like a kid does.

Once when Lori was babysitting, she just happened to 'accidentally' find their stash of weed, so she took a pinch. The next day, while my dad was working, but my stepmom was home, I went over to her house, her parents were gone with her siblings. She told me what she had found at Joe and Katie's, and she explained to me how we could "get high."

She broke out the marijuana and rolled it up in a piece of a brown paper bag (a grocery bag) then taped it with scotch tape, lite the end, and up in smoke, it went as we both quickly took one puff off of it and about choked to death. The paper caught fire fast, and the weed fell out of the end onto the floor. We rushed to open the front door to let out the smoke before her parents got back and smelled it. We were both terrified and running around like two chickens with their heads cut off as we fanned the kitchen, opened windows and doors to let the smoke roll out (honestly, it wasn't that much smoke), and prayed her dad and mom wouldn't come home early. All the while, we were yelling at each other, "Oh God! Get the doors opened, open the windows, hurry! Grab the dustpan, sweep up the weed off the floor. Here, wave this magazine by the window to make it go out, hurry-hurry!"

After the smoke cleared, we thought we were high, and both once again got scared stiff (can you say paranoid?) so, she grabbed this big ass jar of pickles (32 oz.) from her fridge and poured all the juice out and split it for us to drink. She told me it would take away our buzz and the smell of pot on us (I didn't smell marijuana, but I did smell burnt grocery bag). Both of us downed that shitty juice so fast then we ate a few pickles. Who knows, maybe we were high and had the munchies for pickles and the liquid.

Her parents pulled in about that time, and I rushed out the back door so as not to be seen.

After I got home, I laid down, and it hit me, up came that pickle juice and chunks of pickles (projectile style). My stepmom, Maudie Jo, assumed I was sick, which technically I was.

Lori ended up telling her mom what happened, and then her mom confronted me but swore to me that she'd never tell my dad or stepmom. I think she kept her promise as I never got into trouble for it. Nonetheless, I've never been a fan of pickle juice since that day.

After the summer was almost over, dad and Maudie Jo put the house on the market and moved to the country — the same town, just a different suburb and school. Now I was going to Napoleon schools. We moved to the Clark Lake area into a small two-bedroom house. My dad had his chickens and dogs and a big spot for a garden.

Soon enough, we met the neighbors, and I became friends with their daughter, Sadie. They had horses, dogs, and cats. Their farmhouse was big, and they had substantial red barns too.

Sadie seemed pleasant enough. She asked me if I wanted to ride to school with her since she had just gotten her driver's license. That was exciting to not have to wait for the school bus anymore. I felt like a grown person riding with Sadie. We'd listen to the radio and sing on the way to school, it was a fun ride, and I cherish those days traveling to school with her. Times like those were few and far between for me, which made them even more special and memorable.

She also let me go with her down the street to babysit. That was fun too. I only got to go once, as Maudie Jo claimed she didn't want me to bother her while she was working. I mean, really. She asked me to come, and she also asked the people if she could bring me. Step-Mommy dearest put the kibosh on that. It seemed like every time Maudie Jo would correct me for something, she'd make sure she told me that her daughter would never have done that as she knew better. That was her daughter from a previous life, another person I could never seem to measure up to.

THE SUMMER THAT I TURNED 12 was my dad's family reunion, and I was very excited to go and hang out with all my cousins. I hadn't seen them for about two years, since before the foster home. It also happened to be my birthday.

My Uncle David, my dad's brother, had the same birthday as mine, and we always teased each other, saying who was born on whose day. Uncle David would win that debate because he was older. We would just laugh and laugh. It was our thing, and it was fun. Uncle David was a taller man with a medium build, and he had sort of an Elvis look going on because he wore his dark hair slicked back with a poof. He typically wore blue jeans and white t-shirts with his cigarettes rolled in his sleeve. Everyone used to say he was so handsome and smart.

As soon as we arrived at the park, I ran inside the building to find Uncle David, and when I did, I was so excited to see him I ran up to him with arms out for the birthday hug, hollering, "Hey old man, Happy Birthday!"

He immediately pushed me away and backed up. Glaring at me, he said, "You stay away from me. I don't trust you. You lied on your brother, and I don't want you lying on my boys or me, so you stay away from them too, do you hear me, you, little troublemaker. You stay away!" He then continued with, "Go find a tree to die under and leave all the other kids alone. No one wants to talk to you or play with you "cause you're a liar!"

With my head down and my sad eyes filling with tears, I walked out of that building, went and found a tree on the hillside, and sat quietly under it. I sat there alone while all the other kids played freeze tag, kickball, and rolling down the hill. Most of the other kids left me alone, and I sat wishing I would die.

Maudie Jo came out to the tree and asked if I was going to eat, I told her no. She got mad and told me I had better eat because there wouldn't be anything else other than this. I shook my head, no. I didn't want to go back inside where all the other adults were, and Uncle David especially. I figured since the other kids were not playing with me, their parents had told them to leave me alone too.

On the way home, my dad yelled at me for crying and not eating, and then he told me I could just go to bed hungry, so I did. The drive from Indiana to Jackson was long, and I fell asleep in the backseat. After that ordeal, I hated family reunions, and I never attended another. I hated Uncle David. I hated Virgie. I hated Donny. I hated Maudie Jo, and my dad was on the list of seriously not liking.

The hate grew more intense, and I wanted so badly to get away from everyone. I never understood why my own family was so evil. What I did know was that whatever went wrong was my fault, whatever went right wasn't because of anything I did, and anyone I cared about—or more so wanted and needed love from—wasn't able to give it, at least to me.

My dad talked negatively about Chelcie and Claude all the time, reminding me of his violent ideas if he found out they were behind my "lying about Donny." This threat always kept me on alert, still holding the secret safe that it really was my mom that said everything and not me. They even gave me a lie detector test when I was in foster care, and because I couldn't keep my feet still (because I was a scared-shit-less 10-year-old), the guy gave up, and that meant I failed. But I didn't really fall short. I couldn't keep my damn legs still, so the readings were off. I was told many times to hold still, stop wiggling, sit still, keep your legs still, stop moving your arms. He told me so much he literally gave up and gave me a failed result. But in his defense, he did tell my lawyer and social worker, "She failed because she can't sit still, and I can't get a correct read."

My family, the ones who should have believed me and helped me, held on to that "truth." I failed the lie detector test, so in their limited, uneducated, backward minds, I lied.

It was after the family reunion event that I thought about killing myself. I thought, *why not? No one likes me anyway, and I hate all these pieces of shit. I'm stuck here until I'm old enough to live on my own, and that will be forever.* I felt there was no way out of the hell I was in, and I wanted out. No one stuck up for me, and I had endured enough crap to last me a lifetime.

I was tired. I was done. I felt there was no more I could take.

My head was about to explode. The tears were non-stop at times, and I hated myself. I hated me because no one else cared. *I must be a horrible person. I just want to die and be done with life, it's not fair and I'm not happy. What is the point?*

LIVING IN NAPOLEON was nice. I met many new friends in school and again, loved being at school as it was always a way to escape. I never wanted to stay home because if I did, I would have been confined to my bed. That happened once when I was sick — high fever and puking all day. Maudie Jo gave me a pail and made me stay in bed. I had to let her know when I needed to pee, which was the only time I was allowed to get up. I hated being sick. I really hated it.

My BFF Daisy had a twin, Tess, and they looked exactly alike. I could tell them apart, though. They were shorter than me by about an inch and had long black hair to their butts. They had their nails painted pink all the time, and their front teeth were a little buck-toothed, not too bad, though, just a tad. They were skinny girls with big boobs for being seventh graders. Well, I thought so, but then again, I was flat-chested like a pancake. When you are in seventh grade, these are the things you notice and think about.

I had a crush on their older brother, Boo. I never learned his real name. I don't think I cared what his name was, he was just cute, and I liked him. I'm not sure the feelings were reciprocated as he would always roll his eyes and shake his head at us girls, then walk away, giggling. He was a senior, and I was not on his level in more ways than one.

Daisy, Tess, and I had lunch together every day at school, we also shared a few classes. We'd sit by each other when we could, and talk. Our science teacher moved our seats after the first day. Our math teacher, Mr. Cane, was a dreamboat, who gave us plenty to talk about. All the girls thought he was the cutest teacher at Napoleon. His girlfriend did too, I bet.

Both the girls went to church, and they were very adamant about me going to church with them and getting "saved." I needed to find

Jesus and be saved, or I would go to hell and burn forever. The old hell, fire, and brimstone! I wasn't feeling the whole church thing. I'd been away from Marylou's for so long. I guess the idea of going to a different church wasn't ringing a bell for me. I loved the church family I had at Marylou's, but that was gone now. I remember going to church with Virgie, and the preacher (who, by the way, I thought the sun shone for) would preach fiery pits of hell, and if you don't obey, God will allow you to burn forever, and Jesus will send you to the pits of hell if you don't follow what he says to do. Yeah, scary shit. I feared God and what he might do to me all the time. Why would I want to go back to that kind of teaching?

I told Daisy in private that I had thought about killing myself, and I told her why, not everything, just a little. I told her about what happened with Donny and being in a foster home and then living with my dad (I summed this up as well as I could). I then told her about the family reunion and that I was sick of my family and wanted to die. She insisted I go to church and that God would help me, she made me promise not to try anything dumb. I promised.

They won. I went. The one and only time I went to church, with Daisy and Tess and her friend Della Jean, was a flashback for me. They were Pentecostal. Therefore, the speaking in tongues and falling out in the Spirit was nothing new to me. I went to the altar and accepted Jesus as my savior and prayed but did not speak in tongues at that time. I was told I needed to pray harder and louder, but still, nothing happened. There was one point I was screaming for God to save me and fill me with the Holy Ghost so I could speak in other tongues. It still didn't happen, which reinforced the theory that I was a sinner bound for the fiery cave of hell with Satan and his cronies. No speaking of the tongues came out of me. I could have faked it, but I was too scared to fake anything at that moment. Besides, that would be lying.

On the way home that evening, Daisy told me that maybe I would get saved next time. I smiled and said, okay, I'll keep trying. We spoke no more of my salvation from that day forward.

VIRGIE STILL HAD VISITING RIGHTS, and I had to go. Things had cooled down somewhat with her, and I wanted to give her a second chance to be a mom to me the way it should have been. Also, Marylou taught me that forgiving people was what God wanted us to do. So, the forgiveness set in, and the second chance began.

I'm pretty sure this wasn't what Virgie had in mind, though. She started laying the guilt trips on me about running away, living in a foster home, lying on Donny, and now living with my dad. She would cry and tell me how much she loved me one minute, then dry her eyes and yell at me for not being there in her home, causing her money to get cut off by the state and not getting child support. This was my fault. I should have known better. I should have thought about her and what my choices would do to her. Blah, blah, blah.

By now, she was married to Richard. His son Carl lived with them, and Carl was actually a pretty groovy guy. We got along well. He was the only reason I felt like I wanted to go back, knowing he was there because we did have fun. Virgie continued drilling into my head every other weekend about how much money my dad owed her. She told me the only way she would get her money was if I came back home.

Virgie cried, telling me it was my fault that she lost her money and that she was going to starve. Then she'd push her food back and tell me she couldn't eat, it was too hard on her heart due to the money lost and me not being there. She continued to badger me with everything she could think of regarding moving back home until I broke. I fucking broke! I believed what she said. I felt sorry for all I had put her through. I knew I was terrible, and I thought I was the reason she didn't get her money.

While at Virgie's one weekend, she explained that if I'd call my dad and cry and scream, he'd have to let me come back and live with her.

So, I did what she told me to do. I called, cried a little, and told my dad I wanted to move back with Virgie. He immediately signed over his rights without any questions. Maudie Jo even packed my bags for me.

I think he was relieved to not have me around any longer. I always felt I caused trouble for him and his wife. Since I knew she didn't want me with them, I thought that Maudie Jo was probably happy now. Truthfully, I thought things might be different at Virgie's, and I sure hoped they would be. I also hoped she would allow me to see my mom, Chelcie, whom I hadn't seen or spoken to since the day at court when I was 10, and now, I was 13 years old. *Three years.* It is a long time to go without seeing someone you love, someone you yearn to be with.

Carl had a small bedroom off Virgie and Barry's room. It was awkward because he had to walk through their room to get to his. This room had been a back porch at one time, therefore, the floor was cement. Of course, they put carpet down for him but no padding. The ants came through like crazy, he always complained about the ants. That room, only big enough for his single bed and a small dresser at the end, had two windows overlooking the kitchen sink.

Three of the four walls were gray cement. The one wall painted white was plain with nothing on it because Virgie didn't want any holes in her walls. So, basically, his room was a small closet, empty and echoey. He probably heard his dad banging Virgie. Ewwww!

I got my old room back, but Virgie had Richard nail all the windows, and the one door to the left side, shut. The only other doors were to the kitchen and to the back porch, which I wasn't allowed to lock unless I had her permission.

In other words, whoever was coming and going into the backyard had to go through my room. What a place. A room with absolutely no privacy. I did, however, get to hang one poster on my wall with tape, and it had better not mess up the paint or else!

I had a poster of Andy Gibbs with no shirt on and wild hair. I would switch it out every now and then with the other two I had; Leaf

Garret with his opened shirt, crazy hair, and headband or the poster of Shawn Cassidy, who was wearing shiny pants, shiny silk shirt, and nicely combed hair sporting a charming smile with dimples. They were the hotties of my days—teen heartthrobs. My posters came out of the magazines I used to buy while at my dad's house with my work allowance. They were 16 x 20 pictures, but they were mine.

I soon became reacquainted with my cousins next door, but it wasn't like it used to be. Partly due to us growing up and moving on with friends and different interests, but I missed it and realized that I had missed out. I loved my cousins very much, and I had always felt I could tell Bobbie Jo anything, and it'd be safe. Not now, though. Bobbie Jo was older, she moved on, things changed, and so did she, just as I had. She seemed to be on Virgie's side. I had to watch myself and my mouth, or I'd get what I used to get. Nothing had changed, but everything had changed.

Richard was banned from seeing his other three kids, but I am not sure why. I never cared to ask since I hated Doris, the last time we were together, I bent her finger back and threatened her. Nonetheless, Carl was around, and he was a jokester. We became close, and I felt that we had a stable stepbrother/stepsister relationship going on. We did things together like ice skating, movies, working in Granny Ally's house and garden for a popsicle. Yeah, she hadn't changed. We only got something if we did something.

But we would have fun and laugh at things, watch scary movies together, he was like the brother I never had, and I trusted him. Until he got pissed at me when he discovered I was growing weed in a little pot in my bedroom window. He was actually pissed because I told him I wasn't going to share, which is when he squealed on me. That fucknut! It was just sprouting and about three inches tall, (and due to the tiny pot, I planted it in, I'm sure it would have keeled over in a day or so anyhow), when his big-ass mouth hollered, "Peggy's growing weed!"

I got the pot plant thrown away, talked to for about two hours straight, and then Virgie said she had to teach me a lesson. She made me pull my pants down so she could spank me with Richard's belt. The leather stopped bothering me years ago. I learned to just block everything out for the moment. But that buckle! It hurt. She decided that I wasn't learning a lesson until I cried. It took a few swats to get me crying because if I faked it, she'd know, but if I allowed some discomfort in, it would create a few real tears, she would see the agony in my eyes, and that was when she decided I had learned my lesson.

As I stood there with my pants down while she was beating my bare ass *again*, memories of my younger years just kept rolling through my mind, and all I could think of was getting out. I wanted to puke. There I stand listening to the whooshing sounds of that fucking belt, while the remnants of my past began hitting me right in the face. I remembered why I hated her so much. And, once again, I wondered why she adopted me. But I knew why, spite. It never really was about me but rather her husband and sister. I was just the fucking pawn in this shit show.

I wished I hadn't listened to her, that lying bitch! Now here I am stuck living with her again, and I just knew history would continue repeating itself. All the pain of knowing she was fucking irrational, extreme, and out of control came rushing over me in a hot second, and I froze. It took a lot to allow the tears to roll, and then they flowed down my face like Niagara Falls.

My heart turned black, cracking into a million pieces, bleeding. I wanted to crawl into a hole and die rather than live like this again. And, the thought of suicide resurfaced once again.

THE VISITS WITH MY DAD started again, as did her checking my pockets, bags, and shoes. What money he gave me was hers by law. By Virgie Law. She also insisted I hate Maudie Jo. It wasn't so hard this time after hearing Maudie Jo talk about my mom, but still, I had to do as Virgie wanted me to do, say, think, and breathe. Virgie demanded that I make fun of her bugle nose. I will admit Maudie Jo has a pretty large nose.

Nonetheless, it was my civic duty to make fun of her and call her Bugle Nose. Of course, the funnier thing was that Virgie had a speech impediment, so when she said it, it came out, "Beau-dee Nose." I tried to let her say it more than me, and then I'd laugh inside and think to myself, *ha-ha, you think her nose is beautiful*. It made me feel good if only for a moment and only for me to know. More so, I just laughed inside at her speech mess.

Virgie told me if I acted right and did all she said, she'd let me see Chelcie. My "chore list" consisted of cleaning the house, doing yard work, watching Richard in case he was cheating on her, telling her everything Richard did, said, who he called, what they talked about, how long he was on the phone, and so much more. The more I did, the more she wanted, but, at last, the visits with my mother Chelcie began... as did the same shit again.

Virgie would call her at midnight screaming, yelling, and swearing to kill me, demanding they come and get me. Chelcie, Claude, and Glenn would then drive an hour in the middle of the night to beg and plead with her not to kill me, hit me, or punish me in any way and she'd laugh and tell them, "I changed my mind, you can't have her, it'd make you too happy, and Ardy owes me money. She's staying." Then she'd kick them out again. Same shit, just another fucking year.

This cycle turned the brick wall of hate into a brick fortress, which I had no idea would take years to come down and dissolve. Often, this type of demolition happens at the rate of only one brick at a time. It's a slow and painful process, but I can see how it is necessary. It's the only way to heal and help others heal. I sometimes wonder if the wall is entirely down yet. I reckon it will be a lifetime of excavating.

In addition to loving school, I loved the library, my favorite place to be. Lost in another world, lost in a good adventure book. Lost in a love story or history. I don't think it mattered much what I was reading as long as I had a book in my hands. I never took them home much as I was too afraid someone would rip them up and laugh at me for trying to better myself. After all, I was the stupid one. I was the one who didn't know anything. I was the idiot. The fool. The liar. The one who no one wanted to be around. These words often rolled off the lips of the people who should have loved me and cared for me, but instead, they scolded, yelled, screamed, called names, and blamed me for anything that went wrong and then some. So, learning and reading became my secret place to be free from judgment and ridicule and abuse. It's what saved me.

When I was 13 and 14 years old, I had a handful of girlfriends with whom I hung out as much as possible. Fortunately, Teresa (Barry's youngest daughter) was the leading player in that group, and Virgie loved her so, if the gang wanted me to hang, Teresa would beg Virgie to let me go, and she'd cave. Even though she succumbed, I'd have to pay when I got home.

Teresa's mom was never home, but her older sister Jane took care of her and Jeffery. Jane was the prettiest girl I'd ever seen. She was short with long black hair and the most beautiful smile ever. Jane made Teresa and Jeff behave and was fair to all of us kids, but we had to be respectful. She was the mom-figure. Although Jane was a very young girl—still in high school herself—she was the boss, and that girl ran her house quite well. Jane once caught Teresa and me with a bag of weed, and she made us flush it. Then she lectured us on the harms of it and how it was going to kill our brain cells and make us stupid. Flushing that bag of weed was painful. Then she dared to take our papers and pulled every piece out, ripping it to shreds and throwing the whole pack of rolling papers away as she lectured us. Jane was like that. In hindsight, best big sister ever!

There were six of us—Teresa, Tracie, Billie Jo, Lena, Brandy, and me. Wherever one of us was, the rest were close behind. Billie Jo and Lena's parents owned a bar in town, and they brought home the cash box every night. Yep, the girls would sneak out a $20.00 or sometimes a little more so we could all go eat tacos and hit the movies or the usual, buy weed and a bottle or two of Boones Farm so we could all go get high and drunk, and we did – a lot.

We had an older friend Della who had a car and would buy the booze and rolling papers for us because we all smoked cigarettes too, sharing a pack when one of us would get a hold of one. Well, I didn't like them, but I'd have one here and there and just not inhale it, I couldn't, or I'd puke. Della let us drink, smoke, and drive her car. She was a trip, kind of wild.

Our shenanigans were plentiful. Many times, we'd pay for one of us to get into the movies, and then the others would be at the backstage door waiting until the one who paid would let the rest of us in. Sometimes it was me. We all took turns doing it. Once in the winter, we snuck into the local college and borrowed six lunch trays so we could use them as sleds. We had a blast going down Victory Hill. The trays were small, silver medal, and they were terrific on snow. Fast as lightning! Being high and rolling down that hill made for a great time!

It was all fun and games while I was partying with my friends – until I had to go home. Then the little dirty pawn would play to the Queen's requests.

The fall of my first year back with Virgie, I re-met Alex. We met at a party, after which he told someone, I was stuck up because I was so pretty. I liked the idea that he thought I was stuck up and more so because he thought I was pretty as I had been told, by my family, I was ugly my entire life. Later, I saw him downtown at the phone booth and called out to him, waving, "Hey, Alex! Just so you know, I'm not so stuck up."

That was all it took. Alex was at my door the next day, asking if I could go for a walk. Good thing Virgie wasn't home or that would have been a disaster. We went. I liked him right off the bat. We became like peanut butter and jelly. A thing. Inseparable. It took us about three weeks to kiss for the first time, and then it was the quickest smooch ever. And that's all we did for a long time, kiss and smoke a lot of weed. I think he woke up with a joint in one hand and a lighter in the other.

After we were "going together" for about a couple weeks, he told me he hated Virgie and that Richard was a stupid-ass monkey she trained. He hated her, and she hated him. She dared me to see him and told me that if I did, I'd be put in the juvenile home, and there wouldn't be a thing I could do. The threats got a harsher the older I got.

I asked Alex to help me run away. I had no plan and no money, but I did have a nickel bag of weed and some papers. (Nickel bags back then were equal to a half-ounce today). His buddy, Joe, agreed to drive us in a car that Alex had purchased, an old yellow Ford station wagon. It was ancient, but it ran well.

We plotted out my runaway in about one sentence and two seconds. Joe and Alex waited for me one night at the corner of my street while I went out of the back-porch door, snuck around the side of the house, and ran down the road to meet them. I took nothing with me, just me and my bag of weed, papers, and a lighter. I was ready to see the world!

There they sat as planned. I jumped into the back seat and yelled, "Get the fuck out of here before Virgie catches me!" Joe pushed the pedal to the metal, and away we went down Ionia St. then back up Superior St. We drove out of town as fast as we could, thinking she was hot on our trail, but she was actually fast asleep.

I told them I wanted to go to my mom's house in Sherwood, but not until daybreak. So, there we were, two teens and a 20-something, pulled over and drinking homemade moonshine and smoking weed until sunrise, then off to Sherwood we went.

We arrived at my mom's farm, which also had a trailer on the property. My older brother James and his wife lived in the mobile home beside my mom's farmhouse, where she had lots of farm animals and raised her own meat and vegetables. Growing up in the hills of Kentucky taught her how to live self-sufficiently and that she did.

My mom was gone, so I went over to my brother's trailer to ask him and his wife if I could wait there until mom got back. My brother's wife, Sandy, knew Virgie well. The whole family knew how she was, mean and hateful, spiteful if you crossed her but loving if you kissed her ass. Sandy told me the cops had been there already this morning looking for me and that I had to leave as she wasn't going to meet the wrath of Virgie. She told me everyone knows I've run away, and everyone is out looking for me.

"Define everyone," Alex said.

"Well, mom and Claude are out looking, and the cops did stop by here."

"So, no one else is driving around knocking on doors looking for Peggy, right?" he asked again.

Standing corrected, Sandy breathed a defeated sigh, "Yep, that's about right."

My brother mentioned them taking me to my older sister Addy Mae's place a few miles away, so off we went. By the time we got there, she had already heard the news. She told me to get inside before someone sees and calls the cops. She instructed Alex and Joe to leave, or they'd go to jail for helping me.

Over breakfast, I told Addy Mae many things, mostly why I had to leave and why I hated living with Virgie. She listened and told me I'd be safe with her. As we were talking, we heard a car pull up. She jumped up and looked out the window. It was my mom and Claude.

They had come to get me, but my mom told me I couldn't stay with her because Virgie would put her in jail for kidnapping. She'd already threatened her and Claude by phone, and as usual, they believed she could make good on her threats. Virgie was extreme enough to do many things, but I know now that that woman didn't have the law in her pockets as claimed. She had most of us conditioned to believe that the police and FBI were on her side, so everyone catered to her.

After pacing the floor trying to figure out what to do next, we decided to go to Granny's. The ride from Sherwood to Homer wasn't that far, but when you have to lay in the backseat with a quilt on top of you in the heat of the summer with no air conditioner and the windows rolled up, it's fucking long. My mom was so paranoid that Virgie would call the FBI and have them arrested, that she made a comment about every car Claude passed, and then told him to go slower than the speed limit. Apparently, she didn't realize driving too slowly would attract the cops. I don't think that either she or Virgie had much logic about anything. They only reacted based on emotions of fear and/or anger.

They dropped me off at the corner of the road about a quarter mile from her house. I began walking up the road to Granny's when my cousins came riding their bikes and started yelling, "There she is! There's Peggy! Go tell!" which is precisely what they did. They rode their bikes back home and told my aunts, who lived side by side down the road from Granny.

I made it into Granny's, where she fed me soup beans and cornbread for lunch, and we talked. I explained to Granny how Virgie treated me and that I couldn't take it anymore. Granny told me she figured Virgie was ruined in the head when she got that fever as a little girl. She said to ignore her because she didn't know what she was doing. Well, easier said than done. How the fuck do I overlook getting the shit beat out of me? I looked at her dumbfounded. *Ummm, sure, lady. Why didn't I think of that before? Thanks for the insight.* She was clueless as to how this trauma affected me, most likely because that was the norm in my backward family.

My Aunt Opal called up to Granny's house and talked with me. She asked me why I would run away and scare Virgie like I did. I shared many stories on the phone that day about how I was treated, some she had known, some she hadn't. They all failed to realize that by running away and then reaching out and telling Granny and Auntie how I was treated, I was asking for help in a teen's way. Especially a teen who wasn't taught what to do with—or even allowed to have—feelings. I had no idea how to come out and say *help me, please!* So, I ran away and then tried to explain why. Auntie told me she knew how I had been treated was wrong and Virgie was mean and hard on me but she claimed she didn't know what she could do. Granny threatened Virgie when she came to get me that afternoon, but it didn't help. And nothing changed. Again.

I went home with Virgie that day. I was locked in my room with all doors and windows nailed shut. Thank God there was never a fire.

I HATED LIVING WITH VIRGIE. I was sick of the treatment I grew up with, and it only got progressively worse as I got older, with my dad well, I grew to hate living with him too. He was a hard guy to be around because of the Donny's ordeal, and it was evident that he didn't like me too much.

I felt like I had no one. I wanted to live with my real mother but couldn't, and I regretted my conversation daily with the judge. My mom never contested the judge's decision. I'm not sure why, but she never did. I genuinely believe that she didn't understand all the laws. Regardless, she didn't fight for me. My dad just handed me back over to Virgie without even trying to talk to me about it, he just signed over custody, and off I went. He didn't fight for me. And Virgie made it clear every day that she didn't want me other than to use me to hurt the rest of them.

So, there you have it. I was alone in a family of hillbillies. Sad. Truth.

My return was nothing short of a good reason for Virgie to be really pissed and give me shit just a little worse as if it could even get worse. She had been quiet for a few days, but I knew it was coming, I just didn't know *when*. She always exploded, so it was inevitable. Well, it didn't take long.

About a week later, I sang a song by Jefferson Starship, *Runaway*. The ditty was popular, a big hit with many kids my age, and I sang it a lot. I was singing the song out loud and pounding on my legs and stomach like I was playing the drums. Virgie watched me for a moment and then concluded that I had had sex and was patting my stomach because I was pregnant. I hadn't even had sex then, so I was definitely not with child.

She began yelling and telling me I was going to burn in hell like both my parents for having sex and getting pregnant before I was married. I tried to tell her I was listening to music and just playing the drums, but she wasn't believing me and ended up chasing me out of the house. I ran to Bobbie Jo but was told to go home because Aunt Marie didn't want any trouble with Virgie. Whenever she tried to help me, Virgie would tell her brother, Micky, Aunt Marie's husband, and they would fight. Uncle Micky was a drunk and would hit Aunt Marie "if she needed it," so he said.

I hated the thought of going back to that house again. I knew she was pissed, and for what? A fucking song? A fucking song!! Really?! Who gets pissed because their kid is playing the air drums and using their own body to make drumming sounds? I guess she does. I scampered off into the lilac bushes, waiting and hoping that she would calm down. Sometimes she'd calm down and forget, but most of the time, she'd calm down and then get pissed all over again when she saw see me.

After about two hours in the lilac bushes hiding and hoping it would blow over, I decided to give it a try and go back inside. I went through the back door that led into my room, and there stood Virgie. Standing. Waiting. Smirking. And she was holding a wooden baseball bat. She held it high and told me she couldn't deal with me and my lies and a baby too. She told me she was tired of being "done wrong" and was going to "end it all." She spoke calmly at first, but then, as the conversation moved on, she got louder and more violent.

She had a good grip on that bat, and with both hands holding it tightly, she swung it at my head. I ducked quick enough to miss her swing, and yet it was all in slow motion for me. I thought I could hear the swooshing of the bat going by my head and hitting the wall. As she hit the wall, it dented the old plaster, and some pieces fell out, which ignited her even more.

"Look what's you's made me's do! You's is gonna ruin my home. This is you's fault!"

As this moment played out, I shoved her away and screamed for help from anyone. "Help me! Someone help me!"

Carl must have seen her with the bat in my room waiting because as soon as he heard me scream for help, he took off right away to get the neighbor next door. As she entered the house, she listened to my screams and Virgie yelling at me about being a 'cherry' and me yelling back, "I didn't do anything!"

There she was, hovering over me in the corner with the bat. She held it above my head, screaming, "I was cherry until I was married. Why did you's do this to me's? Why? Yous'll burn in hell with them's two."

I sat there hovered in the corner holding my hands above my head, waiting for her to just bash my fucking head in. I seriously thought she was going to kill me. And, I think our neighbor thought so too based on the look she gave and the way things panned out.

She stepped in between us and grabbed hold of the bat while telling Virgie, "It's not worth it! Give me the bat!"

I had never been more thankful than at that moment. The look in Virgie's eyes told a story of horror and hate, and I honestly thought she was going to end my life.

The neighbor took the bat to her place and told Virgie to go to her mom's house and calm down. She told Virgie that I probably wasn't pregnant and not to worry. She could make me have an abortion if I was. Virgie went next door to Denise's to try and settle down. I was told to get to bed, of course.

Virgie and Denise left, and Carl came into my room and sat with me, and we talked. He told me he was sorry for all I had to go through. Carl said I should take off rather than put up with all this bullshit. He was right, and I knew it.

Later after she had calmed down a little, she came into my room to let me know I was grounded for the rest of the year. I couldn't see "that dirty boy, Alex," nor would I be able to visit with Chelcie or my dad until she, Queen Virgie, said so because she was my boss, and I was going to straighten up and do as she said or else. After she scolded me some more, she left to go to Granny's finally. Carl came back and told me she was gone and that if I wanted to get up, he wouldn't tell anyone. So, I took him up on his offer, and I left out the back so Denise couldn't see. I ran up to Alex's to tell him what happened.

I told Alex that if I didn't get away, I was going to kill her, or she was going to kill me. I hated her. I wanted away from her more than anything. The hard truth was, though, I couldn't go live with my mother because she'd never let us have any peace. I couldn't go back to my dad's as I didn't feel welcomed. Maybe I was, but at that time in my life, I didn't feel it. So, what were my options? I thought I had only one, and I wanted out so badly I just didn't care anymore.

Alex's older sister and her boyfriend lived on a migrant farm in Bryan, Ohio, and that's where we planned to go.

Later that night, Alex was once again waiting down at the corner in the station wagon with Joe. I rolled up a few clothes in a blanket, took my pillow, opened the bedroom window that Carl had helped me "unnail," and out I slipped down the street carrying a bundle looking like a thief in the night with her goods.

I rushed down the street, swung the car door opened, threw my bundle in the back, and jumped in. Joe was hot with the foot, and off we went out of town, out of sight. We made it to the migrant farm early the next morning and set up with Alex's sister. She had already spoken with the landowner and asked if we could stay and work.

III
I'D RATHER
BE HOMELESS!

WE LIVED IN A BIG RED BARN that had been made into two- and three-bedroom apartments. The three-bedroom apartment had a small fridge and stove and a sink for dishes but nothing regular-sized and nothing special. The floors were cement and cold. The walls were old wood and not insulated, but the rain didn't come in. This barn was where most of the Mexican migrant workers lived, and the rest lived in tents behind the barn. There was a big bathhouse that had individual shower stalls as well as toilet stalls, but they were all in the same building, and everyone shared, men and women as well as kids. Not ideal.

It wasn't so bad, though. We worked the fields from sunup till sundown every day but Sundays. After work, everyone went to their own little rooms and had their private dinners, mostly tacos every day. After dinner, many would gather outside at a fire pit, and one old white guy would sing and play the guitar. There was a puppy that sat by him one night, and he kept grabbing the pup's ears and shaking them, making the pup scream and cry.

I kept telling Alex to make him stop, but he did nothing about it, so I walked up to that old rustic looking shit head and grabbed his ears and shook his head and yelled at him. Then, picked up that puppy and snuggled him until he ran off. Poor little thing, he just wanted some love. I didn't like that old traveler, he reminded me too much of all I had run from, dysfunctional bullshit and people.

We are working on this farm for about a month, then I got an infection and needed a doctor. I was in so much pain. Burning. Stinging. The feeling of needing to pee every two seconds. I had never experienced this before, but after explaining to Alex's sister what was going on, she told me I probably had a bladder infection and would need some medication to get rid of it.

Well, we couldn't go anywhere as I was a run-away, and I'd be sent back to Virgie so, I called my biological mom. She told us to get to her, and she'd help me, but we had to come at night. We left that night, hitchhiked a short while, then Joe picked us up at a meeting spot. We didn't want him getting into trouble, so he dropped us off about a half-mile down the road from my mom's house. My level of paranoia was at an all-time high. I feared Virgie so much that I felt her eyes and presence everywhere. I was afraid that she had the FBI and all her minions watching. There was no one watching me, not even her.

We arrived at my mom's, and she rushed us into the house, acting as if someone was watching. (See where I got this paranoia?) She had gone to her doctor and gotten these big yellow pills that were the size of a quarter and told me I had to drink lots of water and take the pills three times a day for seven days, and my infection would go away. They were hard to swallow and turned my pee a burnt orange color, but they did the trick, I felt much better after a few days. I've no clue how she got these pills or what she told some doctor to get them, but she made it happen. I think she must've lied. Wasn't the first time wouldn't be her last.

We stayed at my mom's house for a week, and within that week, Alex had contacted his parents to let them know he was okay and where we were. His parents wanted to see him, so they came to visit, and it was then my mother began her scheming, and the three of them conspired.

ALEX'S PARENTS AND MY MOM sat and talked about how to keep us safe from Virgie. My mom had Alex's parents convinced that Virgie would put Alex in the juvenile home if she found out that he'd helped me run away again. They believed her, so did I.

The plan was for the three of them (Stanley, Nancy, and Chelcie) to get us both to Kentucky and 'married off' so Virgie couldn't touch either one of us. So basically, these three adults decided that us kids needed to get married. And these adults pooled money together and gave it to Vickie Sue, my sister, and her husband Robert, who we called, Red Rooster because his hair was a bright red and there were two Roberts in the family. As to not get them confused, we gave them Knick names (it's a family thing). My brother from my mom had very curly afro hair, so we called him Curly-headed Rob.

I don't think Vickie Sue's Robert ever worked a day in his life. He claimed he was disabled, and Vickie Sue had dishwashing and cook jobs at truck stops.

Two days later, money in hand, we took off with Red Rooster and Vickie Sue to Kentucky to get married. I am not sure how I felt at that moment about getting married. Neither Alex nor I were asked if this was something we wanted, but it was certainly something the adults wanted—probably to cover their asses. All Alex and I knew was that we were crazy in love with each other, and we wanted to finish school so we could make something of ourselves. Shit, we were only 15 years old. We were babies.

The four-day trip to Kentucky and back was grueling for Alex and me. At times, I wondered what we were doing. One thing was for sure, my mother had me terrified that Virgie had the cops, the FBI, and her people looking day and night searching—in her words, "high and low"—to bring me back to her so she could beat my ass. I was freaked out. I also knew I didn't want Alex to get into trouble for helping me, and I sure as hell didn't want to go back to her after the baseball bat incident. So, we kept going.

As soon as we pulled out of the drive and began down the road, Rooster put in his eight-track tape, Earl Scruggs Bluegrass banjo-picking music. We had to endure that same tape over and over and over all the way there and back. I've nothing against Bluegrass music, but holy shit, not the same one for days and days, hours and hours. I sat in the back seat with my head in my hand. *Just shoot me now!* Rooster drank coffee continuously and chained smoked. I'll bet his mouth smelled like filthy sewer ass. Vickie Sue wasn't a light smoker either, she smoked and drank Pepsi the entire trip as well.

Alex and I were allowed one pop to share because they needed money to get coffee for Rooster as he was doing the driving and pop for Vickie Sue to keep her awake to help Red Rooster watch the road. They bought us one meal a day at McDonald's, and that was the extent of our food and drink supply for four days. Meanwhile, they both got whatever they wanted from McDonald's whenever they wanted it and kept themselves stocked with an ample supply of smokes, coffee, and pop.

We drove straight to Red Rooster's brother's house in Teaberry, Kentucky. His sister in law was a Christian woman and told Alex and I that we couldn't sleep together. Alex had to sleep in the car, and I was allowed to have the couch, but only because she slept on one end and I the other so she could keep an eye on us since we were "living in sin."

She fed us, though, and her cooking was so excellent. She made a huge breakfast, Alex and I both ate as much as we could stuff in our hungry bellies. She made pork chops, biscuits, sausage gravy, eggs, bacon, tomato slices, goat cheese, fresh corn on the cob, and cornbread with soup beans. Yes, that was just breakfast! It's Kentucky folks, and they feed ya. If you go away hungry, it's your own fault.

After breakfast, we left and went to the courthouse a few miles up the road. Red Rooster told me to go in and ask if I could get married here. I had no clue what I was doing, so I asked him to come in with me, which he reluctantly did. As we were walking into the building, I told him I didn't know what to say, and I confessed to him I wasn't sure I really wanted to get married. He told me I had to or go back and live with Virgie.

I walked in, went up to the counter, and said to the lady, "Can I get a marriage license?" When she asked my age, I lied, telling her I was 16 while Red Rooster said nothing and just stood there like a mentally disturbed creeper with a cigarette hanging out of his mouth and the pack crinkling in his hand. She took one good, long, hard look at Red Rooster and asked if he was my daddy. He said yes, standing there looking like a dim-witted moron. She looked at both of us, shook her head, pursed her lips, and said to me, "Good thing you look like your mama, honey. Are you pregnant?"

I shook my head no, and she continued, "No, you can't get married. Have you even finished school? Go home, study, graduate, go to college or get a job and move out of your daddy's house."

I liked her. I smiled at her. She smiled back at me, gave Red Rooster a dirty look, and told us the door is over there, pointing at us to leave.

We got back in the car, and Red Rooster told Vickie Sue, "Well, we can't get 'em married off, so we might as well go back home now." Vickie Sue and Worthless basically had a short, all-expenses-paid trip to visit his family. They both lied and told my mom and Alex's parents that they drove us all over Kentucky trying to get us married off, but no one would let us get the license, and they believed them. What a couple of dishonest, thieving, cheating, fucknuts. And when we tried to tell our parents the truth, no one understood us. Hillbilly logic: We were old enough to get married but not old enough to be believed.

AS WE PULLED INTO MY MOM'S DRIVEWAY, she and Alex's parents were waiting there for us. Once we were unpacked, the three adults began plotting our future once again. They decided this time to drive us to Lima, Ohio, and ask if we could stay with Red Rooster's brother, Bud, and his wife, Juju.

This was another short-lived dead-end trip with Red Rooster and Vickie Sue and that god-awful music all the way to Lima. When we arrived, we all went inside and sat down in the living room where Vickie Sue explained they were trying to get us "married off" and that I was a run-away because of how Virgie treated me. Juju knew Virgie, and that set her off. She jumped up off her couch and pointed towards her door, shouting at Alex and me to get out of her house "right now!" We were not allowed inside. "Never come here again!" she screamed.

By this time, it was cold outside and raining like crazy. Worthless Red Rooster refused to give us the car keys to have shelter from the thunder, lightning, and harsh freezing rain.

"I don't trust you, youngins. You might run off with my car," he scoffed.

We were too scared and exhausted to drive off. We just wanted to be out of the weather. Juju told us we could wait in her garage until the rain stopped, but then we had to get off her property, or she'd "call the law" on us and turn us in. Vickie Sue and her husband stayed all night inside a warm house while Alex and I sat on a cold, wet cement floor, trying to cuddle with each other to keep warm while the rain was coming into the garage. Juju left the garage door open all night, so the cold rain was blowing in. When we asked if we could close it, she screamed like a wild woman reminding us she was doing us a favor by letting us stay on her property.

"And," she explained, "in case the law comes, I can say you broke into my garage."

We found a big old dirty piece of plastic and sat down covering up with it until Bud, her husband, got home and took it away telling us it was his and we couldn't use it. They all had dinner and were warm and safe inside while Alex and I froze in a wet garage, hungry, on the cement floor with just each other.

Late the next morning, which was sunny and full of hope that it might be a better day, Vickie Sue and Red Rooster came down and stated we would be leaving after lunch to return to my mom's house in Michigan. It was a long ride home. We were wet, cold, hungry, and pissed off, but we made it. I told my mom what happened, and she blew it off as if I wasn't appreciative. It did not turn out to be a better day.

You'd think by this time I would have gotten a clue and walked away from the situation, from them all, *but* ... I was stupid, young, and needed help. I didn't know what I was doing and didn't know what to do. Scared, cold, and homeless, we continued to do as we were told.

On the next attempt to accomplish The Plan, my mom took us back to Lima to Red Rooster's sister, Jacie. She was married to a guy named Brian and had a little girl. They lived in a small house, but they allowed us to put a cot in their bathroom and stay for a week if I cleaned, cooked, and Alex did work on the house, and my mom had to buy our groceries. My mom paid Jacie $25.00 a week for food and a tiny cot with no mattress, just a quilt to lay on in their shitter where they hung a sheet between us and their toilet. If they needed to take a shit, they felt free to do so without telling us to get out. It was fucking nasty.

The house, located in a lower-class neighborhood, was white with blue shutters and a small yard. Inside, the back door opened to the kitchen where there were cabinets on one side and the sink, fridge, and stove on the other, with one small window above the sink. She had a small, four-seat table in the kitchen, a 1960's silver-legged round table with red checkered seats on silver metal chairs.

Right off the kitchen was the bathroom, which, by the way, had no door for privacy. It was a big bathroom, there was a shower & tub to the right side and the toilet right next to the tub and sink right next to the toilet. On the left side was shelving, where they had food stored, boxed meals and canned foods. On one end was the hot water heater, and in between that and some shelves was where we put the cot.

The living room was small with scuffed, was-at-one-time-white walls and a couple of pictures, one of Jesus and the other, an outdated floral print. The big window had two sheets as curtains, but the door window remained bare. To the side were two other rooms we weren't allowed in, I figured they were the bedrooms.

Jacie was tall with olive skin and short black hair with a crooked smile that looked good on her. She wore tight jeans and tiny tops. She wasn't big-chested, but she was pretty. Brian, on the other hand, was an average, skinny, simple-looking man who wore his pants loose and a belt that kept them up practically to his pits. He always had dirty nails, and his hands seemed black all the time. The little girl was a cute kid who looked like her mom. That was probably a good thing, too, since Brian was rather ugly.

We lasted two nights there, and then we packed up in the middle of the night and left. We took what was ours, which was a change of clothing and a brown paper bag, and we also helped ourselves to two bags of chips, a box of crackers, and two Pepsi's. We had no idea where we'd go but knew we needed to leave that house. Jacie and Brian were nasty people and living in their bathroom wasn't okay with either of us.

As we ventured out into the night, walking and trying to keep quiet, we noticed a girl about our age. We asked her if there was a park nearby. She asked us why, I was upfront with her and told her we needed to find a place to sleep for the night because we were on the run. That's when she offered to help us out. I'm sure God was looking out for us and sent this young girl. She was 16 and lived in an old school bus in the backyard of her house.

This girl was gorgeous and exotic looking. She was half-Mexican and half-black, and her nickname was May-May. She was taller than me, skinny, and had massive boobs. We were quite a sight, one sixteen-year-old and two fifteen-year old's hanging out in an old school bus getting high and drinking wine. She loved to dance and sing, we enjoyed her music and, after all those banjo-playing', crazy-ass road trips with old people trying to dictate our lives, we had some much-needed fun with her in that old bus.

She allowed us to stay there a few nights and told us that when everyone left her house, she'd leave the back door unlocked, and we could go inside and shower. So, we both went in and took baths. We came back out to some Pop-Tarts and Mountain Dew, she had left us on the bus, now that's a friend!

After a couple of days, May-May let me use her phone to collect call my mom, Chelcie. She insisted we go to Red Rooster's other brother's house in Lima and stay with him and his wife. And she came down to make sure we did. We were to meet her at the address she gave us, which was ironic as it was right down the street from May-May.

Red Rooster, another brother, Charles, had a two-story, old, beat-to-shit house, the worst-looking one on that block. His wife, Jomaa Lea, was crazy (technically, she had a psychotic disorder). We were told Charles married her because the state would pay him to be her caregiver, and then he wouldn't have to work and could just sit at home and drink his shitty, mule-piss beer, and watch T.V., which is precisely what he did.

When we got there and went inside, Jomaa Lea was sitting in the living room yelling at the T.V., but it wasn't on. She was a big woman with black, long, greasy hair. She wore dirty, stained-up clothing and had on high heels with sweats. The shoes looked like a child had been playing with them and had broken down the heels, they did not look stable enough to walk on. Charles, on the other hand, was a very tiny, frail-looking man who wore jeans and a plaid shirt, both of which were filthy and smelled terrible. He had a comb-over and looked as if it wouldn't budge in a hurricane due to all the grease.

The front porch was somewhat large and broken down. The railing had missing spindles, and the paint was chipped, looking as if it had three coats of various greens. The screen door had no screen or handle, but it was there, not sure why. The front door had one window that was broken, and a piece of cardboard was taped on it with an excessive amount of black electrical tape. Just the porch and doors were enough to make my skin crawl, I grabbed my mom's arm and told her I wasn't getting a good feeling about this place and didn't want to stay there.

She retorted with, "Well, there ain't nothing I can do. I'm trying my best, and if you don't get off the streets, Virgie will find you and make you come home, and you know she'll whoop ya now." Fucking scare tactics. But I genuinely believe she would have done that or worse had she caught me, us.

This house was nothing but a horror film in the raw. As you step inside, you are in the living room, which had a big window facing the front porch. There was a rebel flag hanging like a curtain in the living room. There were two dirty chairs with dirty foam coming out and spilling onto the floor. In front of the two chairs sat a broken makeshift coffee table that was two large grey cement blocks with a piece of plyboard on top supporting a very overflowing ashtray and about 20 empty beer cans. The floor was gritty and looked as if it had never been swept or mopped. The walls were a smoke color with yellow streaks, and the ceiling was the same, I'm assuming from all the years of chain-smoking.

Through the living room was the kitchen, which housed a stove and fridge. Through the kitchen was a bathroom with a toilet, a small sink, and a shower but no running water and no electricity. The oven was gas, and that worked, but nothing else. Those crazy-ass hillbillies had the T.V. hooked up to a car battery and rabbit ears on the back for adjusting the picture. I am not sure how it worked, but that is what I saw.

In the living room was a door that led upstairs. That was the room we would live in or the filthy space for which my mom paid them $25.00 every two weeks. There was a seriously gross smelling stained up mattress on the floor that looked like it came straight out of a whore house and had been used for years. The stains and smell were enough to knock us over. No curtains on the windows, no blankets, not much of anything other than a place to hide, and honestly, we both couldn't believe what we walked into. Or more so, what my mom wanted us to stay in! Extreme filth with a chain-smoking drunk and a crazy bitch.

I wasn't so sure how I was going to live with no running water or electricity, but hey, we survived thus far, so I figured we could make it a little while longer. But I wasn't sure why we still had to hideout. And I wasn't sure why my mom was insisting on us getting married other than to keep Virgie from making me go home. Which I supposed was reason enough. Even though no one even asked us if we wanted to either get married or go back and face the music, I honestly would have rather died at the time than go home and meet Virgie again. I knew it would be the same old shit, just another fucking day of trying to survive while dealing with crazy.

In the two weeks that we stayed in the crazy house, we learned a few things. We knew that if we were kind enough to the neighbors in the back, they would let us use their bathroom to take a shit, but only a couple times. We also learned that help from others always has limits. After a few times of hitting them up to use their latrine, they started telling us no and to go home. The girl with the bus got in trouble for helping us and letting us come in and get food and a bath, so that stopped after two baths each, back to smelling like street rats.

Alex met an old man two blocks over and did some work for him to earn $10. 00,, so we could have food, but, as soon as he got the money, he wanted to go find weed to get high, which is what we did. Dirty and smelly with greasy hair and filthy clothes, we started hitchhiking. Alex was asking the people who stopped to help if they knew where we could get a bag of weed. I just stood there, not saying anything. I was sort of scared and somewhat annoyed with him as I wanted a fucking sandwich or something to eat. By this time, we hadn't eaten any kind of good food in about three days, and I was about 75 pounds soaking wet.

Nonetheless, three guys in a pickup truck picked us up and got us high as hell and a little drunk too. They were just good ole boys, and the driver asked if we had any place to stay and clean up. I think it was a polite way of saying, Y'ALL STANK!

The driver's name was Robby. He was tall and cute with curly brown hair. He had dimples and a smile that would melt your heart. The guys told us to call the big one, Goat. Not sure what his real name was, but he was tall with a sturdy build, and his hands were bigger than my whole head. He was a teddy bear of a guy though, simple but friendly. The third guy introduced himself as Ray. He, too, was tall and had a bigger build as well but not as big as Goat. They were all accommodating and decent.

He took us home to his house, where he lived with his mom. As we stepped inside the house, his mom greeted us right away.

"Howdy, I'm Darla, and who are y'all?"

She immediately asked if we were hungry, and I stepped up and said, "Yes, Ma`am, I am hungry, and my name is Peggy." I didn't have to be asked twice. Thank God she could cook, it was so good.

Darla was short but taller than me, thin-framed with short brown hair and a mole on her left-side cheek. She had false teeth that she kept clicking as she cooked the cornbread, soup beans, fried potatoes, fried chicken, and greens. Darla apologized that it was such a small dinner, but I didn't know what she meant. A Southern woman usually cooks everything in the house for a meal, and this was no exception. I told her I was so happy with the beautiful meal, and I thanked her over and over. She talked to me a little while at the table, and I told her the truth about being a run-away and everything else. I told her about Virgie, living in a foster home, and off and on with my dad. I told her I wanted to live with my birth mom but knew that couldn't ever happen due to the family being the way they were. She listened patiently as my life story poured effortlessly from my mouth.

Darla offered me a shower and washed my clothes while the guys smoked pot on the back porch. She combed my hair and put it in a braid. She told me if I wanted to, I could stay with her and she'd take care of me until I was old enough to marry her son, Robby.

Hmmm, well, that was a tempting offer but a little too much Steven King (He's one of my favs by the way) for me, so as soon as my clothes dried, I told Alex we had to leave. Robby, my new future hubby, gave us a ride about six blocks from Charles and his crazy-ass wife's house. Not sure why he dropped us so far away, but kind of glad he did.

We were near a Goodwill store when it started raining. It had one of those big metal bins that people can dump clothing in. We climbed inside and hung out while we listened to the thunder and watched the lightening. We laughed and smoked more weed and thought nothing of the fact that we could die if that tin box we were in got struck by lightning. Nope. Didn't faze us at all.

We ended up back at the psycho nasty house, but the Goodwill bin became an every-other-day thing to do. We learned we could get inside, dig for clothes, and change into a new outfit since we had no way to do laundry. It was better than wearing the same things for days. We also learned to go into gas stations and wash up. I learned how to steal a bar of soap and the small shampoos from little stores. I took toilet paper from gas station bathrooms and sometimes their soap too. We had some bad habits, but this two-week thing turned into about two months, so we did what we had to do to survive. The money—so Charles claimed—stopped coming, and he required payment, or we had to get out. I called my mom, and she said she didn't have any money but to have Alex's friend Joe bring the station wagon and title over to her so she could sell our car and use that money to feed us and get us a place to stay. We did as we were told.

My mom received the station wagon and title, but we didn't get any money for food, nor did we get a place to stay. I honestly thought she sold the car so she could help us, I had believed her.

For the next couple of months, we learned how to walk into a store, snag two slices of bread, bologna, and cheese, eat the sandwich we had just made, and a drink all while walking throughout the grocery store. On our way out, we'd steal a candy bar or an apple for the road. This became a daily habit at a variety of stores so we could eat. Times were hard, and we were famished.

We used the park fountain to clean our feet and legs sometimes. We'd also bend down and wash our arms and face if need be. As for the psycho house, they never kicked us out, but we stayed as little as we could manage. Sometimes outside under the stars was a better place to sleep than inside their roach-infested shithole. And, sometimes, covering up with a plastic bag or box was cleaner than lying on a filthy floor. I am confident the streets were more sanitary than their house. We were two run-aways learning street smarts and survival techniques that no kids our age should ever have to learn.

FALL WAS UPON US, and the weather started turning a little colder, leading to thoughts about moving to Florida. We talked about it, but before leaving, I called my mom in one last-ditch effort to get the help I had asked for two months prior but never got.

She came through. My mom drove down with Alex's parents, and they decided they were going to get us married that weekend. Alex and I had taken our birth certificates with us when we ran away, so we went to the local library and changed the 3 on the year 1963 to a 0, so it read 1960 to make us look like we were 18, in hopes that we could get a job and get married. Getting a job was a far-fetched idea because of the way we were stinky and dirty looking, we never would have been hired.

My mom and Alex's parents arrived and took us to Goodwill. Alex got a $5.00 suit and me, some new $0.50 flip flops. Then, they drove us downtown, Lima, Ohio, to the courthouse and told us what to do to get a marriage license.

Of course, I asked my mom to go in with us, which she did willingly. As we entered the courthouse, a blind man was greeting us. She grabbed my hand and said, "Don't talk to him, he's watching you two. He knows you guys are run-aways, and he will call Virgie!" She really had me (as my granny would say) buffaloed. I believed every word she said. I didn't look at him. I dropped my head and turned away. Alex laughed and told her she was fucking crazy to think that and that he was just a blind candy man. That didn't go over well.

We entered the hallway to the records department where we had to go to get a marriage license. We had no problem at all getting our business taken care of. The marriage certificate was $5.00, and you could get it right away, the same day, so we did. Our lying wasn't even an issue. It certainly wasn't for the adults who told us to. We explained to the lady what we wanted. She asked to see our birth certificates, which we promptly showed her. She approved and filed our papers, then handed us a marriage license giving us a lecture that it had to be made valid within 10 days or else the certificate would no longer be good, and we'd have to pay $5.00 for another one.

My mom and Alex's parents dropped us off once again with Vickie Sue and Red Rooster right back where we started, at Bud and Juju's house. That bitch had kicked us out in the cold-ass rain, and we had to go back and endure her again. Unbelievable.

The reality was, she hadn't changed her mind about us, we weren't allowed to step foot inside her house. However, she allowed us to get married in her backyard, so that's what we did. Vickie Sue and her chain-smoking, non-stop coffee drinking, no teeth, yellow-tongued, comb-over strands of hair, goofy-looking motherfucking hubby found a preacher woman who married us for $5.00 in Bud and Juju's backyard. (Now, let me tell you how I really feel about Rooster).

The preacher was a tall, thin, black woman with concise hair. She brought her three little kids with her in a van that was parked in the dirt drive, the holy ground on which we stood and said our forever vows. I felt as if we had nothing short of a backyard shot-gun wedding.

We didn't have wedding rings. There were no flowers. No music. No hairdo. No pretty shoes, nor was there a real person to stand with us and celebrate our day.

There was just my hillbilly sister who wore black polyester pants with an oversized flowered t-shirt and her pink slippers, smoking her cigarette the entire time. Classy. She was my maid of honor, I guess. Red Rooster, in his polyester pants, silk paisley shirt, black shoes, yellow striped socks with his coffee cup in one hand and a cigarette in the other, stood up for Alex. Truth. What a hillbilly wedding. Picture it: Alex and I stood at the edge of the drive with Vickie Sue next to me (smoking) and Red Rooster next to him (smoking and drinking a cup of coffee), the preacher lady in front of us and her van two feet away. Did

I mention her kids? Three little kids jumping in and out of the van (van doors open) screaming and hitting each other like kids do, and then the guy next door starts mowing his lawn. Oh, yeah.

As the vows were spoken, I realized this was "until death do us part." Until that moment, I had no idea. Not that it really mattered. This shit show did not diminish the fact that we were two, young, 15-year-old kids who thought they loved each other even though neither one of us had ever spoken of getting married. As I look back on this situation, I feel as if I dragged Alex and his family into my private hell with the dysfunctional family that I was in. I often think he must have either been silently scared of Virgie and believed all the hype about juvie and jail, or he really loved me. I'm going with the notion that he loved me because I need some kind of mental peace if only in a thought but, I do believe he loved me.

After the ceremony, Juju said she made us a bologna sandwich, but that was all we could have of her food, which she claimed was plenty for us. She scolded us about how it wasn't her responsibility to feed us and that the extra food we'd eat would cost her too much money, so we were each generously given half of a bologna sandwich (insert eye roll). Oh, and a glass of water to split as well. After we celebrated with our wedding feast of a ½ bologna sandwich and ½ glass of water, she kicked us out again. She said she was cooking dinner for the grownups. This time, since we were legal, I guess Red Rooster felt we had no reason to run, so he let us sit in the hot car while they ate a nice dinner and drank a full glass of water each. Fuckers.

After they ate, it was the same ride, same shit, same music, just a different day. Even though Vickie Sue and Rooster were still annoying to ride with, I felt happy. I had always wanted to live with my mom, and now I was going to.

THE RIDE HOME SEEMED SHORTER. I think it was because the danger of Virgie making me go back home with her and sending Alex to juvie was over so, I was just happy about that. It was as if I took a big, colossal shit. Ya know, that feeling of being constipated for a long time then finally pooping. Hell yeah! It felt *good*. I had been emotionally constipated, and now I felt relieved.

When we arrived at my mom's, it was business as usual with the farmhouse and people. Nothing much had changed. She still had animals, and the trailers—one next door and one in the backyard—both lived in by my siblings—Bonnie in one and Curly Rob in the other. Mom and Claude were still in the main house, a simple home.

As the rhythmic crunch of the dirt driveway slowed down, I saw the back porch and the side door that led into the kitchen. I stepped into the kitchen, looked around, and took it all in. The kitchen was smaller than I had remembered, having only one window looking to the backyard and a four-seater table sitting right next to it. The farm sink faced a wall, and the cupboards were old and painted a lime green that was chipped and dirty. There was a small pantry door to the left where mom kept her freezer and her home-canned foods on a shelf. The walls were an off white with many dirty little handprints and scuffs all over. The brown stove and fridge were the same but a little more worn looking. My mom had put a brown animal border along the top of the walls in the kitchen, it didn't exactly belong. It was peeling off in places, barely hanging on. I snickered to myself at the similarities which that border and I shared. *I know how you feel, Wallpaper Border. Keep holding on, you got this.*

Stepping out of the kitchen, I walked into the dining area where the wood stove took up a significant portion of the corner of the room.

Mom had chairs sitting around the woodstove for the company to sit and keep warm during the winter. Behind it was mom and Claude's very tiny bedroom. Their bed and dresser fit in there, nothing else. To the left was the bathroom with enough room to shower and shit. There was no storage space but one small sink, a tiny pink bathtub, and a white toilet with a green shag rug. Got to love the 50's and 60's decorating styles.

Through the dining room to the right was the living room entrance and through that, another small bedroom. I wandered through the door next to the bathroom, which led upstairs to two bedrooms. The ancient plaster walls were cracking and chipping, some material had fallen off the ceiling. I wondered if the roof was going to collapse and kill us all.

I sat on a bed and put my hands over my face. Taking a deep breath, I tried to wrap my 15-year-old head around what was happening. *I just got married, and now I get to live at my mom's house.* It was all so surreal. As I sat thinking of everything we had just gone through, my head spun, and I allowed—for the first time in a long time—some tears to trickle out, it felt good. It felt good to let go and breathe!

Through my blurry tears, I peered out a window at the large front porch completely full of house plants and flowers. My mom loved her plants. She had a green thumb, of which most people wished they could have a fraction. The front porch was so packed there was only enough room to walk in a line either way to water her plants. I swear she could grow anything, and she did, almost. Mom and Claude had a vegetable garden that was about a quarter acre. The other vegetable garden was about an eighth of an acre of corn, the same for her strawberries and grapes. She canned everything and froze the rest. They ate from what they grew and raised.

She had hogs, goats, cows, chickens, ducks, rabbits, dogs, cats, one pet raccoon, and one pet deer. She made her own butter, ice cream, pickled corn, pickled eggs, pickled green beans, sauerkraut, and whatever else you make on a farm. On her side porch off the kitchen, she had a few old churns containing sour-smelling stuff in them almost all summer long. There was always a smell of soured something fermenting. It was a smell that took some getting used to if you weren't around that type of stuff a lot. The pickled green beans and sauerkraut were good. I never ate the other pickled crap, it always grossed me out but, everyone else loved it.

Alex and I were ready and eager to help and get back to living life, not as run-aways but as productive members of society. And to be able to shower daily and eat well was a bonus. We felt as if we were in heaven, at least for a week or so, we did.

My mom was still convinced that Virgie could put us all away and make me go back home with her. Which wasn't accurate since we were legally married, at least that's what I thought. She began to ask Alex's parents for additional cash, which she'd been doing all along to help pay for Alex and me to stay in the lodging places she'd find for us while we were on the run. Which were total fucking shit holes but, at least we were off the streets. My mom felt we needed to sneak around like double 007's or something. She got this bright idea to have Claude drive her into town every other day to use a payphone and call Alex's parents to give them an update on us, but she said she needed to use a secret code. Alex and I became "tomatoes and or potatoes." She said the phone people were listening in and would tell the cops if she mentioned our names. My poor mom was so paranoid.

When she'd call and talk to Nancy and or Stanley, she'd say things like, "The tomatoes are rotten today." Which meant Alex and I were not having a good day. (I never knew we had bad days.) Or she'd say, "The tomatoes are good. Nice and ripe today. You can come and get some later." Which meant they could visit, but really in other double 007 terms suggested, she needed more money to help pay for our food and the extra hot water we used taking baths and such. She had requested we bathe every two or three days, which "was good enough." Oh, well, it was better than what we washed prior.

Stan and Nancy always gave whatever money they could provide. I never realized until recently how much of a scam artist my sweet mom

184 · Peggy Watkins

really was, but, fuck, she sure was. We stayed with her for three weeks until Alex told me he was sick of not being able to do anything or go anywhere, and he was sick of getting up at the crack of dawn to do the farming. He told me he was going to go crazy if he didn't "get the fuck away from these crazy hillbillies." I agreed.

We conspired out by the barn one day and agreed that we'd leave next time his parents came to visit. So, we waited until the "tomatoes" were decent. Then, we sprang it on my mom that we were leaving to live with Nancy and Stanley in Albion. My mom was confused as to why we would want to go, but she didn't argue. Nancy was happy about it and Stanley too. We packed our stuff and left.

Funny how all my life I wanted so badly to live with my mom, and then when I did, I couldn't wait to leave. Maybe it was all I'd been through that'd changed me or her expectations of Alex and I contributing to the farm life. Perhaps it was Vickie Sue and that red-headed pecker-faced dude still there and annoying us. Maybe it was just time to go.

Nancy and Stan lived two blocks from Virgie's house in Albion. I didn't give two shits about how close I would be to her. I just wanted to leave my mom's farm. Even though I was finally around the family for whom I had always longed, I wanted to get away even more than I had wanted them. I didn't have a relationship with my mother I had imagined in my mind. Nothing was turning out the way I had dreamt it would be. My mother loved me, I don't doubt that. It was just a different kind of love for me than her other kids. I know that now, and I'm okay with it. I almost feel as if she longed for me so much and for so long that the pain broke her too.

In addition to loving me, the only way she knew how she also showed me how to get what you want by lying. I wasn't impressed back then, and I'm sad about it now. Sometimes, I still want to cry today about all that happened or maybe more so because of the way things went down. Perhaps my sadness is rooted in the thought of a bunch of adults pawning a child such as they did.

I am grateful to Mrs. Martin, who taught me a different way than lying and cheating, one lesson I'll never forget. It was a lesson that I have referred to (and still do) repeatedly throughout my life as I watched everyone around me manipulate and hurt others by lying and cheating. Thank you again, Mrs. Martin, for instilling the value of honesty in me!

"PEGGY, LISTEN TO ME KIDDO, this is a pivotal point that means you stay or go back. Have you had sex yet?" Officer Lentz repeated.

Okay, now he's getting personal, and I'm going to get in a lot of trouble for doing it. I sure as hell wasn't admitting to a cop that I had sex. I mean, I was married, and that's what married people do, but still. I knew I wasn't supposed to be doing it, and I knew he would tell Virgie, and then I would really get it for having sex. Recalling past issues and a baseball bat made me think long and hard, which caused him to repeat the question. I was scared shitless.

"Peggy, have you – "

"NO! No, we haven't."

"Peggy, it's okay if you have. Now listen to me, kid. If you tell me you did not, you'll have to go back home with Virgie, and she's going to have your marriage annulled, canceled because you've not 'consummated' it which means, you and Alex had to have had sex to make it real, to bind it, make it legal. You get it now? So, if you tell me you have—and it's perfectly OK to say to me you did have sex—then Virgie can never bother you again, and you never have to go back to her house again. So, kid, what –

I interrupted, "Yes, ok. We've done it a lot. Every day and sometimes two and three times a day." I wanted to make sure we had 'consummated' enough, I guess. I was angry, yet terrified out of my mind, worried that I'd have to go back and live with her. Dealing with all of them again was more than I could bear. Not anymore, spawns of Satan! Move the fuck on!

Officer Lentz looked at me, and with a chuckle, he said, "Ok, kiddo. I get it. And, you don't have to go back to her house, she can't make you do anything ever again. You can tell her no or call us, and we'll help you. You got it, kid?"

My eyes welled up with tears, "Really? I never have to go back again?"

"No. No, you don't but, you should get back in school and get your education so you can get a decent job and have a good life, okay? Promise me you'll go back to school?"

"I promise. I want to be a nurse and help people. I need my diploma first though then college," I rambled. "Yes, I promise I will go back to school."

Officer Lentz smiled and, with a nod, handed me back my marriage license and walked to his vehicle. Before he reached his patrol car, he walked to Virgie's car once again and said something. He must have told her I had sex and to drive away and leave me alone because as she spun out of sight, she yelled, "I'll be back, and you's will get it, little girl. You's hear's me?" She shook her fist out the window and drove away with Donny and Denise following behind.

Watching them drive away gave me a sense of freedom I had never known before.

I was FREE! My heart lifted, and I felt light as a feather. I had never smiled so big in my life … all while trying to ignore the nagging, deep-rooted feeling that she'd be back.

But just for now, this time…**I won.**

Sadly, even though I was on my own, the four horsemen never quit their ways… until I stopped mine!

IV

MARRIED

AT 15

A COUPLE OF MONTHS AFTER the whole ordeal with Virgie and her posse, Alex and I got our first apartment. Stanley and Nancy encouraged us to sign up for a government handout. The plan was to start collecting checks and get our place, which is precisely what we did. Part of me was excited, but the other side was sad to move out of their home, I loved living with them. They were the parents I never had—you know, the kind that takes care of you—and I had longed for that kind of relationship with a mother and father my whole life. Lord knows Ardy & Virgie never provided it.

We moved into a three-story, top-floor apartment, two bedrooms with a kitchen, dining area, living room, and bathroom. Big enough to allow Alex's cousin to move right in with us. He didn't stay long though, just a month or so. Then he got one of the apartments on the second floor. Funny thing, Nancy and Stanley also moved to the first floor, and that made one family renting three out of four flats in the same building.

We lived, acted, and partied like teens. Because we were teens. In our living room, we had a big cloth hanging on our wall with a giant marijuana leaf. We had nothing else on our living room walls—just that, right over our couch. We had beads (many missing from the strings) hanging from the doorway into the living room and kitchen— real teenage hippies from the early '70s style. Everything we owned was either hand-me-down or garbage-picked.

We were excited to be on our own and have money that was our own, but neither one of us liked being on welfare. Nonetheless, we were 15 years old, what were we to do?

I registered at school under my married name, so I could get back to my education, but Alex said school was too boring. He was an all-A student and never had to study for any test. I, on the other hand, had to research everything and study hard. I was an A, B, and C student, but I had to work for it. I had common sense skills that many others lacked, just not book smart. Not that I am dumb, but I would instead learn a skill than read about it. However, I loved reading. But...I only wanted to read books about adventures and thrillers (I think I've read *maybe* two romances in my life). A good Steven King book was my kind of reading.

Tenth grade, which I started as soon as we returned from our runaway adventure around the end of October, was brutal. We had gotten married in September 1978, and by December, I was pregnant. Classes became a little more complicated as nausea started hijacking my mornings. It was tough going to class and having to sit and raise my hand and ask to go to the bathroom. Often the teacher's wastebasket was the best I could do. And of course, teens being teens, once they knew I was pregnant, the teasing began.

It was suggested I go to the alternative school for moms in Battle Creek. I enrolled, but they said I had to have the baby first, then I could attend. I tried explaining to them that the other school was driving me nuts, and I was going to drop out due to all the kids picking on me, but they stuck to their guns.

Well...so did I.

I dropped out of high school as soon as my pregnancy began to show, about mid-April. The kids had been teasing me about being pregnant *before* I was pregnant, so I could only imagine what it was about to be like. But then again, I came back to school as a married woman who was 15 years old. I get it. I was prime material for picking on back then, and probably still today. Nonetheless, I quit.

We were still on welfare and didn't have much money, but we did odd jobs to get extra cash. In the fall, we raked, bagged, and mowed lawns. When winter rolled around, we used our old-fashioned shovels to clear sidewalks and driveways. In the summer, we weeded onions at a local farm. I also babysat a couple of kids here and there and cleaned houses. Alex wanted to be a mechanic more than anything, so he fixed cars, often in trade for a bag of weed or $20.00 bucks here and $30.00 there.

My mom, Chelcie, was very happy for us that we had our apartment and were getting along well. She called us at Nancy and Stanley's about once a week to talk and see how we were, which meant everything to me. I was empowered and free in the physical sense, and that felt great. Yet, Virgie and her minions still had this control over me and a hold that will undoubtedly take me years to break free from.

Virgie would also call, but not for a friendly chat. She screamed and demanded that I come and clean her house. Or she would call and tell me that she was sick and needed help because I'd run off and gotten married, leaving her so that now she doesn't get any more money from Ardy for child support. She'd say that made her heart act up, therefore, her being sick was all my fault.

As usual, she continued with threats of telling Denise and Donny how I was treating her, and she made sure I knew that they'd teach me a lesson. This repetitive often threat came after I'd tell her I couldn't go and clean her house that week.

A few times, I just caved to shut her up. I would walk over to her house and clean, and never once did she even offer me a bologna sandwich while I worked the entire day without breaks. She never paid me or said thanks. She did, however, tell me what I didn't clean good enough or what I needed to clean again "or else."

Once when I was first pregnant, I told her I needed something to eat because I was feeling lightheaded and sick while I was cleaning her house.

She looked at me, disgusted. "Why?"

I took a deep breath and stood a little taller. "Because I'm pregnant, and I feel sick."

She looked me right in the face, pointed her finger at me, pursed her lips, and said, "Yous ain't my a-bil-ty anymore, little girl. Yous got knocked up. Now, yous is PG, and now yous want me to feeds yous and that thing in yous big belly?! No! You finish, then go home and eat. I ain't feedin' yous."

Bitch.

It wasn't like I'd ask for a five-course meal, I just wanted a few saltines or something. Hell, I remembered what it was like trying to eat when I did live with her. I finished cleaning that day and then told her I was never coming back to clean her house again.

She threatened that if I didn't come back to clean, she'd get the FBI after me, and they'd put me in jail. I told Alex, he laughed so hard. So did his brothers. She was a force to be reckoned with, but no one wanted to bother with her crazy ass.

I HADN'T HEARD FROM my dad and or his dim-witted wife at all during this entire time. It was as if they were non-existent in my life again. Like when I was seven, and I asked Ardy who he was when he picked me up for a visit. Outta sight, outta mind.

Denise —the sister who I thought always had my back but never did—contacted me and wanted to be, as she put it, my "big sister." The audacity! However, my starved heart was longing for family of some kind, so I took what I could get, which, believe me, wasn't much of anything from either side of the family.

As for the rest of the family, I'd see them occasionally by chance, and we'd speak superficially. Other than that, there was no intentional contact with cousins, aunts, uncles, or grandparents, and that was okay with me. Life was pleasant when none of them were around, yet, I found myself still wanting the family to love me and accept me. I wanted them. I'm just not sure they ever wanted me.

When I found out I was pregnant, I told Denise right away. I thought maybe she'd offer some sisterly advice on pregnancy stuff but, she didn't. Someone did however spread the news to all with scoff-at-Peggy and taunting. After I was about three months along, Ardy contacted Virgie and told her to tell me he was coming for a visit, and I'd better be home.

I rushed around, making sure the apartment was spotless. I was so excited that my dad and his wife were coming to visit our first home. I had Alex get the coffee machine from his parents so I could make coffee, and we put out some chips and cookies on the old fashion corner dining table sitting in our living room. It was red and white checkered and in fair condition. It's all we had, and we offered it humbly.

I had forgotten one thing to hide before they arrived, the ashtray that sat in the middle of that table. The ashtray was used and dirty, not trashed, but it had a few dark marks from putting out joints, and there was a roach (the end of a marijuana joint) sitting in one corner. First, let me say, as soon as I found out I was pregnant, I stopped smoking weed and drinking anything alcoholic. I didn't even like people around me smoking weed as I was afraid that I'd get the baby high. I didn't want to hurt my baby. So that stuff wasn't mine. But it *was* in my home.

My dad and his wife, Maudie Jo, arrived late. They walked up two flights of stairs—one bigger than the other—and they both complained the entire way up.

I was oblivious to their nasty looks and remarks, I was so used to them. I had learned to accept them and roll with it. My dad's first remark was something about how he'd "not live where you have to walk up all those steps. That can't be good for you!" I asked them if they'd like a tour of our home, they declined.

"We're not here for a social visit," Ardy said as he was somewhat catching his breath.

I raised an eyebrow. *Why the fuck are you here then?* I thought.

As they sat down at the corner table, they both took out a cigarette and lit one. I sat over on the couch away from both of them, and my dad scowled.

"Why are you over there?"

"I don't like the smell of the smoke because it makes me sick to my stomach."

He rolled his eyes, shook his head, and shouted, "Oh my gosh! That's all in your head. You are just making that shit up. You've been around us smoking before, and it never bothered you, so why now?" He took a long draw off his cigarette in sync with his wife, and they both blew it over my way.

I sat in silence while accepting his condemnation and secondhand smoke. It was sad to me that *that* was all I seemed to ever get, disapproval. But at least it was *some* attention.

They smoked about half of their smokes, put them out in the ashtray, and got up and left. They barely spoke to either of us, didn't look around, or anything. They just came, smoked up my house, and went. Shit! Had I known their agenda, I wouldn't have busted my butt to make my home spotless, and I wouldn't have set out a bowl full of chips and a plate of cookies.

I heard a couple days later through the grapevine that my apartment was dirty, and there was an ashtray "full" of half-burnt rolled dope. I also heard we had no food, and the apartment smelled like pot. Denise made sure she told me all about how nasty my home was and what "daddy" said. And of course, I heard all this from Virgie, as well. Neither her nor her daughter ever muddied my doorstep and had no right to bash me, but that is what happened and right to my face.

Bullshit spreads fast and smells dirty.

Hearing this was hurtful. Alex told me way back then (repeatedly) to not let them be a part of my life. He pointed out that none of them treat me right, none of them have ever helped me out, and they never will. He knew, but I didn't want to see or admit it.

Shortly after that incident, my Aunt Opal came to visit, and she *did* want a tour, after which she told me, "You're clean as a pin, Peg-a-Lulu."

She sat down, had a cup of tea and a cookie, and talked to us about moving to Homer into her small two-bedroom trailer by the river's edge. We were ecstatic to move to the country, and the home was perfect. She accepted our Doberman, Pretty Boy, and our kitty, Fudd-lee. I was happy we could take our washer too. It was an old wringer washer, and my aunt had a clothesline outback, it was going to be great.

We were good to go, and the bonus was that I would now be closer to my mom, Chelcie.

OUR NEW NEIGHBORS were an older couple, Maggie and Harold, who rented from Virgie, which was how I knew them. They had always been kind to me. Maggie was a puzzle and gameshow mama, she loved working on her crossword puzzles while watching tv gameshows, which is what she did every day all day, into the evenings. Harold loved telling jokes and drinking beer, and that's what he did all day every day.

Maggie had one daughter, Dena, who was a genuine friend to me. She had been in a car accident with a train when she was younger, and it caused her some issues. Her entire left side was basically of no use, and when she did walk, she limped. Her left hand was slightly useable but pretty much stayed snug to her chest. She visited her mom often and always came over to see how Alex and I were doing, she genuinely cared about me.

On one of her visits, I was hanging laundry, and she rushed to my backyard, hand in the air, yelling, "Put your arms down! Put your arms down!"

Um, what? And why?

The closer she got, the louder she yelled.

"Put your arms down!"

As soon as she got to me, she grabbed the clothes out of my hands and told me that if a pregnant woman puts her hands over her head, the cord will wrap around the baby's neck and pop its head off!

Of course, I was barely 16 at this time and easily influenced, so yeah, I put my hands down and stopped putting my hands over my head and called my doctor, who, by the way, laughed so hard, I thought he would shit himself.

He told me after he was done laughing, it would take a lot to pop that head off. He explained it was a good exercise for me and that I could do laundry, but just let Alex carry the load to the clothesline for me.

I never figured out if Dena was messing with me or if she thought that was actually a true medical thing, but I knew Dena was a good-hearted person. We were friends for a short time before she got married, had a little girl, and moved out of state. I was happy for her. She found true love and happiness. I do hope someday I see her again and get to catch up over a cup of coffee. But for now, she'll remain in my happy memory file where I'll cherish her smile and keep her safe.

After I learned that a baby's head wouldn't pop off for raising my arms above my head, I signed up for driver Ed classes at Albion High school. I was 5 months pregnant in May of 1979.

Alex had already gotten his driver's license even though he was younger than me by four months. He had petitioned the Secretary of State for a "Special License." Since we were both 15 and married, and of course, I was pregnant, I suppose they thought he had a good reason to be able to drive. I felt relieved that they granted it to him, but I needed my own. We lived way out in the country. What would happen if I went into labor, and no one could drive me to the hospital? Therefore, he'd drop me off every morning at the high school for my driving lessons.

It was apparent I was pregnant. My belly protruded like a fully ripe watermelon (or at least I thought so) and I grew boobies. I was still picked on immensely by the preppy girls, but I really wanted my license, so this time, I just ignored them (looking back, I wish I would have used that same tactic and stayed in school). The guys didn't really pick, they just kind of said, hey or hi, and that's about it. I made new friends, and some old acquaintances learned to respect me.

After our classroom work, we had actual driving practice. I was put with Mr. Foust and a group of three guys, there were four of us teens and the teacher in one car. We all took turns driving in and around the parking lot, soon enough, we were ready for the road. The real test!

I had a habit of holding my belly and rubbing it. While it never seemed to bother the guys, the instructor always seemed a little nerved up over me. I recall him saying something to the effect of, "Wow, you're pregnant. When are you due?"

I guess I don't blame him. It probably wasn't typical for him to have a 16-year-old pregnant teen in a driver training class. Nonetheless, I wanted and needed my license, so I endured his nervous behavior and curious looks.

At the end of a driving lesson late in the season, two of the guys whispered something to me. I giggled and agreed. Soon enough, it was my turn to drive, and I was all ready to "get the instructor going."

As I was driving down a back road, I hit a medium-sized bump and shouted, "Oh God!" and grabbed my tummy. I thought Mr. Frey was going to have a heart attack right there on the spot. He grabbed his heart, the wheel, put his foot on the break (on his side), and yelled, "Oh God, not now!"

Every one of us laughed so hard it took a few minutes to pull ourselves together. Needless to say, the driving lessons were over a little sooner than they were supposed to be for that day. I did assure him I was due in August and healthy according to my doctor. And that I would never do that again.

I passed driver's ed with flying colors, I got the highest score out of our group, so he told me.

During our first summer in our new place, my mom and I had a great time together, "yard sale-ing." I was excited to go and see what treasures I might find for the baby. Alex did a lot of auto work for garage sale money so we could get a bed, playpen, and all the things we needed for the baby coming in August.

I hit the jackpot! Chelsie and I were out hitting the yard sales and came across a gold mine. Some lady gave me a 40-gallon plastic yard, and leaf bag stuffed full of baby sleepers, bibs, cloth diapers, burp rags, onesies, tee-shirts, and baby mittens for $5.00. Cute little boy outfits and not one stain on anything. My mom explained I was set until the baby was about three months.

I washed everything in Ivory Snow Baby detergent, rinsed it twice, hung it to dry, and ironed what I wanted to be hung up while folding everything else neatly in my baby's little dresser. The nursery was set up so cute with a few toys and a couple of pictures. My mom had gotten us a used baby bed, and my sister Addy Mae had given us a mattress from her son. I was getting big, and my feet swelled something awful. My boobs went from tiny yokes to cantaloupe in a matter of a few months. It was great. We were young, but we were proud of all we'd done for our baby and home. I tried extremely hard to make it look beautiful with the yard sale trinkets and hand-me-down furniture.

One day, Virgie decided she needed to see what I had. As she knocked on the door, opening it and walking in, she was met by our very big, 98-pound, Doberman, who was growling.

"Yous better put that stupid old dog up, or I's is gonna get Donny in here, and he'll kill it!"

Of course, I rushed in and put him in the back bedroom. It was then Virgie told me that she came to see all the clothes Chelcie and I had gotten for the baby. I thought for a brief nanosecond that she was excited for Alex and me, but then I realized her agenda. As I started showing her, she felt it was her duty to direct me on what to do with the boy's clothes since I didn't know what I was having yet, and Donny and his girlfriend had recently had a baby boy. As she held a few outfits up to inspect them, she told me, "Yous ain't gonna need these. I'll take them for Lewis (Donny's new baby). He needs them, you don't."

Well, welcome to my home, Queen! Come on in and start ruling the kingdom!

I took them out of her hands and placed them back into the dresser and told her. "Those are mine in case I do have a boy, and I'm not letting you take them from my baby."

There were very few times that I stuck up for myself with her, and this was one of them. It felt good. She wasn't happy. She stood up, stomped to the door, grabbed the doorknob, and let me know that, once again, I'd upset her, and she was going to get Denise and Donny to teach me a lesson.

Here I am, pregnant, and she is still threatening me over some yard sale baby clothes, classic!

Well, did I think it would ever be any different? I mean, she didn't even give me crackers when I cleaned her house a couple months ago. When am I going to learn? She doesn't care. None of them care!

IN AUGUST OF **1979,** AT PRECISELY **6:29 PM,** I gave birth to my first child, Alexander J.R. My labor was short-lived and not so bad. Four hours total time from first pain till the actual delivery. I had heard all kinds of horror stories about some women in labor for days and weeks, so I was glad mine was short.

Chelsie had explained that childbirth is painful, but the intense pain only lasts as long as the delivery, and each one seems to go faster than the previous. My mom furthermore shared that, as soon as my baby is placed in my arms, I'd forget any pain. And that was *so* true.

As I lay on that shiny steel birthing bed, the nurse put my son in my arms. I cradled him and smiled at him, and looking down at his little face, I stared in awe that this tiny person was my creation. I beamed with a love I had never felt before. Alexander J.R. was perfect! I now knew what real love was because I was experiencing it with my child. Immediately, the mama bear instinct kicked in, and I was in full protection mood.

Back in 1979, the hospital would keep women for about a week after delivery. During my stay, I only had a few visitors, Alex (of course), his parents, my best friend Teri, and then—surprisingly—Denise.

Alex brought me a bundle of wildflowers, a new outfit for his son to wear home, and a teddy bear. The flowers were beautiful. We could never really afford to buy them, but he had stopped alongside a country road and picked me a nice handful as he had many times before. Teri, my best friend at that time, brought Alexander's first Pooh Bear, a Venus Fly Trap plant, and a card. Nancy and Stanley came bringing a toy and lots of hugs and kisses. Nancy was the huggee-kissy kind of person, and Stan was too, he just didn't gush as much as his wife. I was just glad they were there.

Denise also came to visit. And believe it or not, she was actually pleasant. Denise stayed about 5 minutes, long enough to sneak in and hold Alexander, give him a kiss on his forehead and leave. It was these moments of seemingly genuine effort on her part—to be nice rather than condemning, accepting rather than accusatory—that made me wonder if she had a twinkle of humanity shining through. When she would act that way, it would always give me hope, albeit a give-and-take-away nugget of hope, which they would toss to me every now and then. I would find myself clinging to that nugget of hope, thinking that maybe—just maybe—this was their conscience talking to them. Perhaps they realized how hurtful they were? Yeah, and pigs fly! I would come to learn that these far and few between moments of flash-compassion never lasted. Never.

No one else came to the hospital.

Virgie was right in the same town, about a 4-minute drive away. Ardy lived 20 minutes from Albion, and Chelcie was about an hour away, not one of them came to see the baby and me. However, Virgie and Ardy raised hell and acted as if I was supposed to bring Alexander to *them*. Hardly an indicator that they cared.

As soon as I got home, though, Chelcie, my mom, came right over to visit and see her new grandchild. She brought me a new bag of cloth diapers and told me they'd be great as burp rags. She brought me a nursing bra and showed me how it worked. In her basket of goodies was also three little receiving blankets and a big handmade quilt she had made for when he got bigger. She taught me to always have a receiving blanket with me so I could drape it over my shoulders when I needed to feed the baby. We sat and talked for hours. She told me a few things about nursing and taking care of myself that I was never taught before. I was lucky to have this time with her, and it made my heart feel loved.

We had many friends stop by to see the baby and visit with us within the first month that Alexander was born. It was nice to have so many friends and family (Alex's family) who showed and honestly did care.

I was given a phone message from Aunt Opal, that I was to go and bring the baby to Denise's house on a specific day at a precise time, so Ardy and his wife, Maudie Jo could see him. Alexander was about three weeks old at this time.

Well, Denise lived about 33 miles away. We were two 16-year-old kids who had a shitty car and little money for gas, but we were expected to do as they demanded, so we figured out how to pull it off. We borrowed five dollars from Alex's parents for gas, and off we went to for our visit. We were kind of excited, and both thinking that maybe they would surprise us by having a nice gift for the baby.

We were definitely surprised.

When we arrived, we walked into the kitchen where Ardy, Maudie Jo, Denise, and her husband sat at the kitchen table playing Euchre. We were not greeted at all by anyone! Not one of them stood up to offer a hello, hug, nor did they even stop talking amongst themselves about the card game and or whatever their conversation was at that time. They continued as if we were not even there—all four of them.

I said a couple things, and Ardy laughed and kept talking. Dim-witted Maudie Jo kept scowling with her pruned-up face, rolling her eyes and sighing loudly. It was as if Alex, I, and the baby were intrusive and annoying.

I mean heck, *they* demanded me to come so they could see the baby! One might believe, at the very least, they may perhaps want to, *maybe*, look at him or possibly even hold him. There was nothing. Call me strange, but that hurt. I felt so discarded. So sad. So alone. Unloved and unwanted. Although that feeling wasn't new, it didn't make it any less painful. It had always been with me, and at times I didn't even notice it. It was my reality. But *that* day…I noted.

It was feeding time, and Alexander Jr. began to fuss. Denise directed me to the kids' room to nurse him. I came out after about 20 minutes to see Alex sitting in the living room playing Star Wars with my nephew and niece, the only two people who would talk to him. I no sooner walked out of the kids' bedroom when Denise let me know it was nice of me to come all this way so they could see the baby, but the door was opened for us to leave because they were ready to eat dinner.

Numb and feeling out-of-body, I picked up our diaper bag and walked out the door. Before the car door was shut, Alex began venting about how wrong it was that not one of them held the baby or even wanted to look at him after they demanded that we bring him to visit.

"Why couldn't they even offer for you to sit down?!" He raged. "They kept playing cards and didn't even engage in conversation with us! They don't deserve to have you—us! —in their lives, and you should never speak to them motherfuckers again! I HATE THEM!"

I hate them too. But I have to. You don't understand, I thought as I stared out the window, holding back tears.

A big part of me knew he was right, but that part of me, the part that had been conditioned to listen to them and do as I was told, had kicked in high gear and overruled the logical part of my brain, so, once again I had been at their mercy.

BECAUSE WE WANTED to be closer to Alex's parents, we moved out of Aunt Opal's trailer shortly before Christmas and went back to Albion. We moved next door to the first apartment we had, which was also with the same landlord. He was nice to us, and Alex did some work for him, which helped with rent costs.

Alex's parents also moved around a lot, and we seemed to follow suit. I would say, on average, during the first few years of our marriage, we shifted about every three months. It indeed was a never-ending thing. We'd get all settled, and then there would be a cheaper, better place, and we'd pack it up and move again, just as his parents did.

When Alexander was about five months old, Denise and her then husband, came to Alex and I and offered to "help" us out. They claimed that they wanted to give Alex a job working construction in Gladwin, MI—where they had moved to—and Denise told me I could help her around the house until the baby got older, at which time I could go back to school if I wanted to. She knew that graduating had always been a big deal to me since none of my siblings had graduated.

We listened, accepted their offer, and packed everything up. We stored some things at Alex's brother's house, took just want we needed, and moved our baby and our Doberman, Pretty Boy, to Gladwin to begin a new life. Fudd-lee found a new home with Alex's family.

We were excited to have this opportunity. We appreciated Denise and her hubby for the offer and wanted to make something of ourselves. This was our chance, we thought—a short-lived thought.

We arrived in northern Michigan late on a cold January night. There we were, two teens, a five-month-old, and a 98-pound Doberman in an old shitty pickup truck that had broken down on a back road. We sat there for about 30 minutes trying to get it started, which led to the foolish choice of getting out and walking to the nearest house with the baby and dog in tow.

We came to a big farmhouse, and of course, they had a dog that came charging at us in the road. Both protective dogs began tearing into each other. The owner rushed out the door wielding his rifle and yelling at us to get off his property. Alex threw his hands up into the air and yelled that we needed help and had a baby. Somehow, Alex managed to convince the guy not to shoot us.

Things settled down, and we were able to talk calmly with the people. They ended up being very understanding and were nice enough to give us a ride five miles up the road to Denise's house—even after our dog had ripped out the eye of their dog. I suppose folks up there have an understanding that that's part of owning a dog in the country. All I know is that their compassion for us was more prominent than their anger about the dog. We also offered to somehow make it right by paying for the vet bills, which probably helped calm them down.

After we finally arrived, Denise had us all sleep in the living room the first night. The next day, Alex started work with Larry, Denise's husband. I took our bags of clothing up to my niece's room as they had moved her into their son's room. Once settled and unpacked, Denise took me over to see my dad and his wife, who lived in Gladwin at that time as well. They owned a small bait shop and lived in a trailer right next to it. Their neighbors on both sides seemed nice, two single guys, one on the right and one on the left. Alex became friends with Eric fast because Eric had the weed. He worked and was a functional weed smoker, too, so they did hit it off.

Denise told our dad and Maudie Jo all about the truck breaking down and the dog fight, and then, of course, it began. It was my fault. They all three sat and belittled me for being with Alex and having a Doberman (which was a "killer dog" who obviously eats little babies and just attacks other dogs for "no reason"). After they grew tired of jeering me, we left and went back to her house. She told me her kids would be home soon, and I needed to make them a snack for after school while she went next door to "visit" the Realtor, Fred.

Starting that night, I made supper, cleaned up after everyone, did the laundry, vacuumed, dusted, and cleaned whatever else needed cleaning. This became my routine, every day and night. Alex went to work with Larry daily on the same schedule. Every morning at daybreak, they left for work, and every evening around dusk, they'd return.

After a few days, Alex fixed our truck himself and got it over to their house. It was at that time when Denise and Larry decided that our Doberman was not safe to be around their kids (even though he stayed upstairs in my room unless he needed to go out) and told us he had to be put outside in the doghouse outback.

We worried about putting Pretty Boy outside in the cold winter. Even though Alex made sure he had plenty of straw and a blanket to block the wind from inside, it was still a weak-ass doghouse and not what our boy was used to. Our Pretty Boy cried, barked, and hated it. I am sure he was confused and wondered what he did wrong. I hated them for making me chain my inside dog up *outside*. I never liked dogs being on chains. It's just not right!

After three solid weeks both Alex and I had had enough of them, and we wanted to move back home. They did not pay Alex for his work. Well, they did but they kept the majority for the vet bill and our rent and board, therefore, Alex and I received $45.00 for two of the weeks, and the third week he was paid $20.00 in silver dollars and told to take his dog, shitty truck and leave without me and the baby.

We knew what was going on. Denise, my dad, and Larry were fucking with us, and it wasn't just with the vet bill. Every night after dinner while I did the dishes, Denise would bring every dirty—or not dirty—plate she could find. She'd laugh as she put them in the dishwater and look at me and say, "I just keep finding them."

Larry worked with a friend of his named Aaron, who thought I was cute. I guess he had a crush on me and was interested. What came next proved that neither my sister nor her husband cared that I was married and loved my husband.

Alex was told to leave because the silver dollars were being saved by Denise and he was accused of stealing them, which he didn't do but, honestly, we both should have and left together nonetheless, it didn't go that way.

Alex packed up the truck with his clothes, our dog, and off they went to Albion, leaving our son and me behind. I was pissed off at all of them. I was pissed at Denise and Larry for kicking him out at ten o'clock at night. And I was pissed at my dad and stepmom, who got involved and kept saying what a thief Alex was and how wrong he was for "stealing the dead baby's headstone money." They carried on letting me know how he's ruining my life because his parents are drunks. The rest of his family was a bunch of drunks and pot smokers. The whole family is terrible, they yelled at me.

Meanwhile, Larry invited Aaron over to dinner that very next evening. We ate, I cleaned up, we played euchre, and then I put Alexander to bed. I knew Aaron was behind me, following me up the stairs. My heartbeat faster. I walked into my room, then stopped, turned around and looked him in the eye and said, "What do you want?"

He responded by leaning in for a kiss.

I backed up with my child in my arms. "Stop! Why are you hitting on me?! I'm married, and my husband is coming back to get me."

He looked puzzled. "Can I come in and just talk? I need to tell you something."

Naïve me agreed. After I got the baby to sleep, Aaron started in.

"I thought you were interested in me. My understanding is that Alex left and isn't coming back."

"How can I be interested in someone I just met for the first time tonight, Aaron?" I scolded.

He looked embarrassed. "I'm sorry, Peg. I was told you were into me."

And with that, he left the room. I see now that I was fortunate. It could have been so much worse that night. I thought he was kind but that didn't mean I wanted to sleep with him, not at all. Thank God he backed off.

The next day I asked Aaron if he would give me a ride to my dad's store so I could use the phone, I had no vehicle, and Denise said I couldn't make a long-distance call on her phone. Despite our awkward interaction the night before, he was kind enough to give me a ride.

As soon as we arrive, I noticed my dad out behind his store as we pulled in. He looked up and started shaking his head, glaring at me, and mouths the words, "You're sick. This is embarrassing me. You are disgusting." Confused, I get out of the truck and approach him.

"Why are you so upset with me?"

"Denise called and said you slept with Aaron, and now here you are riding around with him?! You're disgusting. You're an embarrassment to me!"

Um, is that like the pot calling the kettle black? Let's think back about 17-18 years ago when you impregnated your wife's sister, my mother. Wow! Say it isn't so, daddy, say it isn't so!

"*What* are you *talking* about?!"

I tried telling my dad that it was a lie, but he kept shaking his head and telling me I was lying, "just like you lied on Donny." Aaron also tried to tell him nothing had happened between us, but it fell on deaf ears. My dad spewed obscenities about how he believes Denise over me. It hurt. At that point, the conversation was over. I asked Aaron if he could take me back to my in-law's in Albion on his way to Jackson. He said he was shocked at how my family was treating me and said he'd be happy to get me out of there, no problem.

Right before I left Gladwin, I realized I was pregnant for my second child. I was 16 years old with a baby, no diploma, no job, and pregnant. When I realized I was expecting, I told Denise, hoping she would give me some sisterly advice. She didn't. She gave me her ugly, nasty attitude and told me how having another baby would ruin me and kill our dad. She kept saying things such as, you don't want to kill daddy, do you? This will kill him, knowing you are pregnant again and only 16. What kind of life will you have? You would be stuck with two babies at your age and no education. She told me over and over and over, "Get rid of it! Have an abortion!" drilling it into my head and making me feel as if the only alternative is to ruin my life and everyone else's by "killing" her daddy. And of course, it'd be all my fault.

IT WAS A FRIDAY NIGHT when Aaron, I, and Alexander Jr. started the two-and-a-half-hour trip back to Albion. When we began, Aaron offered me water or pop and asked if I had diapers for the baby and a bottle. He was very kind, and I appreciated him. We chatted the entire way, and he reminded me again how he felt my family was not treating me right and how it upset him to see the way they act towards me.

In all honesty, the whole thing was a little unsettling. Even though I was married, and I knew I loved my husband, I felt as if I was starting to like Aaron. I wasn't sure if it was in a brotherly/friend kind-of-way or something deeper and more meaningful. What I did know was that he was friendly and talked to me like I was a real person. He never once belittled me or made me feel like I was stupid or wrong. He listened as I told him a couple things, and he replied with thoughtful, sincere responses, it seemed as if he tried to help me see things in a better light. No one had ever really done that before, and I liked it. I respected that he made me feel like a human being and not a piece of shit. I did like him, but perhaps it was only because he showed compassion for a young girl who was starved for positive attention.

He said, if I ever leave Alex or needed help with anything, I could find him through his dad's construction company. He said he'd help me out. We parted as friends.

After he dropped me off, I never really thought much about him again until about 16 years later when I ran into him while partying at a bar in Jackson. We simply shared a couple beers, laughs, a hug, and went our own ways once again. I can admit now that I do like him, but I like him because he is real and a friend. Throughout my time living in Jackson, Aaron, and I ran into each other several times. Often, we would go have a beer, catch up, laugh, and simply enjoy each other's friendship. I appreciated him, and I, to this day, am glad we met. I am pretty sure we both felt a kinship of the sort, but it was in no way romantic. I believe he is a good guy who could see my family for what they were and helped me out of a bad situation. And for that, I am grateful.

As he dropped me off that day in Albion at my in-laws, he told me I shouldn't listen to my sister about the abortion because it was something that would haunt me for the rest of my life. He told me it was wrong, and I should bite the bullet and have the baby.

I shook my head slowly—a*nother person who doesn't understand. I have to do as I am told.*

"Well, my sister told me I should or else this will kill my dad to see me pregnant again at 16," I said matter-of-factly. "I don't want to kill him, you know."

Aaron looked tired. "It will not kill your dad. That is a scare tactic, and you shouldn't allow them to use it on you. She's wrong."

I thought briefly about what he said, but it was overcome by my conditioning. *If I don't listen and do as I'm told, something terrible is going to happen. That is a fact. And besides, I just met this guy. He can't possibly understand.*

Alex and I were happy to see each other, and we talked a lot that evening. I told him all that Denise had said, and he agreed, he felt that another kid would tie us down even more than we already were. We were both 16-year-old kids, what the hell did we know besides nothing?

The next day, we contacted our former landlord and discovered our previous apartment was vacant, so we moved back into the same place we had just left weeks ago. It didn't take us long to get settled in over the weekend. Monday morning, I called and quickly made an appointment in Jackson on Wednesday, January 23rd, 1980, to have "the procedure" done. The flat-toned woman on the other end of the line instructed me to arrive 15 minutes early and to arrange for a ride home afterward.

As we drove to Jackson, Alex smoked a joint. He told me it'd help calm me down if I got high, but I told him it'd hurt the baby, and I didn't want to injure the baby. I even made him roll his window down, so the smell wouldn't affect the baby. Crazy huh? I'm on my way to kill my child, and I don't want to hurt it. What the fuck was I thinking? I wasn't.

When I arrived, they asked for my Medicaid information. I don't know who paid for the abortion, but we didn't pay a dime. Feeling anxious, I told Alex I wasn't sure about the abortion, and what exactly was it anyway? I didn't have enough sense to realize what I was getting ready to do.

As we sat down in the waiting room area, my hands were sweaty and clammy. My heart pounded so hard and fast I thought it was going to come out of my chest. My mouth dried up, and I could barely speak. I was scared. All I wanted to do was run and scream. But, there I sat, frozen in time, waiting to terminate my child.

As the nurse called my name and I followed her down a cold white dull hallway, which smelled like ammonia, my legs felt as if they were going collapse. I was sick to my stomach, and everything was spinning out of control. My mind was whirling out of focus. I kept hearing Denise's voice over and over in my head, telling me that it'd kill daddy if I had a second child.

I can't let that happen.

I followed the nurse to an office where we sat while she "counseled" me. Her method of counseling consisted of a few simple questions, after which she told me that if I were her daughter, she'd insist on abortion. She continued reminding me I was married, on welfare, and already had a baby. She told me that having an abortion is no big deal. Farmers give their cows abortions every day, and we humans are no different than a cow. She explained that we have an abortion, and the next day "we move on, and we're fine." No one even thinks twice because it's not a baby. It's just a blob of cells and fatty tissue. It's nothing.

She handed me a small cup of about five pills and told me to take them, they would help me relax.

"Will they hurt the baby? I don't want to hurt my baby."

She took a sharp breath and stood up taller. "No. You are only three months along, and your baby isn't a baby. It's nothing. Take these pills because I don't want to have to support another baby on welfare."

I took the pills.

Then she led me into a different room where I had to lie down and wait for the doctor. As he came into the room, I tried sitting up. I made it halfway, but I was so dizzy and weak—not to mention scared—that I fell back down. I told the doctor I didn't want to go through with this. I told him I wanted to keep my baby.

He sat down at the end of the examining bed and looked at the nurse.

"Well, what do I do? We don't get paid unless we abort."

"Take it." The nurse replied. "She's high and doesn't know what she is saying."

I do know what I'm saying!

I know I was clear because I spoke directly to the doctor twice, and the second time, I started crying while feverishly saying, *No! No! I don't want to do this!*

The nurse pushed me down on the table and told me to take a deep breath, and "it'd be over soon."

Despite being drugged, I knew what was going on. However, I was weak and not in control of the situation. I laid back and heard what sounded like vacuum suction sound then felt a pulling.

I felt the doctor pulling my child from my body.

The next thing I saw was the nurse holding a clear glass jar. As I dragged myself to an upright position, I saw my child in that jar. Her head was shaking uncontrollably, and her little tiny hand—a fully developed hand—stretched out and pressing against the container. Her eyes seemed open to me. I know technically that a baby's eyes do not open until they are at least 26 weeks in the womb but, it sure looked as if her eyes opened. I can't explain if they actually did or not, but for me that day, that's what I saw. I knew my baby felt pain, and it was enough to make me want to die right there. It wasn't a good feeling at all. It was as if she looked right at me asking, *why, mommy?*

I sat there, shocked, and tangled in my mind as the nurse held the jar up for me to see. With a sinister giggle, she told me it was a girl and then put the lid on the pot to finish killing my child. I watched as the top went on to suffocate her, and as she slipped away, I imagined her closing her beautiful tiny eyes.

I must have passed out because the bitch nurse woke me up instructing me to, get up. They needed the room cleared. I pulled myself together and got dressed, but the tears were unstoppable, and the pain I felt in my heart and the picture seared into my mind would be a reminder every day that I allowed this to happen. *This was my fault.* I did this.

I stumbled out into the waiting room, sobbing while holding my stomach and crying.

"I want my baby back! I want my baby back!"

I wasn't fully able to walk alone, so Alex had to help me as I was stumbling. But even in that state of being, the clinic let me go. They got what they wanted, a dead baby and $250.00.

I remember a couple was sitting in the lobby waiting for their turn, and as I cried and held my stomach, the young girl began crying. She and the man she was with got up and left. Maybe, just maybe, that was a baby saved.

Alex helped me into the car, and I cried all the way home and the rest of the day. I couldn't take care of Alexander for about a week after the abortion. I felt so guilty, so worthless.

I just killed my baby. How can I ever live with myself now? I'm surely going to burn in hell, and I deserve to burn in hell after what I just did. That's what I thought and believed in my heart, and it was on repeat for a long, long time.

My baby girl had been ripped from me and thrown into a glass jar only to be suffocated in her last moments of life, really, her only moments of life. This incident, the abortion, would turn my life upside down even more so than it already was.

They say time heals all wounds. Bullshit! Time does nothing for your pain and suffering. However, with time, you *can* learn to cope better and understand your problems and hurt. And, sometimes, it takes a whole lot of fucking time to deal with certain kinds of pain. I am not in any position to judge anyone, nor will I, but I will say this, if you are in the same situation I was in and you feel coerced, forced, manipulated, or cajoled in any way to have an abortion, please seek help for yourself and for your child. If you are considering abortion of your own free will, please be mindful of your actions. You can't reverse this decision, and you will have to live with it for the rest of your life.

If you have already had an abortion and are distraught over it, please know that forgiveness of self is attainable, powerful, and necessary. Seek good counsel and do the hard work of healing.

You'll be glad you did.

ABOUT A YEAR AFTER THE ABORTION, Alex enrolled in an adult education program through the State of Michigan. He started mechanic classes that were held in Jackson. We moved there so Alex could be close to the training center, and he ended up finishing the program at the top of his class. Alex obtained his state mechanic's license. We were excited for him to get work and support us. We were even more excited when he was gainfully employed at a prominent dealership in Battle Creek.

After he graduated, we moved into an apartment right next door to Virgie in Albion to be closer to Alex's work. The state also had a program for culinary arts, so I signed up. I loved cooking and figured I could make a living out of being a chef.

Shortly after moving back to Albion, Alex started regressing back to his teen years and began partying with a bunch of local potheads, forgetting about Alexander and me. After lots of fighting and arguing about his drug use and infidelity, he moved out and into his parents' place. I kept my apartment next to Virgie. It wasn't ideal, but I felt trapped since I wanted so desperately to finish culinary school and make something of myself. I had dropped out of 10th grade, so I didn't have much education in high school. Nonetheless, I knew I wanted more, and I was striving for it.

I was so pissed at him for cheating and leaving us, I took all his clothes, cut holes in the crotch of his underwear and pants, making them unusable, and threw them into the front yard an hour before he was to stop by and get them. I also poured gasoline on the little pile and threatened to light it on fire. I was really pissed.

What I now realize is that I was feeling abandoned. Alex had abandoned me—us! He left me just like everyone else in my life had.

I was so hurt, the thought of yet another person leaving me was more than my mind could accept at that time, so lashing out was all I knew to do. There was anger and cussing at each other right in our front yard as he threw a fit of rage about what I'd done to his clothes. I didn't care. I felt justified.

The next few months would be yet another trying time for me in my life. Going to school for eight hours a day, five days a week, and caring for an almost-two-year-old taught me the importance of education and sticking to it. I wasn't going to let my circumstances win.

I made many friends in culinary school, and it was a good, positive experience, but trying to keep a household together and take good care of my son while going to school became a little more than I felt I could handle at times. I called Alex and told him I needed help with daycare. I'd already gone through two child-care providers and didn't like either one of them. I figured since traveling daily to his job in Battle Creek required driving past Marshall—where Alex's brother's wife, Jamie, lived—he could take Alexander to and from daycare every day. Jamie and I had already spoken, and she agreed to watch Alexander for $25.00 per week.

I also felt it was fair for him to pay for it since he was making good money and not paying child support or helping me out in any way other than potential daycare. Thank God, he agreed.

The summer was a long one, and watching Alex run off to party with all those potheads was hard. I knew he was sleeping around, and we were still married. I wanted our family back and made that very clear to all the chicks he hung around. I wasn't going to allow them to break us up—even though we were already broken up and some of them had already slept with him. Those girls didn't care. Making my presence known only motivated them to be even more whorish than they were. It was nothing but a challenge to them.

During that summer, Alex and I fought like cats and dogs over him sleeping around and not being here for his son. He was awful to me, and I was horrible to him. Despite our conflict, he'd pick up Alexander every morning and take him to Jamie's for daycare. When he'd drop our son back off to me, I'd invite him to have dinner with us and watch movies or just hang out, but he was never interested. He'd leave, and I'd cry, and we'd start over again the next day. This went on for six months.

All of us in the S.T.O.P program (Special Training Opportunity Programs) were excited for graduation day. We'd been learning to cook, wait tables, put together menus—and much more—while we practiced serving the public. We schooled in a real restaurant that had classrooms upstairs. I loved culinary school. I cherished my newfound friends and the chefs who taught us.

Graduation night was only for our family since the students were cooking, waiting, and providing full restaurant service to the people we invited to celebrate with us. I was so proud of myself and could not wait to share my accomplishment with my family.

I told my dad and his wife about it with a gleam in my eyes and pride in my heart just knowing they would be happy for me that I'd finished my education and was fully employed now as a chef in Jackson. I was so proud of myself for doing something that I felt was bettering my and my son's life. I figured my parents, of all people, would want to share this special occasion with me. I mean, come on, I was now a real honest-to-God chef. I did it!

I asked my dad first.

"Well, I don't know, Peggy. It's a long drive from Burlington to Albion, and it's not that big a deal, is it?"

The drive was about 30 minutes. I was stunned. *I made something of myself, aren't you proud of me?* His words forever stuck in my head, as did the disgusted look on his face when I offered the invite.

I managed to stammer out that we were cooking and serving, then they would do the graduating ceremony. It made no difference to my amazing dad. He told me no, right away, and that was his excuse. It was a long drive and no big deal.

Thanks, dad, and fuck you too.

I then invited my bio mom, Chelcie, and stepdad but was told she had something to do and couldn't make it. When I asked what she had to do, she said, "Oh, things come up, ya know."

I was crushed.

I never planned to invite Virgie, and I didn't. I had had enough of her shit for a lifetime and living next door to her was a challenge as well. I didn't want to subject myself to her any more than I had to.

I begged Alex to babysit Alexander that evening and told him if he'd watch him, he could come and eat for free, and then after my ceremony, he could go out drinking with his friends. He agreed.

My gratitude didn't last long.

That night, Alex came in with two huge hickeys on his neck. I mean bright purple and red, they stuck out like a sore thumb, and everyone noticed. No one at school knew I was living in a broken marriage, so many assumed that I had done that to him. Later that evening, I made sure everyone knew we had been broken up and that my lips were not making marks *anywhere* on his body and hadn't for a while. Not a proud moment, but it was courtesy of the anger that had been building quietly, tucked away just as it was in my younger years.

Nonetheless, he was there to watch me get my certificate and graduate. He and my son. I was so proud of myself and not willing to allow his 'sucky' slut marks, or my parents not coming, destroy my night. I'd made it, and to me, that was something.

After graduation, I began working in Jackson, but two weeks later, that kind of fell through. They had hired me for the top cook position but then started me out as a waitress making $1.71 per hour plus tips. They explained that I could work my way to cook, which I accepted but

222 • Peggy Watkins

soon learned the cook wasn't retiring for at least 10 more years. I didn't go to school to be a waitress. I wanted to cook, so I found another job and quit.

I would soon begin working with Alex's older brother, JR, at Little Caesar's Pizza in Marshall. Shortly after starting there, Alex and I would give it one more shot at being a family.

We moved to Chelcie's property in Sherwood. She had her house and three mobile homes on one acre. The small, two-bedroom trailer became our new home, and I was ecstatic to live next door to my mom. Finally, we can be together. Maybe this time it will be better than last.

Alex and I both had jobs, and life was looking up. We both worked in Battle Creek. The drive was about 30-minutes Sherwood. I had free childcare, and all I had to do was bring home a pizza to my mom every Friday. She loved her "pete-cies."

Living next to mom was a dream come true. All my siblings would show up, bringing all the grandkids. The whole family would gather at mom and Claude's place and laugh and share meals. It was all I'd ever wanted, a family. My own family. Finally!

Mom and Claud had chickens, goats, a couple cows, pigs, and rabbits, of course, barn cats and a dog. Oh, and how could I forget the two geese. Those assess waddling, big white, annoying geese that shit all over the yard and would chase anyone they felt like chasing except my mom. She called them Daisy and Donald. I hated them as much as I hated chickens. I'm not sure what geese taste like with BBQ sauce, but those two came close to me finding out!

Mom and Claude brought over fresh milk every other day. We had fresh eggs, homemade butter, and had a huge garden, all from which my tiny family benefitted. We appreciated her so much, and I was the happiest I'd ever been in my life living next door to my mom. My real mom!

We'd spend so much time together laughing, and she taught me many things about cooking, canning, and even how to skin a chicken (which totally made me want to throw up), but all the other lessons were incredible.

On a side note: Do y'all know that when you chop off a chicken's head, its body runs around! Um, yeah, it does. Mom laughed at me when this happens and told me it was looking for its head.

It was genuinely the best years I'd ever had in my life.

Until it wasn't.

One evening I was waiting for Alex to get home from work, but he never made it home that night.

I got a phone call about 1:30 AM from the hospital asking for permission to operate on him. I rushed next door to my mother and Claude's, asking them to watch Alexander so I could go to the hospital. Of course, my sister was there, so she babysat while we three rushed to Battle Creek hospital. Before we left, I called Nancy and Stanley, and they met us there too.

He had been out partying with his cousin, and they'd hit a telephone pole. The pole snapped in two and bounced on top of the car, trapping Alex in. His cousin got out with a few scrapes and was okay, but it would be a whole different story for Alex.

He'd broken his femur bone, ruptured his spleen, and had many bruises, cuts, and bangs all over his body. However, he was a lucky man. After they got him out with the Jaws of Life, he was rushed to the hospital to have surgery, removing his spleen. He recovered for a week or so then underwent another surgery to repair his femur and to stunt the growth of his other leg. Implanting a metal plate to hold his femur together prevented it from growing anymore, so therefore stopping the other leg was a necessary procedure.

After Alex had been in the hospital for a few days, I contacted some of the guys he went to mechanic school with, hoping they would come to visit and help cheer him up. I called one of his best buddies, Tad, in Jackson.

Tad told me his car was being repaired, and he had no way to get there but wanted to see him. He accepted my offer to pick him up if he paid me for gas. So, one evening after work, I went from Battle Creek to Jackson (about 45-minute drive) then back to the hospital in Battle Creek. After the visit to the hospital, I called my bio mom and asked if she could keep Alexander a little longer so I could take Tad back to Jackson. She told me no! So, I drove with Tad from Battle Creek to Sherwood (about a 40-minute drive) to pick up Alexander, and when I got there, I was dog-tired. I asked Tad if I could just get up early and take him right to work, he agreed as it was about 9:00 PM at night.

I was getting my son ready for bed—snack, brushing teeth, book reading, and tucking in—when I heard strange chanting coming from outside the trailer. I finished my story quickly and went to the living room where Tad sat watching TV on my couch. I looked at him, and he looked back with big eyes.

"Um, I'm not sure what's going on but, why are your mom and stepdad walking around the trailer with a lit candle and a Bible praying?"

(I swear I can't make this kind of shit up, I'm just not that creative!)

I looked out the window only to see that he was telling the truth. There, in the cold, snowy winter, was my mom holding a candle and stepdad, Claude, holding a Bible, and they were both chanting prayers to rebuke the demons out of me.

I closed the curtains and started laughing so hard I almost wet myself. Tad was cracking up, too, we couldn't help it as we tried to figure out *why* they were doing this.

My nephew, Hamilton, who at that time was staying at my mom's but hanging out at my house, was laughing with us as he explained what he knew.

"They think you are going to have sex with this guy, so they are praying to God, rebuking the sexual ruin out of you." He told us.

I couldn't believe my ears! I stood there, dumbfounded.

What the fuck did you just say? Are you kidding me? Seriously?

I told Tad to just ignore them, and we got ready for bed since we both had to get up early and go to work. I gave Tad the plush, old, rickety couch to sleep on, and a pillow and blanket. I went to my room and continued to hear them walking around my trailer for at least another 30 minutes, praying the evil out of me so I wouldn't cheat on my husband whom I loved and was in the hospital fighting for his life (well, he *was* in pain).

I put a pillow over my head to drown out their voices.

Good Lord have mercy, Mother Mary of God and heavens above- take me now because I can't take any more!

The next morning was no better. We woke early, and I got Alexander all ready and took him next door to mom's since she was my sitter. I got inside, and she was gone. I asked Claude where she was and if I could leave Alexander because I had to drop Tad off in Jackson, then get back to work in Battle Creek. He told me no, Alexander couldn't stay.

Rushing back to my house, I called Alex's brother's wife, Jamie, and asked if she'd help me out. She always helped us out. Jamie is a great person, and she was a wonderful friend, still is. She babysat Alexander while I went to culinary school, and yet again, she helped me out at the last minute.

Okay, here was my conundrum, it was 8:00 am, and I was in Sherwood. Jamie lived in Marshall (45 minutes northeast of Sherwood), and Tad needed to get to Michigan Center/Jackson (1-hour east of Sherwood), and I need to be at work by 10:00 am in Battle Creek (15 minutes west of Marshall). I may have lost ya there, but the bottom line is, it was a lot of driving. I opt to go to Jackson first, stopping at the gas station to fill up where I am promptly confronted by my birth mom and three siblings who are yelling at me for disrespecting our mother on her property and having Tad in my car.

What a total reality T.V. show moment it was, I'm sure. There I am, pumping gas with my little boy in the backseat, Tad in the front, and I'm getting screamed at for sleeping with someone I never even slept with, nor did I want to. Tad was our friend.

I shouted back at mom, telling her she was just like Virgie, and that struck a nerve with my sisters who yelled back, letting me know I'd be sorry. I finished pumping the gas, went inside to pay, and drove off, leaving them all there watching us drive away.

I drop off Tad, headed to Marshall, dropped off Alexander, then headed to Battle Creek to work. I work a double shift because someone didn't come into work, and I needed the money. After work, I drove from Battle Creek to Marshall to pick up my son then another 45-minute drive to home. Alexander is sleeping. It's about 10:00 PM, and I am beat.

I have my son wrapped in a blanket in my arms, ready to put him into his own little bed and snuggle in myself to get some much-needed rest. It has only been about six or seven days since my husband's accident, so he was still in the hospital during all this commotion.

I get to the door, but I couldn't get in. My damn trailer had a padlock on it! The place I rented, my house. I had been locked out of my own home.

Why?!

I walk next door, baby in my arms, tired as hell and now pissed off, only to hear the words spew out of my own mom's mouth, "Well, I can't help it. You have to talk to your sister. She owns the trailer, and you owe her rent."

First off, it was on my mom's property, and she owned it. They weren't fooling anyone but themselves if they thought I didn't know that horseshit!

Secondly, my rent was $35.00 per week, and when Alex got into that wreck, my mom told me not to worry about rent and just think about Alex and the baby and myself.

Thirdly, we paid our rent monthly, and the rent was paid in full for a couple more weeks. I didn't owe a damn dime! I couldn't believe my own mother did this to me. I was confused, to say the least. I had thought our relationship was going perfectly, and when she had said, "no worries about rent," I actually thought my family was going to be supportive during our hardship.

There I go again, thinking, hoping, and getting nothing but shit from them. I have HAD it!

I told my mom that "it's late, I am tired, and if you don't remove that damn lock, I'm busting in since I don't owe you or anyone else a damn dime."

And, that is just what I did. I walked back to my side of the property, put my sleeping baby back in my car, grabbed a crowbar and broke the fucking padlock off the door of my paid-up-to-date rented trailer, and went inside my home.

The next morning, I called Jamie and JR and told them what was going on. I didn't even have to ask for help. They immediately told me to get boxes and pack up everything we owned, JR would be over with his van to load it up, and we'd leave.

I did just that. All-day, I packed and took care of my little boy while dealing with rantings and ravings from my family, the family I desperately wanted to be close to and live by.

Yet, one thing misconstrued turned into a chain of events that could have been avoided had they listened to me and understood or offered a helping hand. But, no! Instead, they thought they knew it all and decided I was evil, and sex crazed. Jesus, help them.

ALEX'S RECOVERY WAS A LONG AND HARD ONE for both of us. We stayed with JR and Jamie for a few months until Alex got his body cast removed and was doing rehab for recovery. On a good note, his employer kept his position for him, and once he was up to it, we moved to Battle Creek into a small two-bedroom house, which worked great as we both worked in the "Creek."

We weren't rich, but we had a lovely house, good jobs, and weed. We took good care of our son, and we loved each other. His family treated me well, as usual. Often, we'd have someone from Alex's family move in with us, and yes, it crushed our lifestyle somewhat, making things difficult at times, but we made it through and became stronger.

During this time, I had stopped speaking to Virgie, Denise, Ardy, Donny (I despised him anyway), and my mother and siblings as well. We stayed away consistently without words, visits, or issues for about a year until one day it was full-on contact again as if none of them had done anything to me, and I was the one who needed to straighten up and stop this silent spell.

The first to contact me was my brother, Glenn. He wasn't a part of the whole mess with the trailer and pad-lock issue. He just wanted his little sister around, and therefore, he reached out, and I felt hesitant but responded.

He lived next door to our mom in one of her trailers. After we agreed to reconnect with Glenn, Alex and I started visiting him. As soon as mom saw us pull in, she began to cry, and we reconciled without any apologies or words, we just hugged and said, I love you to each other, and the issues were over. Well, at least forgiven and dropped, never forgotten.

Even though there were issues with my mom, it seemed as if they were simple things that we could and would eventually work through. I'm not letting her off the hook for praying the sex-evil out and the trailer-padlock thing. I'm just telling you how I felt back then. I needed her to be my mom. I wanted her to be my mom and love me, and she did love me the best way she knew how.

Moving to Battle Creek and Alex's accident resulted in a significant improvement in our relationship until he went back to work and started hanging out with John and Jeff, or as I called them, Mutt & Jeff. Those two 'boys' started making our family life miserable. Well, at the time, I blamed it on them but, now I can see the problem indeed was Alex— and maybe me too. The partying began again, and it was a nightly thing. Soon enough, we broke up again, and this time I moved out and left. I moved across town into my own two-bedroom apartment with my son. I was still working at Little Caesar's, but it wouldn't be for much longer.

I started working at Meijer's photography lab, which was called Smile America. I loved my job, and I quickly became an Assistant Manager. I also was employed once a month, bartending at the Sugar Shanty in Battle Creek. I felt things were looking up and was proud of myself once again.

I held the photography lab job for a couple months until they closed the doors without notice. One day while I was bartending, I was crying that I didn't have enough rent money and needed another job. Turns out that my boss who owned the bar also owned many homes around the Creek that he rented and, just as luck would have it, he needed a rental manager and offered me the job with the proper training, so of course, I took it.

One of the perks was getting to live in one of his rentals as part of my pay, and it worked for me because my apartment was sort of a shit hole, but a clean shit hole. I packed up my son and moved into an apartment a few blocks from where we were, and things were looking up. I still bartended on the weekends, and I loved my day job as well until the ultimate offer was made that changed many things for my son and me.

Alex was busy partying with his friends, and even though he'd visit with Alexander on the weekends, he wasn't much of a father figure. Hell, maybe I wasn't much of a mother figure either. We were so young. Nonetheless, while Alex was living on one side of town doing well, I was on the other side in the city not necessarily struggling but could have had been more comfortable with some help.

The bartending job allowed me to meet many good people, some drunks too, but more often, just good people. My boss, Ed, had male strippers one weekend a month. I loved it. And, I made so much money tending the strippers they each tipped me a fifty-dollar bill at the end of each night, making me a whopping $500.00 in tips in one weekend. Yeah, I felt as if I was rolling in the dough!

This is when and where I met Ruthie. She came in one evening with a group of ladies to watch the guys, and we became buds right away. She was a female stripper. Ruthie kept telling me how much money I could make and "stop all this working two jobs shit" and breaking my back not getting anywhere. She was a good friend, but rough. She told it like it was, and she also walked around with a straw up her nose (she did a lot of cocaine). She treated Alexander and me well, though. She never did any drugs around me when I had Alexander, which was a lot, so I rarely got exposed to that part of her life.

One evening as I was wrapping up the office and getting ready to leave to pick up my son, Ed came in. He'd been known to hit on his female employees, and it was said that he'd pay them to sleep with him. He'd never hit on me, so I wasn't worried about it, and I figured the other girls in the office might be lying, I didn't know.

Ed was a taller, dark-haired, thin white man with a big nose and a silent laugh. His eyes were brown and seemed to be half-opened all the time. He usually wore a suit, a longer dress coat, a nice hat, and leather gloves. He always had cocaine and weed. Not only did he have it, but he would also leave little gift baggies on our desks with a note that read, "Thinking of you, Darling!" He left me a couple, and I just handed it over to the other girls. I'd never done cocaine and wasn't interested. Ed dressed nice, and he seemed like a great guy. He was an ugly man, though, in looks nonetheless, he'd always treated me well, and I was happy with my jobs.

Our offices were inside the big hotel he owned that was fully operational. He told me he needed me to come with him to his office upstairs. He had the top floor as his office and home.

As we entered his 'office,' he closed the door behind us and locked it, asking what I'd like to drink, offering me a beer or wine. I declined while laughing and told him I don't drink a lot because I'm a lightweight.

He came and stood by my chair in front of his desk and then started telling me what a great job I was doing and how lucky I was to work for him. He continued by explaining how other girls, who he helps, show him gratitude while stroking my long reddish-blonde hair.

He smiled at me then, excused himself, went into the bathroom, and came out naked with a bulging hard-on and said without blinking an eye, "Take off your clothes, and we'll fuck!"

What the hell?!

I was shocked. Stunned. Freaked out. Scared. Screaming inside silently with flashbacks of Donny. I froze. Glaring. Waiting. Waiting for what? I wanted to run, but my body wouldn't allow me to move. I wanted to scream something, anything, but my mouth refused to open, and my voice shut down once again. My heart was pounding so loud, and hard I could not only feel it, but I heard it loud and clear. My hands were sweating. My body was going into shut down mood, yet my mind was screaming, *run Peggy, run!*

With all those emotions rolling, I managed to yell.

"No! No, we will not fuck!" Then I stood up, rushed towards the door, pushing him out of my way, nervously unlocked it, then quickly walked out with my knees shaking so fast and hard it was a chore to even walk.

Monday, I dreaded going into work, but there I was at 8:00 am and making calls and filing rental contracts, doing my job. I needed my jobs. I had to support my son and myself.

Ed struts into the office as if nothing ever happened, goes into his back office, and calls me on the phone, instructing me to come to talk to him for a minute.

As I step through his door, he begins with, "Ya know Peggy, all the girls that work here know they wouldn't be anywhere without my help, and you don't seem to appreciate it. Why?"

I was shaking. I figured Ed was either going to advance towards me again or fire me. I blurted out, Do I have to fuck you to keep my jobs? He cocked his head sideways, smirked, and said without batting an eye, "Yes."

Nodding my head, my only response was, "I see."

As I turned to walk out, he asked me if I was going to be obedient or not. I turned back towards him, gave him a shit-eating grin, hands on my hips, and said, in no uncertain terms, "Ed, go fuck yourself. I quit!"

I went back to my desk and began clearing out my things. A couple young girls who overheard came over to my desk and said, "Peeeeggg, it's just a fuck. You should do it, and he'll give you a raise."

I slammed a book down, glaring at them. "I am worth more than that moldy old bastard can afford, and I have more respect for myself. I don't need to *fuck* my way anywhere."

I wasn't sure what the laws were regarding sexual harassment in the early 1980s, so, at the time, I just accepted the situation for what it was and left.

The unfortunate thing was not only was I employed by Ed with both jobs, but I also was living in one of his rentals. I knew I'd as well just look for a new place and get to moving. I figured he wasn't going to be friendly, and I was right. That afternoon he called my home and told me to pack my shit and move within three days, or he'd padlock the door and keep my stuff.

Hmm, been there, done that before!

I immediately packed everything I could, loaded the crucial stuff into my trunk and backseat, and called my friend Ruthie. She knew some people who knew some people, and I literally got a house that day to move into. She was a faithful buddy and would help me out many times during the next few years.

THE JOB SITUATION was what made my skin crawl and bothered me so much. Where was an uneducated young mother going to find work at a decent wage? What kind of work was I even qualified to do?

My sister Denise was in the process of moving back to Jackson. And, since things were somewhat okay between us, I figured I'd reach out to her. I knew she had divorced her hubby. My dad, Ardy, and his wife had sold their little store in Gladwin and were now living in Burlington. When I reached out to her, she shared an idea she had, which sounded exciting, and I was all in.

Denise claimed that many factories would hire without a high school diploma and that they paid well with benefits too. I was willing to give this a try, hell, what did I have to lose, right?

So, we got together and began putting in applications to factories and looking for a place to rent. We found both employment and a house that we both agreed to move into and pay 50/50 rent and utilities, even though she had one more kid than I did, and dogs. And not to mention she'd get the master bedroom, and my son and I would have to share a bedroom while she and her two kids all got their own. This felt unfair to me, but for some reason, I agreed anyway.

Honestly, I look back on it and wonder, was I really this stupid? Yep. Yep, I was.

I started working at a small factory in Jackson and soon realized that I needed to get moved and settled, find a sitter and everything else that comes with a new town and job. I rented a small flatbed trailer. I boxed everything up *again. H*owever, this time I had help. I'd met a guy named Kent at work, and he offered to help me move, which I readily accepted.

Denise called and said she had secured the house we wanted in Rives Junction and today was the day we were to meet up at Virgie's place where I'd give her 50% of the deposit and 50% of the first month's rent in exchange for a key to the new house. We were to meet up at 1:00 pm.

I had me and my son all packed, house cleaned out, and ready to move into our new home that I'd been telling my little guy about. I told him how we'd have fun in the yard and ride bikes, all that fun stuff you say to your kids when there's about to be a significant change in their life. There we were, car and trailer loaded with everything I owned, which honestly wasn't much at all, but it was mine.

As my son and I enter Virgie's house, it seems that everyone is there. The place is packed with people, and Denise is there with a new guy I had never seen. She's sitting in the corner chair...on his lap.

Right away, I knew something was up but wasn't expecting (and fuck me, I should have anticipated) something this drastic.

Andy is his name, and Denise wastes no time in letting me know Andy would be moving in with her, and there wasn't going to be any room for Alexander and me.

I stand there speechless with my little boy in Virgie's living room next to snickering Donny, smirking giggling Virgie, and snarky Denise shrugging her shoulders and giving me the who-gives-a-fuck-about-you look. I glare at every one of them, laughing and joking about my loss.

"You've got to be kidding, Denise! I have nowhere to go and a rented trailer I have to return today and not much money! Are you kidding me?!"

She sat there on Andy's lap, shrugging her shoulders.

I turn around, take hold of Alexander's little hand, and together we walk out as they sit and laugh and say nothing. They just laugh.

Devastated. I had nowhere to go, a full trailer, a backseat full of clothes and toys, not to mention a hungry little boy, tried, and now, confused. I thought for a quick minute, then went to McDonald's, got Alexander a Happy Meal, and headed to the park where I could think about my next move. *What can I do? Where am I going to go? What the hell am I going to do?* I called my friend Kent, he offered us his couch.

I called my dad (Ardy) and asked if I could store stuff in his garage until I figured things out. I told him what happened, and he told me I needed to get my shit together and yelled at me for something I wasn't even sure what the fuck he was talking about. Despite his lecture, I drove from Albion to Burlington (40 minutes) and unloaded the trailer alone in his dirty unused garage. Returned the U-Haul to Battle Creek (40 minutes), then we headed to Kent's in Concord (about 55 minutes).

Kent hooked us up with his couch, a hot shower for me, a warm bath for my boy, and a nice warm bowl of goulash followed by ice cream. His mom agreed to babysit Alexander while watching Kent's daughter, which was so sweet of her to do, especially with a moment's notice.

During one of our evening talks, Kent told me about a program at the local community college, Jackson Community College (JCC). It was the beginning of a nursing program. He explained that if I had a place to live, a grant would pay for my education, and even though I'd be on welfare for the two years, I'd get childcare, tuition, and books, all while working towards a nursing degree. He went on to explain that once I finished at Jackson Community College (JCC), I could transfer to a four-year university and become a Registered Nurse (RN), and then I would be able to do very well for myself and my son.

This idea sounded so amazing to me. I was excited, just thinking about it. Also, it'd been two weeks, and I had managed to get myself fired from the factory. And, I could sense that Kent was getting a little tired of us at his house. I don't blame him. He was doing us a generous favor, and I so appreciated him. He was a nice guy, and we had become good friends.

As I tried my best to find another job and a place of my own, the idea of going to college and becoming an RN made stars in my eyes and stirred up big thoughts of becoming something my parents would be proud of. I was more excited about that than anything, and it was as if I could feel the books in my hands. I just *knew* my mom or dad would want this for me and would be willing to help me in any way they could. I needed a place to live and childcare while I would go to classes, that's it. I would be able to pay for our food with food stamps and, I'd be able to pay rent. I couldn't have been happier about going to college, finally.

I went to my mom and Claude's first to explain college and ask if they would allow me to move in and use the two bedrooms upstairs. I also told mom that I would get childcare payments and would give her my food stamps if they would just help me out, and yes, it'd be two years, but then, I'd be self-sufficient.

Mom told me she couldn't allow anyone to move in, or she'd lose her food stamps and what little money the state gives her, and Claude would also lose his social security benefits, so no.

Now, that was a messed-up answer. Mom always let people (her kids and their kids and spouses) move into her house and stay for periods.

Why not me? Why can't you help me, mom? I want to better myself rather than stay on welfare! What the fuck?

Broken but not hopeless, I went to my dad's. I figured I had nothing to lose. I gave them the same explanation of my opportunity, asking for help. Showing my eagerness for college and gaining an education, to become somebody. But once again, I was told no.

"Oh, Peggy! Think about what you are asking? We can't let you stay here. We're happy with just us two, and we don't want to watch a toddler three days a week while you go to school. Isn't there something else you can do? You need to go get a job in a factory-like your sister, why can't you be like Denise?"

Why did I expect anything else from him?

I was hurt. Let down. Once again, my ideas of bettering myself were stupid. I should do what others do and not what I'd like to do. Be like my sister!

I knew I had to do something, though, and quick. My job search continued, and then, I stepped into a bar in Jackson called The Club. They had an ad for a cook and were paying $4.00 per hour. Back in the day, that was pretty good so, I jumped on it.

The parking lot of the dark building had only a few cars, mostly parked in the back. As you stepped inside, there were five or six steps into the upper bar, or you could go down five or six steps to the lower level, the basement. It was your typical bar with mirrors on the walls and dirty, stinky carpet on the floors. As I stepped down into the basement level, there was a large wooden bar made of a dark wood that looked expensive. Stools lined up along the bar, and behind it were two ladies, one older and one younger. Right in front of the bar was a pool table and beyond that were bathrooms and two other small rooms labeled, Dressing Rooms. At the end of the bar was a swinging door that led into the kitchen. I stepped up and asked for the manager, and that's when Belva turned around and asked me why and what I wanted.

She handed me an application, and as I went over to an empty table and filled it out, she followed, pulled out a chair, and sat on it backward in one swift motion. She began asking me questions, and as I was sitting there answering them, this girl walks out with nothing on but a G-string, high heels, and lipstick! I tried to act natural. I failed.

Um, what the hell? What kind of bar am I in? (Hmm, you'd think the name, "Club" might have tipped me off but, nope, sure didn't.)

I stared at her breasts and ass with my mouth hanging open long enough to make her giggle and ask me if I liked what I was looking at. Still, in shock and catching flies, I looked down and said nothing.

Belva told me the cook position was taken. I finished filling out the app, looked at her, and almost started to cry. I needed to get out of Kent's place. I needed a job. I didn't want to file for welfare, but now my choices were not looking good. I had figured out factory work was something I wasn't able to handle. There were no decent cook jobs around, and waiting tables paid about $1.40 per hour plus tips. Back in the early 1980s, the minimum wage was about $3.35 per hour, so a waitress would earn less than half that and depend on tips to finish her pay. There just wasn't a promising outlook for me as far as I could see.

I told her I really needed a job. She said she'd call me if the cook didn't work out. She smiled at me then said to me that she could give me a job and I'd make more money than any cook in Jackson. I stood there looking confused, wondering for a brief second what she was talking about. I heard her out as I felt my options were slim, and I was running on fumes and an empty pocket.

What I was hearing got my attention.

V

UNEDUCATED,

UNEMPLOYED
AND HOMELESS.

THE NEXT DAY I went to the store with my last twenty bucks and bought a thong (a G-string). I dressed in my cutoff blue-jean shorts, a cute button-up top, a pair of black ankle-high tie-up boots, and my black hat. Off I went to The Club.

I had no clue what the heck to do so, I arrived a couple hours before I was supposed to so I could watch and really consider doing this...as Belva called it...audition. I was able to watch a couple different dancers on and off stage before I went up. I needed to know what to do, so I watched, gasped a few times, thought to myself, *holy cow,* and learned what to do. I also learned what I would *never* do, no matter how good the money.

As I sat in the dressing room conversing with the other dancers, I soon learned that they, too, were somewhat like me. Uneducated. Single moms. Working. Going to college. One stripper told me she planned to get her degree in law, then move out of state and start fresh. I liked the sound of a fresh start, and I loved the idea of moving out of state.

Most of the girls were encouraging and friendly. Not what society makes them out to be, as a bunch of whores who just want to take off their clothes, have sex, and snort cocaine. They were like me. Just wanting to stay off welfare and give their kids and themselves a good life.

Oh, don't get me wrong, there were some tramps. I met and worked with a good number of them over the years. Those were the ones who all the men knew well, and all of us dancers knew what they would do for twenty bucks out the back door. Those girls didn't get booked in suitable places due to their promiscuity. There were a few clubs with a bad reputation that secured them but not the classy ones. Not many good business owners wanted a status of employing whores. I didn't

242

like working with these girls either as the patrons would assume you were easy too, and then you'd have to set them straight with a slap across the face (if needed) or call the bouncer to take care of the issue if they got out of hand, which was rare but did happen a time or two.

Carlos was the bouncer. He watched out for us girls. Carlos would kick ass when needed. He was a big guy. His arms were the size of my waist, his neck was like a tree trunk. He was the most solid man I'd ever laid eyes on. He stood about 5 foot 10 or so and was a brick house built to last and kick ass. Black hair and gorgeous eyes, he was *the* man! We all loved him, he really was remarkable and helped the staff feel safe and protected. I met him as soon as I started working at the Club and liked him immediately.

Despite the protection of Carlos, that I had but of whom I had not met yet. I was uneasy. Scared. Confused. Creeped out and wishing I was rich, so I didn't have to do this. However, I knew I had a little guy to care for and not many choices for a job. About that time, Belva stepped into the dressing room, asking if I was ready. The girls didn't flinch at the cocaine on the mirror, nor did Belva. As a matter of fact, Belva teased them, asking, "Where's mine?" then she and the girls all did a line. That first night, I too accepted a line of cocaine for the first time ever.

Belva told me to hurry up and go pick my music. I snorted my first line of cocaine, a little up each side, then one of the dancers took a dab on her fingertip, told me to open my mouth, then she rubbed it on the inside of my lip.

I picked, *Stop Dragging my Heart Around*, and *Leather and Lace* both by Stevie Nicks. Yes, I am a huge Stevie fan! Still to this day. Hence, my black hat and boots.

I was relieved it was only a small handful of guys. I had never danced for people but only with or around folks and definitely not this kind of dancing. As I stepped up on that stage, all the feelings I had earlier rushed my body and I felt as if I needed to puke. Nonetheless, I

244 • Peggy Watkins

stood looking at the crowd as the music played. After about 45 seconds Belva waved her arms at me to begin or get off the stage.

Knowing I had no choice right at this minute and my pockets were light. I started dancing. I stood in the middle of that stage, looking down, one hand on my hat and one on my hip, I bent my knee and tried to look sexy. I had watched the other girls, so I knew a little, and I'm pretty sure the cocaine was creating an attitude.

I closed my eyes and pretended no one was there. I began moving my arms through the air like I was floating on clouds. Tapping my feet from toe to heel with small kicks in front, I popped my legs back as if to kick myself in the butt. Tipping my hat with twirls. Smiling. Winking. Swaying. Blowing a kiss here and there, feeling like Marilyn Monroe. Strutting across the stage like I was in gym class again. Utilizing every corner of the platform, I pranced like an enchanted swan spreading my wings to the pleasurable tones emerging out of the jukebox.

I had to or else I'd be homeless in the amount of time it would take these two songs to play, I slowly unbuttoned the first couple buttons on my shirt, leaving my chest covered while offering just a slight peek of my cleavage.

It felt strange. I felt odd. A big part of me wanted to run off that stage, but there were no other choices at that precise moment. I either had to keep going, or all would be lost. What would happen to my son? Who would care for him if I had no money to care for him? Would Social Services take him? Yes. Yes, they would.

The thought of my son going into the system burdened me like nothing ever in my life. I wanted more for my child. He was better than me, and he deserved the best experiences in life. I knew this was all I could give and do at this nano-second in time, so I carried on.

Unzipping my jean shorts (half way), I pulled them open, side to side, to show only the very top of my red G-string while leaving my entire bottom covered and safe. As song number two started, Belva motioned me off the stage. I stepped off slowly and began instinctively walking to each table for a tip. I took my hat off and turned it upside down and allowed the money to be dropped in my cap. Fully dressed and not baring what was expected to be shown, I moved from table to table, collecting money in my hat. Classy!

Two songs. Two hundred bucks in less than 10 minutes. **I was sold.** Belva offered me the job and told me I could start the following Monday. And with that $200.00 and the next week's take over $700.00, I had enough to pay the first month's rent, deposit, buy groceries, and a toy for Alexander. I had gas money and enough left over to buy a couple of used outfits for work. Back then, that was a lot of cash, and that's what hooked me. I'd never had that kind of money before, and it seemed to me that not taking every stitch of clothing off as the other girls did, made me more cash, so that became my gig. I'm not saying that I never did. I'm saying the majority of the time, I didn't need to.

Although my stage name was Taylor, some of the girls I worked with called me the 'Nun' as in, I never 'got none.' And others nicknamed me, 'baby girl.' Nun because I didn't want to pull a one-night stand with anyone who came into the strip club. I mean, what kind of guy is that? What kind of girl is that? *And, gross!*

They called me a baby girl because I was so innocent and had no clue about that kind of life. Either way, most of the girls were nice and helped me. There were a few who would steal you blind, and I learned who they were, of course, afterward, but I learned. And Belva herself wasn't a true-blue bar manager either. When I first started, she told me to not count my tips as it would take up too much of my time but instead just hand them over to her, and she would add them up and change the ones for fives and tens or whatever. I learned quickly, however, that she also kept half of what I earned as payment for doing me this "favor" she offered, which Belva failed to mention she charged for.

That thieving, lying old wrinkled up bitch.

Soon enough, I was learning the ropes and earning more money than I knew what to do with. Alexander had nice clothes and the He-Man collection of figures he wanted. I acquired many things, too, along with a nasty potty mouth and an attitude that most take a lifetime to achieve.

Dancing was a fun job. I don't mean taking off my clothes in front of a bunch of horny men or a bachelor party. That wasn't fun, but the people I met along the way were great. People like me. They became my friends. Just working-class women who looked at this as a job and not anything else. A means to get by for now.

I did, however, surrender to the occasional line of cocaine and slamming shots of tequila while dancing, as many others did. Fortunately, I never did drugs around my son, that just wasn't an option. I'm not proud of it, but I did do them occasionally to get through the task at hand.

When Ardy found out that I was stripping, he did his best to make me feel like a worthless whore. Of course, this was after I had asked for help, and he refused so, what right did he really have? I recall only visiting a couple times while I worked as a dancer, and all he would do was sit at his kitchen table, shaking his head while looking down and say things like, "How could you do this to me? You are such an embarrassment to me, are you trying to kill me or what? Why can't you be more like your sister? She's not doing these things! She would never do the things you do!"

I stopped going to visit, calling, or even thinking about him. Of course, they never visited me at any of my homes other than once when I was newly pregnant if you could call that a visit. They hardly ever called me, maybe once every five or six months, he'd phone to say hi and ask how Alexander was, playing the concerned grandfather role. Ha! My ass!

I told my mother and Claude as well. Their reaction wasn't so bad, but she did ask me to be careful. I'm not sure what exactly my mother thought I was doing other than getting paid to dance. Claude understood, though. He never belittled me, but instead, he told me he'd pray and ask God to guide me and then told my mom to pray and ask God to help me get a job that I could build a career from. Claude said to me that he loved me and was proud of me no matter what I did. He said I'd always be his baby girl no matter blood or not. He loved me like a real father the best way he knew how, and his best was honest.

By this time, I'd completely stopped going around Virgie, Denise, and Donny, but they all knew what I was doing too. The family gossip runs fast and deep on both sides.

My dad gave me so much bullshit about dancing that I hooked up with Ruthie and decided to move to Florida. I wanted to get away for a while just to see what it was like. When I told my mom, I was leaving the state, she cried and asked me not to go. I told her I needed to get away and that I'd call at least once a week and keep in touch. I asked her to keep this between us. She kept her promise. She was a great secret keeper. Later in life, I would find out just how great of a secret keeper she really was.

I sold everything but our clothes and Alexander's toys and loaded up my 1977 Camaro (candy apple red), and off I went to Fort Lauderdale. Ruthie was already working at a very prominent strip club there, so I got in right away. I also got a condo on the beach, Atlantic Avenue. My backyard was the ocean, and **I loved, loved, loved it!**

Even back then, it was expensive, rent, deck parking, plus a charge for air/heat, and a monthly water taxi pass for two all came to around $1000.00 a month. Oh, Gawd, was it worth it. I made good money, so affording it was easy for me.

Alexander and I would go for walks almost daily on the beach. He had his little bucket and would collect shells. Often, we'd take a water taxi out and go sightseeing just for something to do. And we ate out a lot. I had a babysitter who doubled as a housekeeper, Maria. I am not sure if she was legal, but at the time, I honestly didn't care. I trusted her, and she was a good housekeeper, but more importantly, she was excellent with my son. Oh, and let me say this, she made the best homemade tortillas ever! Warm with melted butter…yum!

I made friends quickly and enjoyed life on the beach. The weather was great, the people were beautiful, and life, in general, was perfect. There was no one to threaten me. No one to make me feel like I was nothing. No one to belittle me. No one around to treat me shitty. And funny thing, Denise lived in Jackson when I moved, but she never even knew I'd left. No one knew. No one came to look for me at my old apartment or my workplace, nothing. No one called my phone. Not one family member.

Even though I absolutely loved working and living in Fort Lauderdale, I really did miss my mom and Claude. Even though I will always remember Fort Lauderdale as one of the best times in my life, I got homesick and eventually moved back to Michigan. When I returned, I picked up right where I left off. Got my job back at the Club and my old apartment too.

After I was back for a couple months, Denise came to the bar and asked for me. I figured she must have needed someone to hang with. She wondered why my number was disconnected, and I told her I just changed it. Oddly enough, we began hanging out but only on the weekends and only to go to the bars and get drunk.

She never invited us to her home for a visit or dinner but only asked to hang out when she needed a weekend buddy to party with. I was outgoing, a great dancer (with my clothes on as well), and she had no one else, at least for a while. Soon, as she made new friends, she dropped me like a hot cake, and that was that. I was the fill-in. I was a convenient human when needed. I was the one on whom she could depend, and she knew it. She always took advantage of my love for her. I wanted a big sister. I wanted a real relationship. All I got was her phony self. That was me, though. I hung in there thick and thin, just hoping for a significant sister relationship, but all I got was used and abused.

While dancing at the Club, there was a guy who continually bugged me to go to dinner with him. I refused all the time. I thought, *Why I would go out with you, ya loser!* Meeting a guy in the strip club was not what I had in mind. He persisted for a few months, and he seemed fun, so I finally gave in for dinner and a movie.

Marcus, worked in a local lumber company, was 6'3", skinny, with short, dark hair, and very handsome. We ended up laughing a lot together, and eventually, I began dating him seriously. Marcus and I had dated for about six months or so when he was offered a chance to relocate to Flint, MI. He asked me to stop dancing and move with him. I was ready to give up my "career" and have a real family, so I accepted.

Soon after we drove into the parking lot of our new apartment with a loaded U-Haul and a hungry, tired kid, we started unpacking and hauling things up to the third floor. A couple hours later, our butts were dragging, and we were all starving. Marcus had some of the guys from his new job helping us with the big stuff, which was much appreciated.

I had noticed, as we drove into the complex, there was a 7-Eleven right around the corner. I told Marcus and Alexander to just keep working, and I'd run to the store and grab us a few groceries. What should've taken 15 minutes took an hour.

My first public experience in our new town was pulling up to a robbery in the process. Yep, you heard me right. As I pulled into the 7-Eleven parking lot, I was parked front and center outside the store and looking dead-on at two masked men with guns. I had no clue what to do, so I laid down in the front seat and prayed they wouldn't notice me. I was parked right out front, how could they not see me?

I heard loud voices yelling, two-car doors slamming, and wheels squealing. I stayed hunkered down since I was crying and thought I'd shit myself (I didn't). The cops came and questioned me, but I had nothing to offer, and I went home with no food either. Luckily, Marcus had found some cereal and milk, and they had both eaten while I was gone.

A few months after moving, Marcus asked me to marry him. We decided on a small wedding with family and friends. A real wedding. I'd never had that the first time. I was excited, to say the least.

Off to visit my dad to ask if he'd walk me down the aisle. I figured he'd be supportive since he seemed to like Marcus, even though my dad hardly called, and not once did he visit. But still, I was hoping my dad would give me away. I thought some kind of normalcy would be nice. I should have known better.

I arrived at his home, and we had a few minutes of small talk during which he mostly watched TV as I sat trying to tell him about my family, job, and our wedding plans. I also thought he'd be happy I was working a decent job and not stripping anymore. He kept watching TV, and every now and then, he'd look over at me and say, "Oh," and a head nod and a smirk that looked as if he was constipated.

When I asked him if he would walk me down the aisle, he grumbled in his familiar annoyed voice, "Oh Peggy! My back hurts, and I don't feel good now, and I don't think it's gonna get better by then."

Yes, he did. Six months before my wedding day, he decided he would not be well enough for that one day and couldn't do it. White-hot anger and hurt rose up inside of me. Remembering how much he hates my stepdad, I shot him with words.

"That's ok. I'll just ask Claude to do it."

He laughed. "Go ahead. He'll just ruin it for you."

I left.

Sometimes people get so love-starved it makes them blind to how they are being treated. I wasn't wanted, yet I kept trying to get their approval when I should have said, *fuck it and fuck them.*

Claude was thrilled that I asked him, he began to cry and hugged me, saying how wonderful it would be. He and my mom both bought a new outfit, and they were there on my big day. It was perfect. I had my mom, Claude, my son, and my sisters (from my mother) stood up with me as well as my best friend at the time, Cheryl. My son was the ring bearer, and he looked so handsome. It was a *great* day.

Shortly after our wedding, we moved to another apartment complex in a suburb of Flint called Flushing. A decent neighborhood and better schools.

252 • Peggy Watkins

One afternoon I took Alexander down to A Mexican eatery on Pierson Rd, and as we sat inside eating and trying to decide what to do for the day, a cold feeling came over me all at once. This wasn't the first time this had happened, my mom always told me to listen to my body, so I paid attention and grabbed Alexander and left. Rushing out to the car without our food, I noticed a man wearing a cape walking into the restaurant with a shotgun. I am not sure all that went on, but the police cornered him on Pierson Road right in front of the restaurant and shot him in the leg to stop him. Later I learned that he called himself Doctor Da.

That happened about a year after the 7-Eleven incident. Even though I had an excellent job at a rent-to-own store and was a top salesperson for over six months in a row, I wasn't loving living in Flint at all. I loved my job, our new home, and friends, but some areas were overrun with crime, and I hated that.

Eventually, I left the sales job and went back to Little Caesar's. It was more money, and I was pregnant, so we needed the extra income. The next few months would be okay, but six months, I started spotting, and the doctor ordered bed rest and no stress for a month. Scared I would lose my baby, I did exactly what I was told. I wasn't about to screw up another baby's life.

While we lived in Flint, my mom and Claude came to visit periodically, and she'd call often. We stayed in contact, and it was perfect. My dad, well, as mentioned before, made no effort. Nothing. Denise and Virgie, nothing. Donny knew better than to ever call me.

Other than the crime, living in Flint was a great time in my life, just like Florida. No family, no drama, no issues. The issues seemed to be steady when Ardy, Denise, Donny, and Virgie were in my life. I'm glad they left me alone for long periods throughout my adulthood. I never missed them, none of them.

One day while relaxing at home on bed rest, the phone rings.

"Hello."

"Peggy Ann, dad needs to know what happened between you and Donny?" says Maudie Jo as if my response was life or death.

Sigh *No, hello, how ya doing? Gosh, we haven't seen you in months or kiss my ass or anything.*

"Um, I'm on bed rest, and I've been spotting. The doctor said I can't be upset or stressed because that could cause me to lose the baby so, please, let's not talk about this now. I don't want to get upset and maybe lose my baby."

"Peggy Ann! Now, this is important, and dad needs to know. Donny is being accused of rape, and we think the girl is lying. Dad needs you to tell him right now!"

"Seriously! I said I don't want to be upset and lose my baby! Thinking it over quickly, I knew she wouldn't stop unless I said something. I could hear him ranting and raving in the background.

"Well, you can tell him that his son did very nasty things to me when I was nine, and I'm done with this conversation. As far as I'm concerned, he probably did rape that girl whoever she is. I'm betting she isn't lying!"

As I was hanging up the phone, I could hear Ardy in the background carrying on about his son going to prison over a lie. I hung up. I left the phone off the hook letting it dangle on the kitchen floor. When Marcus got home, I told him what had happened. He was pissed that they would call and stress me out, especially after I told them what was going on with the baby.

I guess Donny was once again more important than anything else in the world. Because lord knows I lied on him back in the day, and I am sure this poor girl who was raped also lied (insert eye roll). Turns out, Donny and another guy had both raped her. They each served time in prison for it but not enough because he got out a couple years later.

ON OCTOBER 27TH, AT PRECISELY **6:29 AM,** my second son, Jude, came into this world. The best-looking baby in Flint was 8 pounds and 1 ounce with dark curly hair and big blue eyes.

When I was pregnant, I wondered if I could love another child as much as I loved Alexander, but when my baby was placed on my tummy, all those thoughts and concerns melted away while I nestled him and cried tears of love and joy. I loved this little man like no one on this earth would ever love him. It was the same feeling I had with my first, and I thought if heaven had opened, we all could have floated in on my love and happiness alone.

Shortly after Jude, I quit working at Little Caesar's and enrolled in cosmetology school. I was determined to make something of myself no matter what, and now, more than ever with two children, I knew I had to get my education in something, anything. That was my ticket, at least I thought so at that point.

Alexander was 10, and Jude was 10 months old. We lived in a cute little apartment that had an open concept space. The living room, dining room, and kitchen were basically one ample space, and there was a short hall to the bedrooms and bath. The balcony was off the living room overlooking a small strip of grass and a strip of woods. It was usually peaceful.

It's the night before my first day of cosmetology school. I've just been woken up by all kinds of commotion outside my bedroom window. I squint and see that it's 2 am, so I lay back down thinking its teens partying, but the noise doesn't stop. I get up and walk out to the living room slider. I pull back the curtains to find my entire balcony engulfed with flames!

The only thing I can think about is getting my two boys out of that apartment. I rush into their bedroom, grab Jude, throw a blanket over him, grab Alexander by the shirt, and hold on for dear life. Marcus wakes up to me, yelling in the hallway.

"Fire! Get up! FIRE!"

Marcus runs out and opens the main door to exit the apartment, black smoke rolls into our home so fast it's unbelievable. I scream at him to shut the door, and then I haul the kids back into their bedroom. Standing there barefoot in pajamas with my two kids in tow, I push the window open and kick the screen out with my foot. I look down from our second-floor window, hold tight to my boys, and we jump.

I literally landed on my feet and didn't hurt us at all. Not one scrape, scratch, or bruise. Nothing. Marcus looks out the window and hollers.

"What are you doing?!"

"Jump, you idiot!" I yell back.

What a sight! A young mom jumping out the bedroom window with two kids in tow.

The office manager was kind enough to let us use an empty apartment for the rest of the night. Marcus stayed home the next day, and I went to my first day of cosmetology school. I only had a few hours of sleep, but I was determined to go!

We lost some of our canned foods from the high heat, but nothing else. I talked with a friend who suggested I throw out all of our food, even what was in the fridge and freezer. It wasn't much, but it was all that we had, and now it was gone. Fortunately, Marcus's co-workers took up a collection for us, and we used it to restock our food with plenty left over. It was a wonderful thing they did.

About halfway through my classes, I learned that the lady who lived next door started the fire. She was a nurse at one of the hospitals in Flint. Apparently, she had left work, came home, and bashed her husband's head with a hammer and then set her apartment on fire and went back to work. Wow! I was shocked. They had been discreet people. I never heard much of anything from them through the walls.

One never knows who they are living next door too, until they do!

I enjoyed the cosmetology school. I made many friends and learned a great skill. I even won first place at a cut & styling competition. I loved doing hair. Helping people look beautiful and feel good made *me* feel good—a win-win situation.

As students with a certain number of hours under our belt, we could offer services to the public, we never received payment, but we could accept tips. I had the sweetest older lady who came into the school every week for an up-do of her brownish-grey, thinning hair. Virginia was 77 years old, and her 5' 6" frame was thin, she was fit as a fiddle, though. She always asked for me, and her weekly tips were consistent.

Her 'do' was $4.00, and she usually gave .25 tips. To her generation, that was a lot of money. Bless her soul, she'd talk my ear off, but it was always exciting things she'd share, and I just loved listening to her talk with her Jersey accent. She'd tell stories about her husband going off to war while she was pregnant, him coming home with one leg gone. She shared about their hardships and how they got through it. Virginia was an amazing woman.

At Christmas time, she brought me the biggest granny smith apple (my favorite) I had ever seen. She had it in a Christmas bag with a bow and beside it a homemade peanut log she'd made from scratch wrapped in parchment and foil. It was delicious!

Another time, she made me some of her rice pudding and had it in a little butter dish. I chuckled after she left because the butter dish reminded me of my mother. If you looked in My birth mother's (Chelcie) fridge at any given time, you'd find 10 of the exact same butter bowls, and they each had something in them…but no butter. And, Lord have mercy, how she would know what each bowl had in it was beyond me!

Over the years, I've often thought about Virginia and reminisced about our conversations. I just loved her. She was the sweetest woman and made that season of my life special.

After I finished school, passed the state exam (My mom and Claude drove up for the week so she could be my live model for the state exam), and obtained my cosmetology license, I started working at a classy Salon in town. I loved what I was doing. I felt educated and proud of myself. Now I could bring home the bacon, fry it up in a pan with great looking hair! We had purchased a small house, and things were going well.

Unfortunately, my job at the salon didn't last, and the blissful marriage wasn't blissful anymore. It was deteriorating. There was an issue in our marriage that was taking up too much money and time. Hubby number two had a drinking problem. That issue resulted in drinking away much-needed money, a time we couldn't get back, and a whole lot of memories that were not joyful.

I was not able to live with this situation any longer. I tried for a few years to ignore it, hoping it would stop, but it never did. What it did do was develop into a deeper problem. A problem that I did not want to deal with. I grew up around a bunch of drinkers, so why would he be any different? I gave him an ultimatum, Stop drinking within six months, or I will load up the kids and move back to Jackson.

His drinking continued. He became harder to live with, he was always such a cocky prick, and I was just fed up with him treating me like a second-rate citizen. He had been drinking on his lunch hours and was usually loaded by the day's end when he would drive home. I had to make $35.00 a week stretch to buy groceries for four, diapers, and gas for me to get back and forth to work.

He had been in charge of paying bills. When I stepped in and took it over, we were three months behind in our mortgage, our propane tank was as empty as was our cupboards, and our sump-pump wasn't working along with other household things that needed to be repaired.

Shortly after that, I quit working at the salon because booth rental and daycare cost more than what I was bringing home. I needed what little money I made for food, so I quit and went back to dancing. It was fast, easy money. Great money! With everything falling short and almost facing repossession of the house, I felt as if I had no choice once again.

I rented a room in Jackson for a week at $65.00 and stayed there while I worked at the strip club. In one week, I made enough to get our mortgage almost caught up, fill the propane tank, buy a few groceries, and stock up on diapers with enough left over to go back for week two and make a little more to tide us over and start saving.

I booked myself again for the next week. I was hoping that once I got things caught up, I could just do it here and there to keep up on things. I also was hoping no one would find out. I thought my secret would be safe because we lived in Flint, and I was dancing in Jackson, and there was rarely any contact with the goof troop (Ardy, Virgie, Denise & dip-shit Donny). I was right, and yet…I was wrong.

After about a month of this new schedule of mine, Marcus told his mother that I was back to dancing. They had never known I danced in the first place, but they did after that.

It was my week off when his parents came for a visit. His folks were nice, clean, and upstanding people who usually treated me and my son, Alexander, well. However, during that visit, his mother sat in our living room and wouldn't stop questioning us about our problems and my "career." I kept quiet as Marcus was a mommy's boy, he was talking with a different tone and running his mouth non-stop! I just stared at him.

She kept looking at me, pursing her lips, and cocking her head disapprovingly as if I was some whore. Finally, I spoke up.

"Our business is none of yours. So, unless you plan on supporting this family, where I work and what I do are none of your business."

That wasn't received very well, they got up and left. Marcus was upset with me, and it was at that point that I entirely made up my mind. I knew I was going to leave him, it was just a matter of time and money before I could getaway.

A few days later, as I was cooking dinner, Marcus and I had a big fight. He said things and I, well…I *did* a thing.

Our house was 990 square feet. The side door either led to the basement, or you could turn to your right and walk up three steps up into the kitchen. It was a tiny kitchen with barely enough room for the four-person table. Beyond the kitchen was the living room, small, but enough room for us. After walking through the square living room, you had simple options of stepping one way to the bathroom or stepping the other way to our bedroom with the boys' bedroom right there as well.

Marcus had come home and was half-cocked with an attitude from hell. He started yelling at Alexander about the way he made his bed. Marcus liked the covers to be tucked in on the sides and the pillows to be perfectly straight and smoothed out, no wrinkles. Well, Alexander was eleven, and this wasn't the army. His bed was made, and I felt it was fine the way it was. Marcus, on the other hand, was pissed.

"You little bastard, go back and make that goddam bed right, or I'll kick your ass, you little mother fucker!"

Anger boiled up quickly. No one talks to my kid like that! No one! I'd had *enough*. Enough of him calling my son names, badgering him, and treating him like he wasn't adequate. Enough of his cussing. Enough of his spending money we didn't have. Enough.

I had *had* it.

When he walked into the kitchen, I picked up the frying pan that I was cooking fish in, dumped the fish out in the sink, turned around with that hot cast iron skillet, and whopped him upside his fucking head.

The skillet hit him, and he hit the floor. I stood over him with a skillet in hand, and at first, I thought I'd killed him, but, as luck would have it, he moved. He was only knocked out for a brief minute, if even that, and then opened his eyes. Lucky for him. And me, I suppose.

By the time he sat up holding his slightly bloody head, I had gathered my senses enough to speak clearly.

"Don't you ever speak to my son like that again! I am renting a truck and leaving your ass."

That POS picked the wrong mama. Ain't no one gonna mess with my kids! I told him when we first started dating, that my son would always come first, no matter what. I guess he forgot that part.

Knowing I had to make my move right then, I sent Alexander to his friends for a couple nights, left Jude with daycare, and called my BFF, Kelly, in Jackson. I packed up on a Sunday and drove back to my old stomping grounds with 100 copies of my resume in hand, a suit, heels, and small briefcase in tow. I told myself I was going to pound that pavement until I had hand-delivered all the resumes and had a job (not dancing), and I did.

That Monday, I went to what felt like a million businesses. I decided to take a break from job hunting and stopped at Ted Nugent's Bow Hunter's World on Michigan Ave to look around and get Alexander a poster. As I was flipping through the poster display, this tall man with very long hair comes up to me and asks if he can help me find anything. I look at him and smile.

"Naw, I'm just looking but thank you."

"Well, if you change your mind, let me know. It's a hot one out there today, huh?"

"Sure is. I've been in this monkey suit all day, and I handed out 99 resumes in this heat. I'm determined to get a job today, but no bites yet."

He cocks his head to the side and scratches his facial hair. "Wait right here."

He walks into an office and shuts the door. A few moments later, he emerges.

"Do you know accounting?" he asks me.

"Yes, yes, I do. I have an accounting certificate as a matter of fact." My heartbeat quickens. *He's got my full attention now.*

"Can I see your resume?"

A few minutes later, I'm in the manager's office for an on-the-spot interview with a nice lady named Lily while the long-haired guy observes the interview. Suddenly he interrupts us.

"Are you a fan of Ted's?

I hesitate. *Oh god. Is this a trick question? Do I need to be?*

"Yes, I love all his music!" I gush.

Long-Hair says, "Really? What're your favorite songs of his? Name a few."

"Um, well, there's…Cat Scratch Fever and that other one…"

Long-Hair looks at me with a furrowed brow. "Do you even know what Ted Nugent looks like?"

I drop my head and shake it, knowing I have just kissed this interview goodbye.

He stands up and holds his hand out to shake. "You're hired! And, by the way, I'm Ted, nice to meet you."

I went back to Flint the next day and placed a hold on a U-Haul rental, collected boxes, and started packing. I packed us up in three days flat while working full time and taking care of two boys and a drunk. I felt like Wonder Woman!

Kelly started looking for an apartment for us and found one right across the street from her house. Exactly one week later, I loaded up my furniture and the kids, and away we drove to Jackson, to our new place.

THE BOYS AND I loved our new place. We had a downstairs apartment with a big front porch. There were three units in the building. I had the biggest and Kelly's brother Jay had the upstairs while an older couple had the backside.

The main front door opened to a somewhat large foyer that leads to my place and Jay's. After stepping inside my apartment, the living room came first, and that showed through an archway to the dining room. To the left was the boys' room, and to the right was the kitchen. There was plenty of space for the boys and me.

It was charming, full of character, and I loved it. Since Kelly lived so close, I was hoping it'd kind of be like old times again. I had met Kelly years ago at the Club when I was a dancer and she a waitress. She had one kid as well, and we became close. After I moved to Flint with Marcus, I lost touch with many of my friends but not Kelly.

Things were a little different, though. Kelly was now married to Michael with two more kids and pregnant with her fourth. I had another child and was going through a separation. Yet, we were still the crazy, fun-loving buddies who would often get together to take the kids to the bowling alley, movies, or The Parlour—a famous ice cream shop in Jackson. The kids loved our outings, and so did we.

A few months after Kelly gave birth to her youngest daughter, we felt we needed a girl's night out. Well, out we went and drunk we got. We had a great time though, we played pool, danced, laughed, we just had a fun time. We got back late, so she decided to sleepover at my house so she wouldn't wake her family up.

We staggered out of the car and made it up the five steps to the front porch laughing and giggling hysterically. We may or may not have peed ourselves. Who knows, we were pretty tanked up. I thought I needed a key to get into the first door, but we didn't. I'm not sure how long it took me to figure that out. We finally made it inside the foyer after figuring out that the door would magically open if we turned the knob. Kelly leaned against the wall and then slid down. She looked like she needed company, so I slid down next to her and passed out—her head on my shoulder and mine on hers—leaving the first door wide open with keys dangling out of my apartment door right next to us. Jay found us the next morning, and we woke to his uncontrollable, falling-down-can't-breathe laughter about what he was seeing.

This wasn't our first time sleeping together, or rather drifting off in peaceful slumber, heads on each other's shoulders.

Once we were bartending at the same little Sports bar and we took a bus trip (of which we were paid to waitress) to the Lions game in Detroit, and we did fine all the way up and then on the way back, I guess it got boring since we kind of, well, fell asleep. Nonetheless, all was well. Everyone got their own beers and eats, and we just slept like two drunk girls, because, well, we were.

However, I'm not sure either Kelly or I found it as funny as Jay did at that moment, but I can have a pretty good belly laugh about it now!

— Soap Box —

What is not funny is driving while being drunk. I wonder how in the hell I drove home that night. I think about how awful it is to drive intoxicated, about the risks, I took of possibly hurting someone due to my ignorance and stupid decision making. I truly thank God I never killed anyone or did any kind of damage. I can't even imagine turning someone else's life upside down like that. Listen, we all do stupid things sometimes (mostly in our younger years), but I just hope and pray that you do NOT drive under the influence of anything! It's risking other people's lives, and it's not worth it. Do not be an asshole like I was. Don't be reckless and put

264 • Peggy Watkins

other people's lives in danger, which is precisely what
you are doing when you make those kinds of irrational
decisions.

As the boys and I settling, I was also getting acclimated to my new
job at Ted's as his administrative assistant. Even though the money
wasn't great, I enjoyed my work. I met a few musicians and stars. Went
to quite a few concerts and I helped book the tour of the Damn Yankees
for 1991-92. I admit, there were a couple times when my title went
to my head. I talked with people at M-T.V., New York Times, record
labels, and other people and places I never would have dreamed I'd
talk to in my lifetime. Ted opened a door of opportunity for me, and I
jumped in.

I will say this about Ted and his wife Shemane, they were truly
good to me. They treated me well. While I worked for him, he seemed
to treat everyone as equals, and never once did either of them make me,
or anyone that I know of, feel small or different. My only issue working
for Ted was the pay. It wasn't stellar, and I sometimes had to work a
different job on the weekends to be able to give my boys a better life
but all in all, the Nugent's were good people to me.

We lived in Jackson for about 6 months when my 12-year-old was
at school on a Saturday for a science project. After, as he stood waiting
for the bus, he was robbed. He said the other kid came up behind
him and said he had a gun, knocked him down, and demanded his
starter jacket. The kid threatened to take his shoes too but left without
following through it.

When he called me at work, I freaked out! My anxiety was so high
that my mouth got the best of me, and I actually yelled at *Alexander* for
the incident. I know I did not handle the conversation the way it should
have been dealt and I have regretted that every day since. He was the
one who was violated and passably held at gunpoint in the dead of
winter, and I was angry with *him*. Gawd! I have a lot of shame over that
incident as well as a few others.

I stepped back after that ordeal and took a good look at myself and what I had done, how I had acted. I didn't like what I was seeing or who I was becoming. For months afterward, I looked in the mirror and found myself hating what I saw. I felt as I had become one of *them*. I would think *I have this amazing little boy, and he's hurt, and all I can do is act like a damn idiot about it and yell. What a mom!*

Something had to change, but what? I felt worthless and selfish for handling it the way I did. I wanted to fix it, but I didn't know-how. I knew I needed to forgive myself and let it go, but what was I supposed to say? *I forgive myself for being an asshole of a mother. I forgive myself for not having enough sense to do what was needed and right like, be nurturing and protective?*

My child was a great kid. He'd come home from school, and a couple times a week, he'd walk down the street and pick up his brother from daycare before I got home. Then he'd clean the house and sometimes he'd cook dinner. He had an enormous weekend paper route. During the winter, we'd wake at 4:30 am, get Jude bundled up, and I'd drive our station wagon with the back hatch open, and Alexander would toss newspapers to the neighbors. He was a great kid and deserved better.

One thing I knew needed to change was to get my son out of the school district he was in and put him in a better one. I began looking for something in the Western School District. Still in Jackson, just better. There were other options, but they were a little more than I could afford.

I finally found a large apartment complex that I could afford, and it was right on the line of Western and Jackson Public. Literally, two buses came through, one for Western and one for Public, and the stops were across the street from each other. I applied for the apartment but was told it could take two to three months, sometimes longer, to get in. I was willing to wait because I needed things to be better for him-for both of my boys.

KELLY DECIDED TO HOOK ME UP with a couple blind dates. She told me I needed a night out, and she was right. However, I'm not sure the dates she picked were suitable for me.

The first guy met me at a local rock bar. I dressed in a somewhat provocative, tight (hey, now, I had a hot body), red dress. The back was open to my waist, and the front showed a nice balance of cleavage and shoulders. It was short—but not too short—and skintight. I thought I looked amazing, even Kelly told me I was hot! I wore black 3" heels, and my long reddish blonde hair flowed seductively.

I was sitting at the bar waiting when he walked in and came right towards me. The closer he got, the more I noticed how short he was, but cute. As he introduced himself and I stood up (remember, I'm 5'3" wearing 3" heels), his head was only tall enough to rest on my chest, and his eyes stayed right there.

We sat at a table and had a drink while chatting, during which he continued staring at my cleavage. It began to bug the crap out of me.

Usually, I charge people to look at my tits but right now, I'm off the clock, asshole.

"Hey. Buddy. I have a face too if you'd like to talk to *me* rather than my *tits*."

That date ended after one drink.

Two weekends later, the second guy picked me up at Kelly's to go to a free Damn Yankee's concert courtesy of my job. On the way, his car broke down at a rest stop. I honestly should have known better to even get in that damn, rusty, old, nasty car. The seats were cloth, which is fine *but*, they were ripped to shreds with a raggedy-ass, beat-to-shit, old towels covering them. And, there was fast food garbage all in the front seat floor, pop spilled all over the middle console, and the interior smelled like farts and French fries.

We each called a few people, but no one could help us, so I snagged a ride to Kalamazoo from a truck driver. I had hitchhiked before, so it seemed like a viable option at the time. He, however, was not impressed with that idea, and at the end of the concert, he got a ride home with someone else. I, with a co-worker. We never saw each other again.

Kelly had to do some talking to get me to agree to the third blind date. Eventually, she wore me down.

George picked me up at Kelly's place too. That became the pattern so that these losers didn't know where I lived. He seemed nice, laughed a lot, joked around. Said he was going through a divorce and had two girls. He lived in Michigan Center, not far from me, and worked with Kelly and her hubby in a local factory.

A couple good things I noticed right off the bat, he was taller than me, and his car wasn't a piece of shit. The bar was being raised.

We decided to do a movie and dinner. The film went well, and afterward, we headed to Red Lobster. Dinner was going well. We had lots of chatter about the movie, his girls, my boys, what we do, where we work, how we like our jobs, etcetera, etcetera. We continued talking, and soon enough, he reaches over the table (we were sitting in a booth), takes my hand, looks me dead in the eyes, and says with a sly grin, "You know, since I paid for the movie and plan to buy dinner, well we could go back to your place, it's closer?"

I was dumbfounded. Stunned. Speechless. Then, pissed.

What a fucking asshole! Did he just ask me to put out 'puss' for a movie and dinner? That fucknut!

I smiled and squeezed his hand back, looked him right in the face.

"Yummm. Let me go freshen up. Give me a few, I'll be right back."

I winked a sexy wink. I got up and walked towards the bathroom, looking back and flirting as I walked away.

Shit! What now?

As I was in the bathroom trying to figure out what to do next. I rinsed my face to clear my mind, looked in the mirror, and took a few deep breaths.

This isn't your first rodeo, Peg, think!

I stepped out of the bathroom keeping out of George's line of sight. When I flagged down our waitress, I called her over and told her that I had a surprise in mind for "my husband," and I'd love for her to help but to please keep it a secret. She agreed enthusiastically to help. I told her we were heading to a hotel for the weekend. I explained to her that I wanted enough food to last us. I ordered three full steak, and lobster meals, three pasta and shrimp meals, six desserts, two things of extra garlic cheesy rolls (those are so yummy), and I told her to send over two more drinks each plus two shots of tequila to my table but not until I had the food to run out to our car. I told her I'd wait and asked if she could possibly rush it. About 15 minutes or so later, I had two big bags of food.

As I took the bags, I told her to go ahead and take the extra drinks over, and I'd be right back in. I giggled as I explained how surprised George was going to be, thanking her for all her help, I handed her a folded up $20.00. She looked so happy to be a part of this special night—poor girl. I do hope he tipped too. She earned it!

I rushed out the door and across the street to another restaurant, Gilbert's, where I called Kelly to come to get me.

I told her to drive to the back of the restaurant where I'd be waiting. As Kelly rushed into the parking lot, I darted out, jumped in her car, and yelled, **DRIVE!** I was slouching down in the front seat, covering my face laughing so hard I was seriously hyperventilating. She was laughing at me and asking what was going on and where was George?

After I pulled it together, I started my story. I thought she would piss herself laughing. We both laughed so hard we couldn't even get out of her car.

A couple of weeks after that date, I was eating dinner at Finley's with a good friend, Harry. I noticed a couple being seated across the room from us. It was George and another one of his victims. I told Harry all about my blind date a couple weeks back and pointed out George to him. I made some sarcastic comments about George and his date, splitting the bill to save herself. Harry suggested I let it go. Fat chance of that, and he knew it!

As we were on our way out, we had no choice but to walk right past them. I had an uncontrollable urge to say hi. As we passed by, Harry kept walking, but I stopped at their table and looked right at the woman.

"Are you sharing the cost or is he paying?" I waited about two seconds as she sat there looking at me as if I was totally insane and intrusive on her dinner date. I smiled, looked her right in the eyes, and said, "Just know that if he's paying, he's going to want pussy for reimbursement."

Then I looked over at George with a wide grin and patted his shoulder.

"Just keepin' it real, Georgie, just keepin' it real!"

WHILE WORKING FOR TED, I realized that if I wanted to live better and be in a better area, I had to make more money to afford it. So, I took a good long look at myself and made a big decision. I talked it over with Kelly and concluded that I looked good and could still dance. It wasn't what I really wanted to go back to. However, I knew the money was good, and the work was hard but also comfortable. This time though, I went a different route.

I applied to the welfare office for food stamps and a medical card since Marcus had taken us off his insurance policy. They wanted info on everything! I mean *everything*: my car title, bank account, a signed document from my employer (which was so embarrassing), and a signed form from my landlord (which wasn't easy asking her to fill out the forms). They needed to know—understandably why—everything about my life.

After jumping through all those hoops, I was denied a medical card (which was the main reason I was asking for help) but given food stamps. Not to mention, it took over 30 days to be approved to receive anything.

I was so humiliated. Every month I had to go to the welfare office and pick up my paper-money. I'd wear oversized sunglasses, a headscarf, and a long dress to disguise myself, and park a few blocks away to avoid being seen. Then I had to sit in the lobby with a bunch of other people and wait for my name to be called over the loudspeaker to get a measly $97.00 in food stamps.

Each month after I'd get my stamps, I'd go the grocery story around 3:00 am to avoid being seen and spend the entire $97.00, which didn't buy much. This lasted three months until I called and told them to cancel me. When my social worker asked why I told her I was too humiliated. Taking a second job sounded far less exhausting than trying to manage all of the shame I had from using food stamps.

I wanted to get away from the lifestyle of depending on Welfare to survive. Today, I look at it differently. I honestly believe government assistance is a needed system and great for those who require a helping hand in tough times. There is *no* shame in getting help. We Americans pay into this program, and no one should feel guilty if they need to use it. Unless, of course, you are like my adopted mother and think the government owes you and you make welfare your lifestyle, that's wrong, and you need to take another look at yourself.

So, I put out the word that I would do bachelor parties. I hired a bouncer to go with me, and I only did a Friday or Saturday night party every other week. I made between $800.00- $1000.00 per party, and it was much better than standing in a line for fake money to buy food and not even enough imitation cash to be worth my while. Fuck that! A mom's got to do what a mom's got to do.

I finally got into the apartment complex I had applied to. There was a mix-up with the address, so I had to use my friend Harry's address to send the boys to the Western School District. I got the boys settled in school, then enrolled myself at Jackson Community College and began taking classes towards a law degree. I was always interested in legal stuff and figured I had been involved with enough issues that I might be able to help people so, the law it was. I immediately registered for classes to qualify me to be hired at the prison where my sister, Denise, was working. I knew she had a good-paying job with benefits, I thought maybe I could get a job there too and continue in college.

I wanted to stop dancing and build an actual career. Not that dancing isn't a real job, but let's face it, with age comes droopy boobs and a sagging ass. Who wants to look at that? Or, moreover, who'd pay to look at that? Ewww. You're welcome for the visual.

AFTER A YEAR AND SIX LAW CLASSES out of the way, I had passed my exam for hire at Jackson State Prison. I was in. I gave my two-week notice at Bow Hunter's World and began at Southside prison school, where inmates could earn a G.E.D or diploma. Southside was also the last stop for many. As the guys came closer to getting paroled, they would often be sent to Southside to earn their G.E.D or diploma to help them hopefully obtain a job when they hit society again. I was hired as the school secretary and started making $9.51/hr., had Blue Cross/Blue Shield, sick leave, and vacation pay, which was much better than my previous employment situations and pay.

I had a few positions at the prison. I worked in the Warden's office as a Kite reader, reading the inside mail from convicts who wanted to be moved to another cell or many other requests. Honestly, it wasn't pleasant. During my six weeks in this position, I declined most requests to move to another section. Especially the rapists.

After that, I went into Central and worked at the Law Library as the psychologist's secretary. Then over to Engler as a human resource office assistant. Lastly, I became Deputy Warden's administrator. Towards the end, I was making excellent money with all the bells and whistles of full benefits.

Once I stopped working for Ted and went to prison, I had given up dancing altogether. I didn't want to do it ever again under any circumstances, and I stuck to that. I did, however, after working at the penitentiary, end up working two jobs for many years, but that was ok with me. I felt better about myself.

Understand me. I am *NOT* ashamed of dancing. I was a good dancer and a decent one at that, I made a living, and that was that. It's legal and no one should be shamed for being a stripper/dancer/exotic dancer no one! It's a damn job!

272

I didn't really have any issues while working at the prison, but I did witness a blow job in the hallway of the library once. Also, a convict came up to me and showed me his penis. I was shocked and terrified when that happens, and I, of course, told. The officer who I told instructed me on what to do when it happens again. I say "when" because it was bound to happen again. It was just a matter of when. It did happen (same guy), and I took the officer's advice.

There I was, minding my own business enjoying a break, when out of the blues, the willie Flasher walks up, looks me right in the eyes, smiles, and whips out his penis.

I stood still, smiled at him, looked down at his willie, then looked him right in the eyes and said, "Aww, does that come in adult size?" Still smiling.

I was scared to do that, but it worked. The willie flasher never flashed me again. I had made rank with the convicts by standing my ground and not allowing them to break me, their standard MO with other employees or guards. Once they break someone down, they get them to do things such as bring in drugs or get information from the outside.

Prison is a wicked place. From my personal observation, it's a fully paid vacation with three squares a day plus snacks, lots of activities, and unique lessons in learning how to go back into the general population and be better at the skills that got you behind bars in the first place.

I'm not saying that *all* convicts are bad, just quite a few of them. And regarding some of them, I wonder why we even allow them to live after some of the heinous crimes they commit! For example, in 1999, the owner of a place Kelly and I used to eat at, *Kip's Taco House* in Jackson, the owner murdered his wife and cooked her up. They call him the 'Deep-Fry Killer.'

Of course, someone showing off their penis wasn't a monstrous offense, and I learned that sort of thing quickly can be controlled by a simple giggle and a few 'tiny' words. I don't know what that convict did to be imprisoned, but I can say he had a very long weenie that he was proud of.

AFTER A YEAR WITH THE PRISON, my limited-term position was up, and I moved on. I started working for a construction company as a payroll accountant. Thanks to one of my BFF's Teresa. She had been working at this company for years and was the Comptroller and she did her job well. She trained me. Heck, she trained everyone there including the owner. Seriously, she ran this place like clockwork, and she was the best boss ever.

Well, this contractor, Ray had (if I recall correctly) three crews of about 6 guys each. They kept track of their hours in a notebook and would turn them into me each week. Talk about chaos!

I had to learn to read notebooks that were dirty, ketchup-smeared, onion-smelling, mustard-colored, taco sauce-trailed with penciled-in notes everywhere, and words written in Japanize and Greek. About 18 of them every week. Trust me, I earned my pay. The guys were kind though, and they learned quickly what I meant by being prompt with their notebooks if they wanted to be paid on time.

That lasted a good while, then I started my own business, Critter City USA, an in-home daycare. I enjoyed the daycare. My boys, not so much, but it allowed me to earn money, stay off welfare, not go back to dancing, and get some college classes completed to work towards my associate degree in general studies. It also allowed me and the boys to have a short vacation to Mackinac Island every year, dinner out every now and then, pizza and movie weekends, and a move to a better home. It gave us a good life.

My relationship with Denise was off and on during the second round of my years in Jackson. She'd make sure she called me at least every other week to let me know that 'daddy' came to visit her and ask if daddy and Maudie Jo had stopped over to see the boys and me. She

276 · Peggy Watkins

knew they didn't, yet she loved rubbing in the fact that her family had a relationship with them but not mine.

Her phone calls were never to ask me about my life or to invite me to anything. We no longer hung out or partied, which was fine with me. There were a few times I asked her and her hubby to go out to dinner with me and the boys, but she'd refuse and told me some bullshit reason. It was probably for the best.

Once I confronted her about one of her lies, and she looked me right in the face and laughed. Said nothing but just laughed at me as if I was the stupid one. Well, I was. I was the stupid one to take her bullshit and keep coming back for more.

Denise and I lived about ten minutes from each other in Jackson, and my house was on the way home for dad, but he always said they "had to get home," or didn't want to stop because he didn't know if I was home. That was a shitty excuse for why they never visited us. I should have expected it, it had always been that way and always would be.

Jude had a lump on his neck and needed a biopsy to make sure it wasn't cancer. I called to tell them about the surgery, and all he said was, "Well, call me when ya know what it is." They never came to the hospital to wait with me, nor did Denise or Virgie. And all of them knew how scared I was about my child, and yet not one of them showed any kindness to him or me during that time.

My mother had just gotten out of surgery herself and wanted to come, but due to her needing rest, I convinced her to stay home. My caller ID was filled with calls from her while I was at the hospital. When I called her back, she cried and said she'd been praying this whole time for her grandbaby and for strength for me. My mother, my real mother would have come but, I was the one to beg her not to due to her just having a triple by-pass.

I wasn't alone at the hospital, though. Marcus and his parents came, which was nice. Jude ended up being fine, it wasn't cancer, it was a lipoma, and they removed it. He had stitches and was told to rest for a couple days. He was cancer-free, and I thanked God for that.

Shortly after surgery, my sitter canceled on me a few hours before my shift. It was a Sunday. I called Denise, she said she couldn't (or rather, wouldn't) because she and her husband had plans. They were going fishing in her backyard. Of course, they had a pond.

I called a couple other people in Jackson but couldn't get a hold of anyone. As a last resort, I called my dad and stepmom and explained to them I just needed someone to come and sit with him during my four-hour shift. I offered to pay them gas money and babysitting money. They came but only after an enormous amount of pleading. You'd think you could count on your parents when you are in desperate need, right? Ha!

I had Jude set up on the couch in the living room with a pillow and blanket, watching movies, resting. He had coloring books, a couple puzzles, and three films. There was more than enough to keep him busy for four hours. I had also prepared his snacks and drinks, so all he had to do was walk to the fridge and get what he wanted by himself.

As soon as they arrived, Maudie Jo came in and went right to the chair in the living room, sat down, clutching her purse, white-knuckled, and puckering her lips while rolling her eyes. This was her typical M.O. It made me feel as if she thought my house was full of cooties, and she didn't want any nasties to touch her. Let me be clear, I'm an immaculately clean person. My home has always been tidy.

My dad stood in the living room and immediately started asking me when I would be back because they had things to do. I asked what things, and he said, "Things!" I explained it will take me 15 minutes to get to work. I have a four-hour shift, and I will leave early if I can. Other than that, I should be back in four and a half hours. He told me, well, okay but no longer because we have "things to do."

I left with my dad looking down to the ground, pacing my floors and Maudie Jo sitting like a pissed off gopher clenching a nut.

I got right back as I said I would. When I walked in, Jude was watching a movie, and I could tell he had had a couple of snacks. Maudie Jo was in the same spot as when I left, and my dad was still pacing the floors. As the bartender, I was also the cook and always came home smelling like french fries, burgers, and beer. After my shift, I rushed home, still wearing my apron that carried all the fresh aromas of bar life as well as my tips in the pockets. As I pulled out a handful of change and dollars, Maudie Jo bestowed me a very foul look and asked where the dollars had been.

I guess the question went over my head.

"In my apron. where do you think?"

She stood up sharply, still clutching her purse. "Well, I wasn't sure if you'd been out to the bar taking your clothes off again for men."

At that point, I froze with money in hand, narrowed my eyes, shook my head, and turned towards my dad, hoping for some help. He gave nothing. He said nothing in my defense, and it'd been a couple years since I last danced. They knew it, too, they both knew it.

I took a deep breath, I offered twenty dollars to them for gas and watching my son. Maudie Jo took it, and they left like two rats rushing to get the cheese.

If they only understood how I laughed at their stupidity. Those two held so much hate inside their hearts, it shone through all their cracks. It breathed. It floated over my head like a dirt cloud covering everything in their presence with filthy dust to remind me that I was less than them. There were times they took more from me than I was able to give, and it left me depleted and exhausted. They took my patience, self-worth, time, energy. And there were times I gave them more than they deserved. Loyalty, more chances, attention, and love.

Their hate turned into their passion, and when hatred becomes an appetite, it holds the bearer captive and dictates their life. Their demons were my demons. They seemed to enjoy and delight in tormenting me, and yet I stayed. I hoped it would change. I wished for more. I was so conditioned to accept this treatment, I'd forget it wasn't my fault. Actually, I can't remember a time when it wasn't.

MONTHS AND YEARS CHANGED, but the people in my life—
my family—never seemed to. Situations would happen, and Virgie,
Ardy, Denise, and Donny would blow them out of proportion. Their
comments to me were nasty, accusatory, they would often twist what I
said. And they would continually remind me that I lied on my brother,
therefore, I make things up and lie all the time.

I tried my best during this time of my life to stay away from them,
and the reality was, none of them were too concerned about us either.
It's not that we didn't see them. We just didn't make any kind of effort
to see each other.

It was a different story with my mom and Claude. We'd call each
other often and go visit them every month, even though they didn't
come over to visit us. At least she phoned.

When I did happen to see my adopted family, they all continued
to make remarks about what an awful person my birth mother was,
and the name-calling ensued. I'd sit quietly saying nothing as if I were
trained to do so because you know, I *was* taught. That conditioning
stuck with me. It lay dormant in my mind and thoughts for many years.

I would hear the exact same stories from Ardy over and over and
over. He was like a broken record that wouldn't shut up. Telling me
how "that bitch and her sissy husband" tried to put him in prison and
how he "busted Claude in the mouth" and wanted to hit my mom too.
Then he'd tell another story of how my Grandma Ally lied on him and
tried to put him in prison. And every time he said these same stories,
he'd remind me that they were my family by saying "that bitch you
call mother" or "them damn no good for nothing bunch of hillbillies of
yours." Always name-calling. Always implying it—whatever "it" was
at the time—was my fault. When he'd tell the stories, he'd make sure

to look at me shaking his head, pressing his lips together, and making a fist.

He progressed from making childhood intimidating threats to adult browbeating oppression. So did the others, but I didn't realize what they were doing. Maybe I was naïve, or perhaps I was desensitized to it.

A few years had passed, and Marcus and I were still married. Honestly, I didn't want to divorce. Not because I didn't enjoy freedom but because Virgie had been married and divorced so many times I feared following in her footsteps. And, I was afraid people would think I was like her. I had already been married once, and one divorce was plenty. I figured we could just live separate lives, date whomever we wanted, and things would be fine until one of us met our soulmate.

By this time, Alexander was 18. At age 16, he'd moved in with his dad, Alex, and his new wife, Jamie, provided he kept his grades up, which he did. Jude was eight and in third grade. He had a good relationship with his dad, but I only allowed him to visit him on the weekends when Marcus picked him up sober. He also knew better than to bring him home if he'd been drinking.

That "rule" started a few months prior when I had stopped him from taking Jude while he was intoxicated.

IT WAS HIS WEEKEND, and he arrived right on time, 5:30 pick up on Friday evening. However, he was drunk as a skunk. I took his keys, sent him to the couch, and he literally passed out within about 15 minutes of arriving. I told him that he could stay all day Saturday and visit with Jude but could no longer take him since he couldn't restrict himself from drinking around him. He resisted, and of course, there was a little argument, but I won, and that was that.

He visited Jude every other weekend at my house from Friday night to Saturday evening and a time or two until Sunday afternoon. He stayed sober the entire weekend, and they didn't leave my sight. If he took him to the movies, I went. If he took him to McDonald's, I went. If he took him to the park, the mall, the roller-skating rink, I went. I wasn't about to let my son's life change because of a drunk.

My how things had changed! I went from driving myself, and Kelly home drunk as all get out to reeling at the thought of my child in the car with a drunk. We really do make stupid decisions in our younger years, and then some of us wake up and realize just how *stupid* we were and refuse to ever put ourselves or anyone else in that same situation again. That's called maturing.

I allowed his visits to pick back up when he showed me a token from AA and proved with several trips that he wasn't drinking. However, there were stipulations which he seemed to follow, as far as I knew.

Soon enough, Marcus started dating a girl he wanted to marry, so he asked for the divorce. I didn't give two shits about their relationship, but I still didn't want to be divorced twice. Nonetheless, I went to the library, had some help from a friend, and drew up my own divorce papers, and represented myself in court.

The whole process was quick and easy. I filed, and two months later, it was final. We were both ready to move forward and legally be free of each other since we'd been separated for years.

Soon after, he and his new girlfriend took off out of the blue to Arizona. I wanted to punch him in the face only because he left without telling Jude.

It was his weekend to have a visit, and Jude was waiting with the suitcase packed and a couple toys in hand on the front porch as he usually did when the weather was nice. 5:30 rolled around, and no Marcus. 6:30 and no Marcus. Jude is now crying, thinking he forgot him, and I am consoling my son, reassuring him that his father would not forget about him. 7:30 comes and goes, and *no Marcus*. Honestly, this was not the usual. He really was always on time, just like clockwork right there to get his boy.

I called his house, his phone was disconnected. I found that very strange. I phoned his work to only find out that he'd quit his job the prior week, and they hadn't heard from him. I called his parents, and they claimed they knew nothing. I had no one else to call and inquire about where he was or if he was okay.

What I did have to do was tell my little eight-year-old that his dad was okay and loved him, and he'd call when he got a minute. I did my best, yet I felt that wasn't enough, because I just didn't know what to do or say. I mean, what if he was dead. What if he never returned? I just didn't know.

Three weeks later, the phone rings at dinner time, and I see on the caller I. D. it's from Mississippi and an unfamiliar name. I answer it's Marcus. He sounded happy and carefree. He told me he wanted to talk to his son. And of course, I gave him a mouthful, a lesson on abandonment, and filled him in on how the last three weeks had gone due to him just leaving and not telling us anything.

He told me that he simply wanted to start over without me, so he left. I asked him if that meant his son, and he told me, no, but Jude would need to understand that his dad moved and is getting married and won't be around as much. He said a lot of messed up crap that day to me on the phone, and truthfully, I don't remember half of what he said, but the gist of it was this, he moved and was starting over, and he didn't feel the need to let his son, parents, or anyone know—especially me. Marcus was right about one thing. It wasn't my business what he did. But my son Jude *IS* my business, and if he does something that affects him, he better bet his ass, he needs to inform me.

I let him know I could not care less about him, but he needed to be a dad to his son and not leave him hanging. He told me to shut my fucking mouth and stay out of his life, so, I did.

I put Jude into counseling as I knew this would be hard on my little guy, and I wanted him to know this was in no way his fault. He went twice a week for six weeks, and he handled it well. His counselor told me he had worked with many little kids who had been abandoned like this, and he felt confident that Jude would be okay. That was good news, but I was hurting for my son. It was hard to watch him go through all the pain and confusion, but it made me glad I had given that bastard his divorce. I found myself wishing I'd had done it sooner and not held out due to my fear of being a two-time divorcee. I cared too much about what people thought, and that was going to change.

VI

LIGHT

AT THE END
OF THE TUNNEL

My daycare business was going well. College classes were about done, and I had gotten mostly 3.0 or higher grades. I was proud of myself. I was on a new mission. I quit the bar and had been putting my applications in a few places out of state.

I had fond memories of my move to Fort Lauderdale years ago and felt things went well for me during that time so, I thought moving out of state with a job I could retire from was a great idea. Besides, with Marcus out of the picture, who could stop my move, right?

During my job search, I found an open position at an insurance agency in Charlotte, NC, and applied. Much to my surprise, I got an interview, so I made a trip to see the office and explore the area.

I was greeted by Paul and his wife, Betsy, who both showed me around the office and town. Paul was a very tall, thick man. He had black hair, deep blue eyes, and a smile that would make you smile back. He laughed loud and was one of the kindest men I'd met in a long time. Betsy was a tall beautiful solid woman with long curly black hair and big brown eyes. She was a great cook and a wonderful person. I loved her southern accent, which was even more profound than Paul's. Betsy had a familiar spirit that made me feel right at home. She loved showing me around to all the "specialty shops," which were secondhand stores for furniture and other things I needed.

They were very friendly and accommodating and even offered to let me rent one of the houses they owned. *And*, they had a German Shepard who had just had puppies. I was in heaven! I asked if I could have one for Jude, they told me they'd reserve whichever one I picked. I was very excited. The plan was to move right after the first of the year. Since Paul would be my boss, it made things a little easier as to when I moved and where I'd live.

I felt great about my new job, the move, and getting my associate degree. I would be moving to a fresh start—new everything. And since I wasn't really dating anyone, that meant I would be free to enjoy life without issues from some bonehead, which was how I was beginning to see most single men.

One weekend when Jude had gone to visit his grandparents (Marcus's parents), I invited a couple friends to come over and have a girl's night. Stephanie and Carrie came over, and we watched a movie, had pizza and wine and laughed a lot. Later in the evening, Carrie left, Stephanie hung around a little longer, and during our deep, late-night conversation, she decided that I needed a man or at least a date since it'd been a while. Of course, I laughed hysterically at this and any thought of needing a man. I didn't need anyone. I had done things on my own, and I was quite happy with my life and the way things were rolling.

She persisted. She showed me this site called Match.com. As we surfed around, she noticed an offer for a free seven-day trial and insisted I sign up, which I did about a bottle of wine later.

She helped me make my profile, which did not consist of my real name or my actual address, as I didn't trust that some crazy psycho wouldn't come to my home and kill me. She agreed.

I claimed to be Taylor, who lived in Ann Arbor. The name Taylor was taken, so I tried adding letters to the end, and to no avail, nothing was available. Finally, after much debate, two bottles of wine, and lots of laughing, I decided to add my bra size to the end of Taylor. Therefore, I was now Taylor36-C.

The profile was all true except, of course, the two fibs. I don't recall uploading a picture, but I may have. The next day I opened my email to find 157 email responses from Match.com. I was blown away! Surprised to see so many men interested in me, I called Kelly and told her all about it. I asked what to do to narrow it down to pick a couple dates. We had a good laugh and formed a plan, I'd deleted 10 and keep one and do this until I have five left. I did have to change up the math a little, but I deleted it until I had my desired number of possible dates. Let the responding begin!

One guy to whom I returned an email let me know he was not impressed with me trying to "hook a man by way of bra size." I chuckled and had not even thought of hooking a man since I knew I was headed out of state. The only thing I wanted to catch was the latch on my trunk on the way out of Michigan.

Now I had skin in the game. Still, all I was considering was dinner and a movie or just someone to chat with here and there, nothing romantic. I will admit it'd been a long time and well, other options could have been considered. I'd be lying if I said anything different. But, if it was going to be any kind of intimacy, the guy had better be a major hottie, or it wouldn't happen! And my past proves I am not a pushover when it comes to demands on getting into my pants for a simple dinner and movie. Just ask George!

The second guy told me he was bi-sexual and hoped that wouldn't stop me from wanting to date him. I told him I wasn't into sharing with the other team and was done over email.

The first two were strikeouts, and I was on to the third. Now, this guy was impressive. We chatted and decided to meet at a restaurant in Ann Arbor, MI. We sent pictures so we'd know what each other looked like. He really seemed like a nice guy, and I was somewhat excited to meet him.

Brad was 5'10" with reddish curly hair, longer to his shoulders (Bonus! I loved long hair on guys), *and* he was nicely built. Kind of puffed up and solid with hard butt and nice teeth. Yes, I did check out the full package well, not that package!

As I walk into the little café, I spot him right away and walk over. We immediately start having a wonderful conversation and eventually order our food. As soon as lunch is over, this very pretty young woman walks up, sits down next to him, and looks at me and smiles.

She was striking with her flowing long black hair, big eyes, puffy soft lips, and slender body with great waves. She was sexy, to say the least. Had I been a lesbian, I'd have gone for her in a heartbeat.

Now I'm wondering who this is and why she just invited herself to sit with us. Was she Brad's sister? They didn't really look like siblings. Was she a friend? Um, probably not. She was too touchy-feely with him to be just a friend. *Who is this woman?*

He speaks up and says he is very interested in getting to know me better and asks me if I feel the same. Before I answer that oddly direct question, I ask him who his friend is because, at this point, she hadn't even said hello or anything to him or me, she just showed up, sat down, and got all handsy with him.

"This is my wife, Katie, and she agrees. We'd both like to get to know you better and enjoy each other's company."

What the hell?

Not sure what my face looked like at that moment, but I'm pretty sure it wasn't a sexy look. Frozen in silence, I sat staring at both, like a deer in headlights. Finally, I spoke up.

"You mean you want to have a threesome?"

Brad chuckles. "Yes! Wouldn't that be wonderful? Two beauties loving each other, and I'd join in and pleasure both of you."

There was a part of me that was a little flattered, but a more significant part of me was shocked.

I stood up.

"No! No! Thanks, but no thanks."

The nerve! I felt set up and *almost* taken advantage of. After my anger settled down, I thought about it and laughed. She was admiring me from afar and liked what she saw, and he admired me up close and liked what he saw, so I must still have it! Ha!

290 • Peggy Watkins

The fourth guy was a charmer. I wasn't into driving too far so, I told him we'd meet for lunch halfway (which was a five-minute drive) at Red Lobster (starting to see a pattern here?). One of my questions to him, while we chatted on email, was, *do you smoke cigarettes?* He told me no, so we kept talking. It's important information, I just don't like the smell, and the smoke burns my eyes.

We arrive at Red Lobster, and the waitress asks where we'd like to sit, smoking or non (back in the day, restaurants allowed folks to smoke). He speaks up and says, "Smoking."

What? I pipe in. "Wait. You told me you don't smoke."

"I'm in the process of quitting."

Hmmm, lie number one already. Not good!

"Well, that's not what you said, and I don't want to sit anywhere near that smell."

The waitress, with the menus in hand, watched the awkward exchange, and then led us to the non-smoking section.

We first ordered a coffee while we looked over the menu. Our drinks came, and he watched as I doctored mine up with cream and sugar.

Then out of the blues, he says, "If you keep adding cream and sugar like that to your coffee, your ass will get as big as my ex-wife's," as he demonstrated with a hand gesture showing me how wide his ex-wife's ass was.

I stopped, looked at him, and shook my head. I stood up and threw down a dollar.

"Well, no wonder she left you. You're a big asshole," I said, with a hand gesture to show him how big of an asshole he was. I walked out, waiting until I got around the corner to giggle.

I can't believe the luck I have with men. I either suck bad at picking them, or I need to just turn lesbian. Something's gotta give!

By this time, I had concluded that I need to move down South, live happy for a while, and when the universe and God are ready for me to find that special someone, he'll find me. Right? Right!

So, this last guy was the fifth and the final. I had already decided that if this one was nutty or messed up in any way, I was seriously done. Not ever again will I date in Michigan. I will wait until I move to NC and start over. Besides, who doesn't want a cowboy? I love Southern men, tight jeans, cowboy boots, and hats, and their love for country music and dancing. And I *really* love that Southern drawl. Moving was only three months away, so no big deal. I can wait for Mr. Raahht.

We chatted through emails and AOL instant messenger (wow, did I just age myself?). We agreed to meet halfway (again, a five-minute drive for me). This time we met at Gilbert's Steak House. (Seeing a pattern here too as my get-a-way place). I arrived first and wait in the lobby for him, he showed up about 5 minutes late. I wore a white side-button top that crossed over my front and a blue skirt (above my knees a little more than usual but not slutty), and blue high heels.

Gary, my date, was wearing a funky plaid long-sleeved shirt with a nerdy checkered vest and baggy-ass jeans. He was nothing like I had ever dated before, a balding, short geek with bozo side tufts *but*, he had sexy eyes and a friendly smile. I was intrigued.

We sat, ordered a glass of wine, and chatted so much we forgot to look at the menu. It took about 30 minutes to even get our order in, we talked so much. Finally, we ordered, ate, and drank more wine and talked for over *three and a half hours*. It was pleasant. Gary was smart, well-spoken, engaging, and kind. And, did I mention his eyes?

Well, saying goodbye gave me goosebumps. Gary asked if he could kiss me goodbye, and I told him, no, I don't kiss on the first date, but allowed him to have a quick hug. He walked me to my car, helped me in, and ask if he could see me again.

Hell yes! We exchanged phone numbers and went on our way. The next day I got home from classes, and my neighbor and good friend, Dana comes walking out with this enormous flower display, it was gorgeous. I giggled and asked her who she had to blow for the flowers. She laughed right back and said the florist had left them with her, but they were mine. She wanted to know who I had to blow to get flowers.

Stunned, I thought, *who? Me? Really? Wow!* They were so big they filled my entire four-person table. They were stunning. The card read, *"Thanks for such an amazing lunch, I can't wait to see you again, G."*

Um, wow! No words can honestly describe my thoughts and excitement at that moment. I was like a kid loose in the candy shop for the first time. I was exploding with a gleam, and it lasted for days, every time I looked at my table cradling this mixture of tropical flowers. They must have cost him a hundred bucks at least.

We saw each other a week later, and in between, we talked on the phone every night and emailed daily. It was like we couldn't get enough of each other. And *he* pursued *me*. He called first, and then he called me every night after. He emailed first, and then we went back and forth on email. We hit it off right from the start, and it was terrific.

It was as if we were attached at the hip. Then after a few weeks, I allowed my youngest son to meet him, and I met his two kids, Stevie and Cami. Which, by the way, was against my rules. I never allowed my kids to meet anyone I dated. It was kind of funny when I first met them, they were at my door knocking, and as I opened the door, there all three stood. Cami was in front, she was five years old and missing a front tooth. She looked up at me, smiled really big, and with a brisk hand wave says, "Hi, I'm Cami. Are you my dad's girlfriend?"

Well, we hadn't really discussed our relationship at this point, but I smiled and said, "Maybe." The kids came in, and all three of them got along right away. Soon, we began taking our kid's places together, it was nourishing to the soul.

Then, about a month later, at the beginning of November 1998, I was visiting his house and asked if I could search for something on the internet with his computer. His email popped up, and it showed an email from a girl named GG who had sent a picture of herself in bed, with a sheet covering her breasts and her legs dangling out. I wasn't too happy to see that, and it scared me because we'd been having unprotected sex at this point. I questioned him about it, and he got really shitty with me saying, "If you are looking for a ring, you can walk out that door now because you're not getting one! I am not looking for a permanent relationship and certainly not anything more than just someone to hang out with."

Yep, he sure did! Well, I shook my head and fired right back.

"I wasn't looking for a ring, and you don't need to speak to me that way. I am concerned because if you are screwing other women, then I need to be informed, don't ya think?"

I grabbed my coat and purse, called for Jude, and we left. I fumed the entire 30-minute drive quietly home.

He called later that night, and I ignored his call. He called the next day and the next and the next. Four days later, I answered, we talked, he apologized, and we moved on just being friends with benefits but agreed to be monogamous. Hell, yes, I went to the doctor. I wasn't about to catch some crotch disease!

IN MID-DECEMBER, I started packing up all my stuff. In one weekend, I had just about everything packed as I was scheduled to start my new job in Charlotte right after New Year's Day. I'd traded in my little teal blue Ford Festiva for an extra-long van and planned to pack just the basics, whatever I could fit in my van, and go.

Gary came to visit one evening and asked me about all the boxes and stuff packed everywhere. I told him about my job waiting for me, and that'd I'd be moving right after Christmas to get settled in my new house. He looked at me with a sad face. I reminded him I didn't owe him notice or explanation since we were just friends with benefits.

He cocked his head and took my hand, looking me right in the eye and said, "I wish you would have told me this before I fell in love with you!"

Wait! But you said... and, you were a matter of fact when you said it! But...what the what?

We continued seeing each other, and a couple weeks later, I asked for a ride to the airport. I was traveling south for a few days to get the ball rolling with my new job and home. As we sat waiting, Gary seemed kind of lost, and I wondered if I was making a mistake by leaving. I pondered if he was, or could maybe be, the "one?" We had a drink, and then it was time to board. I grabbed my carry-on and kissed him goodbye, thanked him again for the ride, reminded him of my return time, and away I went.

As I went down the walkway, my stomach flipped, gurgling, and yelling. My heart raced, and my hands began sweating. These feelings were like nothing I had ever experienced before, and I felt a slight head rush reminiscent of my old weed-smoking habit. I got to the doorway and stopped. I stood staring at the flight attendant like a deer caught in headlights. I snapped out of it when she spoke up and asked me if I was okay. I said yes, but I forgot something. I turned and sprinted back down the walkway and out the door to the waiting area at Detroit Metro. There he was, standing at the window looking out at my plane. He saw me right away and looked confused as he rushed towards me.

"You're going to miss your flight, ya know."

I kissed him (big time).

"What if I'd rather stay and not go? What if I'd rather be with you?"

He grabbed me and kissed me back all the while the lady at the desk kept saying, "The door is closing, Miss. I pulled away from him and smiled at her.

"Close it, I'm good."

IN APRIL OF **1999,** we moved in together and were married in June of 2000. We have had 22 years of a good marriage. We've been mostly happy, but yes, we have had our share of issues. However, we worked through them and toughed it out. Isn't that what a real marriage is? You choose to work it out rather than running and quitting.

I must admit, one of the funniest moments in our marriage was when I met one of Gary's ex's new husbands. She had something of his and offered to drop the items off to us. I was getting ready to go to the grocery store and grab a few things.

We lived in a nice neighborhood in a simple ranch home, three bedrooms, one bath, living room, kitchen, with a full basement and an attached garage.

The overhead garage doors were open, and I was standing in the doorway that went from the kitchen to the garage, chatting with Gary before heading to the store. That's when Gary's ex- and her new hubby pull in behind my car. My back is to the driveway when I hear her husband exit their vehicle and begin talking.

Why do I know that voice?

I turn, and it's…*drum roll please…'cause you ain't gonna believe this…*

GEORGE!

Do you remember Red Lobster, you-need-to-reimburse-me-for-dinner George?? Yep. You read that right. The Very. Same. George.

I throw up my hand, waved, and holler.

"Hey, George! How ya doing?" I was smiling so big and trying hard—I mean hard—not to laugh.

296

The look on his face at that very moment was priceless! He stopped speaking dead in the middle of his sentence and stood there just looking with his mouth open, catching flies. His wife said something, he got back into the car, and off they went. I have no idea how he explained that reaction to her, or if he ever did, and truthfully, I don't care. It's called pay backs, baby! Or watch out from whom you request kitty. Not everyone gives up the goods, and not everyone is going to walk away without making you pay a "red" price. I still giggle at this story; I can't help it.

Later that evening, Gary couldn't stop laughing about the look on his face. He said he looked as if he'd just seen a ghost and was scared to death. Still, to this day, as I write this, I think back to that moment and snicker with my evil, tittering, chin-rolling, head-cocked snorting.

In December of 1999, Gary proposed to me in Boone, North Carolina. He had booked us a suite at a castle in the mountains in Boone, and it was so romantic. He planned everything perfectly.

Gary claimed said, we were getting out of town to get away in case the world collapse, you know the 2000 theories. That evening we just chilled and went around town looking for a nice restaurant to enjoy a lovely New Year's Eve dinner.

Little did I know, he had already made reservations somewhere and managed to pull off getting to the restaurant without me having a clue.

New Year's Eve dinner was amazingly fantastic, even though I thought he was acting strange. I asked him a few times if he was okay, and he kept saying things like, "Yeah, I'm just worried about the computers failing because of my business." Well, that made sense to me.

Little did I know that one of the most memorable moments of my life was about to happen.

We get back to our little romance headquarters to relax. Gary turns on the TV so we can watch the ball drop, and at around 2 minutes to the

298 • Peggy Watkins

stroke of midnight, he pulls out two silver goblets and fills them with chilled champagne, he hands me one. I look at this beautiful, shiny, bubbling, over-the-top goblet, and notice it's engraved, "*Peg, will you marry me?*"

He smiles as I sit there with my mouth hitting the floor.

"Umm, can you say 'yes' in 13 seconds?"

Speechless, I nod then literally as the countdown from 10 begins, I said, yes. We set our wedding date for June 23rd, 2000.

ONCE AGAIN, CALAMITY WOULD HIT, of course, with the beautiful family that loved me so well. In early 2000, Virgie had a stroke. I was called and told to, "get your ass to the hospital and see how bad it really is." Denise might have figured out her mother was a hypochondriac.

She was living a few states away and didn't want to come back unless it was necessary. Hmm, you'd think she'd rush to be by her mommy's side, right? Neither she nor her brother rushed to her side as a matter of fact—only me. I was the one who ran.

I was told that on a scale of 1-10, she had a 9.5 stroke on the scale of severity. I wasn't hurt, nor did I cry. I am not sure what I felt. Nothing. I don't recall feeling anything. I looked at her, lying in bed, nonresponsive, and it was at that moment I remembered the verbal, mental, and physical abuse I had suffered at her hands. I recalled so many experiences, and yet I felt nothing for her. I didn't care if she died. There were no feelings of hurt or sorrow or even anger.

I visited her a few times while she was in the hospital. Quite soon after she was admitted, they put her on a ventilator and asked her kids (Denise, Donny, and me) to decide whether to take her off the ventilator and just let her breathe or let her die. The doctor felt she was going to die since there was no response yet. She had some brain activity but not much—this might not have changed before the stroke, just saying.

Let me say this, the only reason I was included in that conversation was that the doctor came into the waiting room and asked to speak to her children. There were a lot of families in there, and my aunt was the one who immediately said, "That means you too, Peggy." Denise and Donny just looked at me as if, no, you are not her child, but they allowed me to be included.

Denise, Donny, and I all stepped into the hallway with the doctor. Denise looked at Donny and asked him what he thought we should do, he shrugged his shoulders. Then she looked at me (I was surprised) and asked me the same. I explained that I thought it would be best to let her go then watch her suffer for years. It was decided. Unplug her and let the chips fall where they may.

And as luck would have it, she breathed on her own! Part of me recalled when I was younger how I was told that if I did terrible things, God would punish me for it in ways of mutilating my body, mind, and or my kids. For a moment, I thought, *maybe this was God's payback to her for treating me so shitty?*

Just to be clear, I do **NOT** believe God does paybacks, nor do I think he hurts people. I do, however, believe in a higher being, and I refer to him as my bestie. And my bestie makes it clear in His word (the Bible) that we reap what we sow. Maybe she was reaping.

In the next few months, Virgie would be in rehab trying to learn to talk, eat, and walk as she was damaged full body from the stroke. During one hospital visit, I decided to leave for a while because Virgie was sleeping. Denise and Donny were both in the room, so I let them know I was headed out for a bit. Denise started rattling on about her mommy being in this hospital and how it was my fault that she even had a stroke. Fortunately, the doctor was in the room, and he spoke up and told Denise, no one caused Virgie to have a stroke. It just happened. Donny even spoke up and told her it wasn't my fault. And for a very brief moment in time, I saw the brother I used to have when he'd hide us in the closet with crackers and water to be safe. As odd as it sounds, that moment was kind, and I appreciated him sticking up for me, if only for a nanosecond.

Eventually, I stopped visiting Virgie. Then, Denise made the decision to take her to her home and care for her, and I was glad. I was delighted because they were both out of my life, at least for that time.

LIFE MOVED ON FOR ME, and I became a Mrs. for the third time (and you know the Green M&M lady's motto is, *Third Time's A Charm!*) Our wedding was in Florida at Cypress Gardens (Presently Lego Land—insert eye roll) we took our kids with us, rented a house with a pool, and chilled for a week.

The wedding itself was fabulous. We rented a limo, and all piled in on our way to get married. Cami was my flower girl, Ava My daughter in law, my maid of honor, and both my boys gave me away. Stevie was Gary's best man, and Isiah (my grandson) was our little ring man. It was perfect!

We dressed nice but not in sweltering hot clothing, simple sundresses for the girls, and a short white silky one for me—the guys all in blue dress pants but lighter, not bulky, and overhaul straps with white shirts. Ava and I both had a small bouquet, and Cami had a flower ball.

Very short, sweet, and straightforward. That is precisely what we wanted. Perfect.

On the way to the wedding place, Isaiah was in a car seat by the window. Every time we stopped at a red light, Jude and Stevie would tell him to roll down the window and ask the car next to us for Grey Poupon. Well, he did but as little guys are learning to chat and often things don't come out exactly the way they should, Isaiah rolls down the window, looks over and yells (not too loud but little four-year-old loud-so kind of loud), "Hey buddy, you got any grey poop?" Isaiah sits there, just giggling, looking at the guy in the car as the guy is looking over at him, laughing hysterically as well as everyone in the limo. It was a great limo ride, fun times.

After our wedding, Gary's ex was an issue on more than one occasion. I recall one weekend when the kids brought these brown paper bags of food labeled, Breakfast, Lunch, Snack, Dinner, and Late Snack with their names on them as well. They loaded up the fridge with all these brown bags. I noticed it was enough to get them through the entire weekend, so I asked my husband, why? What's going on? But he didn't know.

Later that evening, I made a nice sit-down dinner like I always had every evening before. It was our family time for my kids and me. I made meatloaf, mashed potatoes, gravy, green beans, and strawberry shortcake for dessert. As I was passing the plates around for each person to dig in, I noticed my step kids not accepting anything and just sitting there looking like two lost poodles.

"Have you already eaten?"

They looked at each other, all nervous-like. "No."

"Are you not hungry?"

"Yes, we're hungry."

"Then why are you not eating?"

Cami speaks up. "Mom said that you are putting poison in the food and don't eat it. I'm scared you'll poison me."

I spoke up, "Well, why would I do such a thing? I eat this food too, and so does my son. Are we poisoned? I think you must have misunderstood her. I'm sure she didn't mean that."

Cami was adamant that's what she was told, and Stevie was too. Gary told them to eat if they were hungry, or there would be no brown bag food. They ate.

I felt so sad that they had to be put through such an ordeal. Why would someone say such an awful thing? One would think that if your ex's new spouse treated your kids well that you wouldn't turn your kids against them for no reason.

— Soap Box —

I will never understand ex's who do shit like this. And, honestly, if you are one of them, you need to take a good long look in the mirror and start challenging yourself to be a better co-parent! If your ex is remarried or has a significant other and that person treats your kids well, you should be appreciative. It is *NOT* about you or your ex. It's about doing the right thing and being human and respectful to your children and yourself. You should be happy someone else loves your kids enough to treat them well and not like crap. Show you are a bigger person and not an ass! *Getting off my soapbox now and back to the story. *

Throughout the years, we had other issues like when I fixed Cami's bangs that were totally messed up and jagged one morning before school. I trimmed them and made them straight, curled them up, and sent her off to school. Well, mama bear was pissed that I cut her daughter's hair, and she called my home and yelled at me on the answering machine.

I chuckled when I heard it, let it go, and moved on.

We had a hard go of things for a while, and yes, there were a few times I almost threw in the towel and walked away but, I kept telling myself that things will get better. *You've come too far to allow bullshit to hurt you.* So, I kept pressing on and falling in love more every day. After about six years, I learned how to let it go and not let it be an issue.

Actually, I started going to church and talked with the preacher one Sunday after church, and he challenged me to pray for her every day for 30 days. I thought I would rather die than ask God to bless this woman who was such a pain in my azz, but I did. Every. Day. For. 30. Days.

I noticed this after I stopped thinking about her so much, and things got calmer. I stopped dwelling on somethings she did and smiled about stuff I did with the kids. I didn't care that she drove past my house every morning and would slow down as she did. I waited for her one morning with a coffee cup in hand and waved with a smile as she slowed down. You know, funny thing, I never noticed her driving by again. I guess that old saying is true, pray for your enemies, and they will flee. She'd done flew the coop! As my southern granny would have said.

So, when you hear the first five years of a second marriage is most challenging, it is accurate. Also, I highly recommend counseling before you get married again to make sure you are both on all kinds of the same levels. Even if you think you are, you are probably not! Counseling will help you find these differences and work through them before you get married, so then the sailing will be much smoother. Not that you'll *never* have conflict, heck, every marriage has trouble here and there, but counseling will hopefully help you spot issues first and keep you moving in the right direction. It's really about COMMUNICATION! There's some free advice for you. You're welcome.

Therefore, for many years, we've had some issues with the kids and ex's, lots of laughs, and some tears too. Loss of parents, friends, and a few family members, and we also gained family with grandchildren and nieces, as well as adding good friends along the way.

On Thanksgiving morning in 2001, Gary's dad passed.

I loved Papa Joe. He treated me so well and was a force to be reckoned with. No one had better mess with his family or piss him off. Just an old Polish dude who loved fast cars, beer, his wiener dog, and Betty Boop!

My stepdad Claude passed a few years after Joe, and that was very hard too. I loved Claude so much. He was the only real father figure I had and the only real man that loved me like his own child. He was a gentle giant, and his Dr. Doolittle ways with all animals were unbelievable! My mom suffered greatly after his passing. She was genuinely heartbroken. Which is why I think she passed two years after, in 2005.

I know the toughest of all was in April of 2005 when I lost my mother, Chelcie. That hit me like a ton of bricks and broke my heart like nothing had ever broken it before.

WE WERE IN FLORIDA on vacation when my mom, Chelcie, passed. Right before I went, we had just spoken on the phone. We planned to spend a week together when I got back so she could show me the correct way to plant a few things in my garden. I so looked forward to spending time with my mom. She was 77 years old, and her health wasn't the greatest but not the worst either.

I learned in a psychology class that it often takes between 2-7 years to work through one's grief over a lifelong partner, and sometimes it can be longer depending on the person and the way their loved one passed. My mom was indeed grief-stricken over Claude. He was her whole life. The only man who truly gave two shits about her and protected her was now gone. She never recovered.

The passing of my mother was horrible for me, especially while being in Florida and visiting with Denise. She had gotten the phone call while I was at the beach with the kids, and soon as we got back, she followed me into her guest room, looked at me with a smirk, and said, "Oh yeah, Chelcie died! Boom dead! I got the call a couple hours ago."

I was devastated and trying to wrap my mind around what she just said. Then she continued with, "I wouldn't cry for her if I were you. You know she wouldn't cry for you. Don't mourn her, you don't need to. She was nothing to you. She gave you away, and *we* had to take you. If it wasn't for mommy and daddy, you'd probably be dead somewhere today. Fuck her!"

I was frozen with confusion. Listening to Denise tell me my mother was dead and her saying, "boom dead," then all the rest of the garbage that spewed out of her evil mouth was more than I could handle. I said nothing to her, grabbed my phone and went outside, and called my sister Addy Mae. We talked, cried, and I told her I would come back home right away. The funeral was to be in seven days.

We left Florida the next day and took a couple days driving back with the three youngest kids. It was torture for me to operate a vehicle as the tears never stopped rolling out of my eyes. And they continued for a month afterward.

We rolled into town at about 5:00 PM. I asked to be dropped off at a church I'd been going to. I had a key, so I let myself in, locked the door behind me, and ran to the altar and fell. I cried out, asking God, *Why my mom? Why now? What did she ever do to deserve to die? Why? Why, God, why?* I cried at that alter for over six hours that evening, and funny thing, I never felt alone. There were times I'd dry up my tears a little and sit quietly almost as if I was being hugged by someone big and I felt cradled. I still hurt. I still cried. I still asked why, but I got through it.

Her death brought out the meanness of a couple of my siblings, my mother's other children. I saw them for who they were more transparent than I had ever before. People say death and money make people crazy, and it really does. Even when there is no money, it's the material things that make people act stupid toward one another.

My mother and Claude were not rich, but they did own a little property and many things in the house, such as dishes, knick-knacks. Mom had a few rings, paw had a few old Bibles. Honestly, nothing worth any kind of money, only things of sentimental value other than the SUV and house, which were old and not worth much either.

A couple of my siblings felt that since I was adopted, I had no right to anything. I had no right to step foot on the property, and if I did, they let me know I'd be arrested for trespassing.

I wondered what I had done to them, but since I know those couple act up frequently, I let it roll and spoke only to my brother Glenn who didn't feel that way. I asked him for two aprons, two quilts that mom had made, and two large and two small iron skillets (mom had about 50 iron skillets, seriously). I asked for two each so that I could pass one to each of my boys since they were close to their grandma, and she loved them very much too. I also asked for the items that lay in my memory and meant something to me.

Glenn managed to get me one quilt, one iron skillet, and some pictures. He also gave me mom's red head scarf and little clip purse she loved. That meant a lot to me.

ONE MONTH LATER, TO THE DAY, my older brother Duane passed. He had lived in a nursing home since he was 13 years old. He was never able to walk or sit up on his own, and he had to eat baby food all his life. He could only speak a few words, and "mom" was his favorite word. He loved mom. It broke her heart to put him in the home. But, having all the other kids and then experiencing what happened to me, she felt it was the best decision for everyone. It was hard for her to make that sacrifice, but she made the best of it and visited him often.

Eight days after mom passed, I was standing at my slider door looking out my backyard. It was a soft rainy day, and things were starting to pop out as spring was on its way. Taking advantage of being the only one in the house that morning, I stood there thinking of my mom and let the tears roll. My mind wandered to Duane. I hadn't seen him in years, not because I didn't want to, but rather because no one would they tell me where he was staying at any given time. One thing my mom and a couple of my siblings were good at was keeping secrets.

They were the 'Secret Keepers,' and I never understood their reasoning. Maybe they felt I would tell their secrets to the four horsemen of hell, Virgie, Ardy, and their two spawns. Nonetheless, it was as if someone was standing right next to me, speaking directly to me. The voice was clearly my mother's. Of that, I am positive. She told me, "Go visit your brother."

After I stopped crying, I went to K-Mart and bought him a frog, blanket, and ChapStick, and then I went to see him. My mother's one sister, and I were close, and she had told me where Duane had been placed. A care facility two miles from my home.

I had called the care home and was told I could come to visit. It just happened to be Duane's birthday, April 15th. I was excited to see him yet, I wasn't sure if he knew mom had passed. How does one tell someone who might not understand a word you say that kind of news? I spoke to the nurse about it, and she said no one had been to visit him in two months. The nurse told me she was glad someone finally came. Hearing this made me sad because not only did she tell me *that*, but she also said he'd gotten sick about a week ago around the time my mom passed and wasn't getting any better.

As I went into his room, he lay there sleeping in his bed like a sweet little boy with a five o'clock shadow. I shut the door behind me so we could have privacy, it'd been a long time since I'd seen him, years.

I nudged him. "Hello, Duane. Do you know me? I'm your little sister, Peggy."

He looked me dead in the eyes and then, without a word, turned his gaze to my right side, smiled with the biggest smile I'd ever seen him have, and yelled out, "Mom!"

It was also at that very moment I felt a warmth come over my right side, the same heat as when I stood at my slider and heard my mother's voice. Maybe I'm crazy, but I think it was her, and I'm okay with that.

Within a few minutes of being with my brother, the nurse came into the room and said that she had called my sister who had power of attorney for Duane. She had been told that I was "not" his little sister and was never to be allowed to see him again. I calmly nodded to the nurse, kissed my big brother on the cheek, and told him I loved him and was sorry for not visiting more, but I would have had I known where he was. He smiled as if he understood, but of course, I wonder. I walked out with tears rolling and once again a silent stab in my heart. About three weeks later, on May 7th, around noon, my brother Duane passed away. April 7th, around noon, my mother had died. One month to the day and about the same time. Wow, right? That experience has always made me wonder if there really is life after death. I have many questions and thoughts on this topic, but that's for another book, another time.

There isn't a day that goes by that I do not think of my beautiful mother and wish she was here so I could redeem myself and be a better daughter. There are no do-overs in life. We have to accept things we have done and things that have happened as well as forgive ourselves first, then forgive others so we can move forward and live with some kind of peace within ourselves.

I sucked ass as a daughter, and I blame myself because as I got older, I should have, could have, would have had enough sense to live and learn and do better, but I didn't, and I'm paying the price with a broken heart. It is too late to make amends with my mom, but at least I learned. That price tag is a harrowing one, don't follow in my footsteps.

Not to mention why in the hell did my sister say I wasn't his sister and to not allow me to visit? WTF? Pure meanness. Complete jealousy. Total ignorance.

On June 5th, 2005, Virgie passed. After a few years of Denise caring for her mommy, she made a choice to put her back into a care home in Michigan. I will say Virgie was now walking (slowly but walking), and her speech was never right, to begin with, but now there were only ranting words no one could understand while her throwing her arms up, demanding shit, as usual. She fed herself, but it was as if you were watching a person who had not eaten in years as food fell out of her mouth and onto her lap. She struggled. To be honest, I felt sorry for her having to live like this.

Virgie had caught a cold, which turned into pneumonia, and she couldn't beat it. I visited her in the hospital and forgave her for being such a bitch to me. She passed about 30 minutes or so later.

During her funeral, I looked at her in her casket and felt no sorrow or sadness. I once again felt nothing.

Her parting gift to me was giving me pneumonia. Two weeks later, I came down with it in both lungs, and I was a sick woman for a few weeks with a cough that lingered even longer. I laugh about it now and think to myself, she just had to have the last word. Old. Bitch.

WHEN GARY'S SON Stevie turned 15, he moved in with us. I felt we became a lot closer, and of course, he and Jude got along like two peas in a pod. They always have—and still do—and for that, I'm thankful. I feel very comfortable saying I have three sons and a daughter, and it makes my heart sing to say so.

A couple of years later, Cami would turn 15 and move in with us as well. By this time, Jude was in college, and Stevie was about a year away from college. Cami and I never got close during her time living at our house. There were many times I'd ask if she wanted to go out to lunch and or catch a movie with me, and she'd tell me no, that she and her mom had plans to go see that movie or she was going to lunch with her mom. There was always that one reason why she could not or would not go with me, her mom.

I stopped asking after about five or six offers. I felt crushed, so I just stopped. Or maybe I was tired of fighting for relationships that I thought would never happen, and I just gave up.

However, the last couple of years have been great. I feel Cami and I have connected on a more respectful level and gained a relationship as stepmom and stepdaughter, with closeness and more in-depth understanding, and I could not be happier. We have done a few things together, and it is finally a relationship I can smile about. I love spending time with my kids. Time worked in my favor with her, and I am happy it did.

As the years passed, Gary and I became a close, loving couple, and by that, I mean we grew together, not just physically but in heart and mind. We enjoyed each other's company and travels. Things seemed to be rolling nicely with many aspects of our marriage.

We celebrated our 5th anniversary in Hawaii. Our 10th on a cruise to the Caribbean. We'd made it a thing to go on a cruise about every three years, and gosh, do we love them. Our 15th anniversary, we celebrated in London, Paris, and Rome, spending about five days at each place. Honestly, my life now is unique from what it was growing up and through my 20s.

Over the last 10 years, I have tried to build a better relationship with my dad, Ardy, and Maudie Jo. Honestly, I still don't like her, and I still feel very intimidated when I am around my sperm donor. They only come to my home when I have a big Thanksgiving meal, and others are here too. I also have been having a summer party every year since 2000 to which I have invited them each year, but they have only come about two times.

They come to town all the time for grocery shopping or a simple trip to K-Mart or a garage sale, but they don't come to visit at my house. I am always inviting them, and I tell them often, "Stopover, I'm only two minutes from the store." But they still have an excuse claiming they have something to do and need to get back home. Ironically, they will go to her daughter's home, which is 40 minutes away and visit all day. What does that say to me? What it's always said. I am not important to him, nor was I ever.

I must give credit where credit is due, though. Ardy will call me about once a month, which is way more than he ever has before in my entire life. I often wondered if it is because he wants to put on a good show for my husband since he is a prominent businessman, maybe he thinks that my husband is "somebody" in his eyes? I have no clue, but I promise you the feelings of fear and shame still run through my bones every time I get around him.

I know that he calls his other two kids daily. I know this because he told me so, and he said he worries more about them. I have no idea why he would say that to me, but he did, then he laughed and said they were not as smart as me. I'm sure he said that to play off what accidentally spilled out of his mouth while I was visiting at his home once.

314 • Peggy Watkins

When Ardy was around 87 years old, I'd take him to many of his appointments at the VA in Ann Arbor—an hour's drive—and in Battle Creek, both require a lot of driving, and I have never once asked him for gas money, or anything. It's just the right thing to do to care for my elder father.

I must admit that he paid for gas once and offered a couple of other times. Bought lunch twice and one foo-foo coffee, of which he complained about the price (A latte`). No, I am not keeping track, I'm just giving credit where credit is due. Keeping it real!

During this time, I began trying to help more with things at their home and driving him to and from appointments. Twice a week, I used to make and deliver homemade dinners such as vegetable soups, chili, pot roast, potpies, pork chops, whole chickens, and all the fixings. I portioned it out into little dishes, enough to last them all week, so my stepmom wouldn't need to cook. I did this because she had a stroke and was now using a walker to get around, and I figured this would help her out while keeping them nourished.

I set them up with their medications and made sure they had what they needed. After I spent an entire day setting things up (drugs, home visits with nurses, housecleaners, food deliveries, etc.) the next stop, everything was changed. I was told at that time that Maudie Jo's daughter would take care of things for them. Okay. Fine.

I busted my ass, running him to Ann Arbor and Battle Creek for years and continuously rearranging my appointments and clients to help him. He never asked me if a particular day would be better for me. Ardy would just book appointments, making them as early as possible. I can't count how many times I woke at 5:00 am to get ready and get to his house, pick him up and drive an hour to wherever to be there 15-20 minutes before his appointment because he would have a fit if we were not there at least 20 minutes before. Hmm, well, thanks, Peggy!

When I delivered what would be the last meal to them, Maudie Jo gave me a disgusted look, and her loud sigh then told me that I didn't need to keep doing this, that she was "perfectly able" to cook their own meals and she'd rather I stopped. My dad was standing there, and he agreed with her. I asked them if they wanted my help with meds or anything else. I was told they had it under control and that I didn't need to come so often and not to bring meals anymore. So, I stopped. I did this for about two years, and then in the summer of 2019, they tell me enough. Ok. Fine. I. Stopped.

VII

HE WILL

NEVER STOP!

IN NOVEMBER OF **2019,** I got a call from a distant family member on my dad's side, Karen. She was crying and asking for my help. She told me that she had been molested by my brother, Donny when she was younger. She continued with Donny molested my toddler too.

During the phone conversation, she told me that she thought he had changed, and she had gotten close to Donny and allowed him around her and her child and even felt safe enough to leave him to babysit.

I went limp. Silent. Cold. I wanted to throw up. I felt the anger inside of me like nothing ever before, and I sat still on the other end of the phone while Karen sobbed, telling me she had turned him in to the authorities.

— Soap Box —

First, why, after he molested you, would you even want to be around him even if the fucker did change. And, people like that usually never stop! Why in the world would she allow someone who was accused of molestation in 1974 and then convicted for rape in 1988 and she herself claimed he molested her as well, why? Why in the world would you allow him to babysit? Who does that?

Things started falling into place with this scenario, and my mind took me back 47 years. That night he molested me rushed back to me,

318

and I felt violated all over again. I hated him. I hated what happened. I hated that my dad, stepmom, and anyone who stuck up for him against a little girl who was the innocent one in all that mess.

Karen and I kept in touch over the next few months. Slowly, I noticed this whole ordeal had once again, turned into a nightmare but in some ways, it's been good. Good to get it all out in the open, good to move towards justice, and right to support one another.

I went a step further. I went through my family's social media friends lists and deleted those who (only 3) were friends with Donny. I felt that if they wanted to be associated with him, that was their business, but I wasn't willing to continue with this lie and act as if things were honky dory, so I deleted a few family members, that simple.

Obviously, that action was noticed, and Denise would of course stick up for Donny and tell me how much of a liar and troublemaker I was to do such a thing.

Well, I supposed she could have her own thought and ideas too, but I'll be goddamned if I ought to listen to her shit anymore so, I sure as hell blocked her on all connections. Problem solved! My only thought was, *why didn't I do this years ago or better yet, why did I keep trying?*

Then, that very same evening, about an hour later, Ardy, called me. And, as I sat in my living room chair listening to him throw a fit, shrieking, and roaring about how Donny shouldn't be punished, Ardy once again claimed everyone was lying. With his voice so loud piercing my ear, his bellowing slipped into a far distance, and I sat in silence. My mind drifted back 47 years ago. No one believed me. Many called me a liar. And all who said he would never do such a thing treated me as if I was Typhoid Mary.

He continued without even giving me a chance to speak, he shouted and tried making me feel guilty. Finally, I interrupted him.

"Do you think the girl that claimed he raped her back in 1989 lied too? Because he was found guilty and went to prison for a couple years.

Do you think she lied?" I shouted back through the phone line shaking with anger.

"Yes, by-God, I do think she lied on him!"

"Do you think everyone who has made this same claim lied?!"

"It all started years ago with *you*, Peggy. This is all your fault. Why should Donny have to pay for something that happened years ago?

Hmmm? Strange? Curious why he thinks it's okay to do something, and even if it comes out years later, it's just OK?

Ardy spouted at me that it wasn't right, Donny's changed. He has a house and a dog and a garden. He's doing good. But then you want to kick him while he's down and make him look bad."

Here we go again. It's my fault. (Insert middle finger, eye roll and a deep breath).

"He shouldn't have to pay for something that happened a long time ago, that's not right!" he repeated furiously.

Well, first off, he got away with my molestation in 1974. He paid time for raping of that girl and now he is being charged with raping another young child, now not years ago but now!

I sat quietly for about 10 seconds, then unloaded.

"Fuck that and fuck you! How dare you blame me for what he has done. How dare you point the finger at me over him molesting *me* AND another family member and *then* her child too, not to mention RAPING a total stranger! How fucking dare you… blame me for what HE has done!" I roared as my body trembling with madness.

"It *is* your fault. Had you not started this, none of this shit would be going on today. He shouldn't have to pay for something that happened years ago, this isn't right, it just isn't right!" He bellowed once again.

Without hesitation, I said, "He is paying for the rape he committee

NOW not when he molested me 47 years ago and this conversation is over. Do not *EVER* bother me again!"

I hung up and sat very still as I thought maybe a tear would roll out but nothing. Not one drop of liquid came from my eyes or my heart, nothing. I was cold. Unemotional. Sitting in tranquility like I had never experienced. This was truly a touching moment for my soul. I sat allowing that incident to remind me that this is how he acted years ago, and this is how he took his son's side and turned everyone against me when I was a ten-year-old little girl. I vowed never to forget that again, and I will never forget!

My husband was steps away during this entire conversation. He told me that he could hear Ardy screaming at me and then asked why I didn't hang up sooner.

"Why did you allow him to abuse you like that?" he asked.

"Because it's what I've always done. But no more."

As I sat in my living room chair, I could hear my mother's voice, "The truth will come out. Watch and listen for it, Pooch!" clear as day she was talking to me!

Since the phone call episode, I have not had any contact with Denise, Ardy, or his dim-witted wife, Maudie Jo and my life has been peaceful. I am not worried when the phone rings as I *know* it's none of them, and I'm happy as hell it's not!

OUR FIRST COURT DAY was January 8th, 2020, and of course, I went. I wanted to know what was going to happen to him and if he was going to be punished this time or get away with it as the past showed he typically did. How could he continue being a sexual deviant and get away with it? How could he have molested me—his sister—and now other family members?

Over the next several months, Karen and I became closer than we ever had been. She seemed sincere. Broken. Hurt. Unsettled. I wanted more than anything to help her and be there for her. I wanted to do what I could to make sure this sick bastard goes to prison for life so he cannot hurt anyone ever again, that was my goal, just to help her heal and move forward—something no one ever did for me.

I felt comfortable helping Karen as we bonded and began building a relationship, until we didn't.

Court days …

January 8th, 2020, 11:00 AM Hillsdale, Michigan. (Arraignment hearing)

The trail is set for 11:00 AM in court. The brick building has big windows, and it smells of old, stale tobacco and criminals. The ladies working the front are all behind an enclosed glass protectant with a little microphone to respond to visitors (the sign should say Victims instead of Visitors).

My husband is with me, and we wait inside on this brisk, chilly morning in Michigan. Soon enough, Ardy and a niece, Patty Raye (to whom I am remarkably close—but she is also very close to her grandpa, my dad) come walking towards us in the sitting section.

The seating area in the courthouse waiting room is tiny making for an awkward situation. In the corner by the big glass windows, are eight orange plastic seats with black metal legs. An extremely uncomfortable environment to relax in while you're waiting to experience one of the scariest times of your life.

Relax my ass! I am uptight. Nervous. Scared. I am 56 years old now but still worried my dad will go off on me and yell the way he did when I was 10 when I was going home with him from foster care. That court day flashes in my mind as he takes a seat across from us. He doesn't even look my way, though, not one glance. No, not one.

Patty Raye speaks and says hi. My husband responds to her while my heart races. My hands are wet with sweat like I've just pulled them out from under a faucet, and my knees weaken as I stand up to walk out to the very tiny foyer to wait for Karen.

We've been waiting for about 5 minutes—which feels like five hours. Karen finally arrives with her friend, who came for support. I am glad to see her, and I can tell she is nervous too.

We all stand in the foyer for a few minutes, and now we're wandering into the actual lobby. Everyone is within spitting distance of each other in that tiny space. We check the screen for Donny's name and scheduled time of appearance. It is still set at 11:00 AM.

As soon as the doors open to the courtroom, we file in and take a seat in the third row from the back, made up of the ugly vexing orange chairs. There are only five rows of six places. My niece and Ardy enter last and sit right behind us. Not a word is exchanged between any of us. The tapestry of silence and emotion in the room is so thick you can cut the air with a butter knife. The judge is sitting in her chair straight ahead and in the left corner is a large TV screen that is featuring some local criminals for our entertainment.

Others in the room are in orange jumpsuits, chained together (just like you see in the movies!), and are being escorted by an officer to sit in the front row for sentencing. Donny is not in the chain gang. It is his first appearance, so his debut is on a big screen.

It's now his turn. An officer walks him into a little room somewhere, and he sits down in front of the camera. He is wearing his best outfit, a white tee shirt with his hair looking like it needs a good wash. Despite his appearance, his arrogance proceeds him in the courtroom as it does in society.

When the judge asks questions, he responds with a smug shoulder shrug and an I-don't-give-a-shit attitude. He is letting the judge know that he has an attorney, but his lawyer couldn't be here today. I find that a bit odd but hey, what do I know?

He also says he isn't going to plead guilty and is going to take this to court.

Okay, then.

The next court date is set; January 15th same place, same time.

As we all exit the courtroom, Karen, I, my husband, and Karen's friend walk together as a group. Seconds after we exit, my niece and my dad follow out. As they begin walking down the sidewalk, Karen calls to Ardy and says, "Ardy, I love you, and I just wanted you to know that." She had been close to my dad and his wife, unlike me.

Even though Ardy was once again sticking up for Donny, Karen is trying so hard to be kind and loving. With tears held back, she steps up to him and also expresses her love again. I have a gut feeling this is not going to go well. I step up next to her and brace myself.

Ardy stands there with a grin, shaking his head, looked right at her, and says, "If you were a man, I'd whip your ass right here!"

Well, the shit just hit the fan, and I'm pretty sure *he* started it this time.

I grab Karen with both arms, wrapping them around her trying to move her away as she yells back. (Yes, it is quite a spectacle). He verbalizes more trash discourse, and out of the blue, Karen yells, "Why is it okay with you that your son does this? Why do you think he shouldn't be punished for raping and molesting people? Is it because you *raped Chelcie*? Is that why you've treated Peggy like shit all her life? Is that why you hate her? Is that why you think it's okay because you did it too?!"

Holy shit! Did I hear that, right? Yep. I. Did.

There's no response other than a smirk and a mumble as he walks away with my niece to their car, they drive off as I stand wishing for some sort of reaction from him.

Would he just admit why he hates me and has treated me like shit my whole life?! Would he confess that he raped my mother? Am I a rape baby? Jesus. Seriously, am I?

15th of January. It seems as if the courts waste time and money, taxpayer money when they make all these court dates to only rehash the same shit, then set yet another court date. I promise you it gets OLD!

There are more court dates and many phone calls with Karen. She calls a lot, and I call her as well. I want to check on her and her little one through this ordeal. While things continue to roll in the courtroom, I continue with mine and hubby's plan to go to Florida for a month. We leave the day after the last court date in January 2020.

I'm eager to get away and be free from all this emotional mess. I keep in contact with Karen, though. I want her to know she has someone, and I feel I can be that person for her. My heart bleeds for her.

Seeing the beach and smelling the ocean air does a body and mind good. Just knowing I was miles away from all of them made me happy. It felt right. The memories of living there many years ago filled my heart, and I wanted to rush back to that time and relive the days of glory. If I could, I'd stay forever. I mean, who wouldn't love their toes in the sand and the rustling of the waves rushing up. Finding unique shells and sunsets. Oh, the evenings!

While we are in Florida, we hear of the virus COVID-19 for the first time. We still don't think much about it and go about our vacation as usual.

By the time we arrive home on February 18th, COVID is becoming a big deal, and things are starting to 'get real.' About mid-March, Governor Whitmore pretty much closed the state down.

Gary and I are approaching our 20th anniversary, but with the Coronavirus pandemic happening, I'm thinking we'll probably celebrate being locked down. At least we'll have each other and a bottle of wine. Maybe not toilet paper but we'll have wine. Not sure what the TP craz was all about but, my neighbors are going to get tired of watching me run my bare ass across the lawn due to our TP shortage, but our dogs don't mind! Ha-ha-ha! -I'm kidding-but it's a thought just in case!

Karen and I kept in touch, and things were good. Until, she changed her mind and didn't want me around anymore. I am not exactly sure what triggered this but, it never took much for her to blow things out of proportion and create a scenario that maybe didn't exactly happen or didn't happen at all. So, honestly, who knows?

I know I wasn't going to indulge her with a Jerry Springer moment so, when she demanded that, "I stay the fuck away from her and the courthouse," I was okay with that too. I was tired. Burnt out. Over her and all this trial shit. I was over trying to be a friend to her and walking on eggshells to do so.

I felt overwhelmed or maybe I simply just took a deep breath and realized, I'm better than all this nonsense! I knew at that moment, I was done with everything and everyone in that family. This knowing feeling of, *'I am finished,'* melted in permanence, and I felt a breath of fresh air and said, I'm really over these people and their shit!

I'm over all their bullshit and blaming. I'm not going. I don't care. I did everything I could to help her and be her friend. I'm done being used. I'm not going to speak to her again if she's going to act like the rest of them (that family has always been fast tempered, quick to jump at accusations and accusing others, not willing to listen to any kind of reasoning but jumping to their own opinions without knowing the whole truth or giving anyone a chance to explain).

I sat quietly that morning outside on my deck, drinking my coffee watching the birds and my dogs. No thoughts, just a blank slate rolling through my mind until a butterfly landed right beside me. This beautiful monarch butterfly held her wings up high then spread them open to show me her beauty. I felt it was a sign. A sign that it was time for me to hold my head up high, move on, and spread my wings, and show my beauty for once.

Patty Raye called me on June 8th at about 9:30 AM to let me know it was over, and he had been given 24 months – 180 months (2-15 years). He received accounted jail time, which means they count the time served in jail as part of his sentence too. And this most likely means that he maybe could be up for parole and released in about a year. No one knows for sure until the day comes.

After the phone call, my day was tranquil. Serene. Undisturbed. Giving me the much-needed time to release the last 47 years of memories. It was as if it was another lifetime ago. And, as evening rolled in and the sun started settling, I poured myself a nice glass of mixed red wine, sat down on my back deck listening to the wind softly rustle by taking with it the chaos of my past.

EPILOGUE

WHEN I FIRST STARTED DRAFTING this book in 2017, I just wanted to write about the first 15 years. Then what sparked part two were a couple things, First, my readers told me that they wanted more, and I needed to give more. Secondly, all that shit started again with Donny, so I thought, *yeah, okay, here we go again.*

I have to say, as a psychotherapist, this was extraordinarily therapeutic and highly needed. I found that as I'd write certain parts, I had to stop so I could literally break down and cry. Many days I sat here at home crying my eyes out over things that happened to me in my past that I felt I had worked through, but…I hadn't.

I found a great local Psychologist, Kristin Tenney-Blackwell and she helped me through the most challenging parts of understanding my childhood and coming out of the bondage my adopted family kept me in. Not that I'd been continuously weeping and hating all the years of my life but, the pain and rage were built up inside me, and I had not correctly, *effectively*, opened the gates to release it until this book. In other words, writing this book was one of the best therapeutic things I have ever done.

Throughout this process, I've learned who I am, who I want to be, and I am powering up to be that me. I've learned there are more good people on this earth than evil, and I learned to spot the bad and walk away quickly without remorse of doing so.

I've realized that my husband, children, their spouses, and my grandchildren are the most important people in my life, and that will never change (actually, I've always known this. I know this with an iron fist or maybe an iron skillet). My big brother who I should have grown up with, Glenn, has become someone I can trust, and we are becoming closer than ever and that alone makes me cry happy tears. I finally have 'MY REAL' big brother.

I have a few nieces and nephews, who mean the world to me, always have and always will. The friends I have made over these years have come and gone, and some returned. I would be lying if I said I love everyone. I do not. But when I do love, I give my all.

During the first few years of my life, I never understood all that was happening. Virgie and Barry fought all the time, and, at first, Donny was a good big brother. As I told in my story, I felt he was protecting us from their fights by hiding us.

I started seeing the evil come out in Donny as we got older. And in my counseling mind (yes, I'm analyzing), I must wonder if he too fell into the trap of 'learning what you live.' First, let me say by no means that I am giving him an excuse for what he did. Oh, hell, no! I'm just looking at this from outside my box and thinking about it with a theory.

Did he hate me because his mother did? Was he mean to me because he was told or trained to be? Did he hate me so his mother would love him? Was it the fear that made him hate me? Or really did he learn what he lived and quickly he too became the hater. I'll never know the answers to these questions and at this point in my life, I don't have time to give a rat's ass, so I don't. He is getting what he deserves, prison time.

And one thing that makes me smile is thinking that maybe right now he is trading his anus for a snack cake or pudding!

(**Update**: On February 23, 2022, he was released from a Michigan prison facility). Isn't our justice system wonderful?

As for Denise, as I look back at all the things she did, said and her actions, it seemed that she too might have been a victim and fallen into the trap of hating me for her parents. Unfortunately, she has caused me so much pain and hurt that I will never allow her in my life again, ever!

One of her favorite names for me was, Piggy. She'd call me, "the little Piggy" then laugh and turn around and say, "Chelcie is the big fat Pig." I hated it. That hurt deep and I had to keep my mouth shut. I refuse to keep my mouth shut, ever again!

332 • Peggy Watkins

As for daddy (Ardy). Well, now I do believe I understand why whenever I'd go around him, I felt scared, threatened, worried, fearful, anxious, and felt as if I dare say a word. I wanted to think my dad was my hero and that he was proud of me and loved me like he did his two spawns. Now, that my eyes are wide open, and I see his true self. I have accepted or maybe finally realize that I was nothing, to him. He would never be there for me. Never be proud of me. Never love me.

He's one of the four horsemen that will never again have a chance to hurt me or anyone I love. I gave so much of my life to him with hopes. I gave all that to a dad who NEVER deserved it and was nothing but a dad to me.

And, then there is Virgie. Mommy Darling. I am not sure she was ever in her right mind. As I look back, I feel the saddest for her. I'm not giving her a pass either, just trying to logically look at this shit storm and wade through it the best I can. I'm doing awesome by the way. I believe Virgie was mentally challenged, then losing her hearing and some cognitive worthiness when she was struck with rheumatic fever as a small child set her back in life, I theorize. Nonetheless, she did know right from wrong, mean from nice, and she was nothing like a real mommy to me, ever. I never experienced the mother-child bond. I did however experience, her revulsion towards me. Well, no more. May her next life be that of a happier more joyful one so she can experience happiness and peace in her soul.

The real hurt comes from not being able to grow up with my mother and siblings. I can't dwell on it nor allow it to hinder me from living, loving, and being happy today. I'd like to say it's just a twinge here and there but, it is more than a pang, it is a lasting hole in my heart but something I have learned to live with.

Over the last couple of years, I have reconnected with Addy Mae on social media. I have also gotten a little closer to my brother, Robert as well. I wish I could say the same for my two sisters, Bonnie, and Vickie Sue but, truth is, I've tried a little, but never received any response. I'm not sure a real sisterly bond will ever happen but at least I can say I've tried and now the ball is in their court. (Just to clarify, I never felt like a pawn to my other siblings, maybe more so just, not one of them, and I so desperately wanted to be).

As a child, I used to dream of living with my mother and having that big family around me all the time. I dreamed of me and mom working in the yard making beautiful gardens since we both love flowers so much. I'd daydream about our gardens and the little tea table we'd sit in the middle and have lunch, laugh, and be together, like a real mom and daughter. I dreamed of us cooking in the kitchen since we both again, love to create things. Really, I just wanted my real mommy!

I'd see her when Virgie allowed us to see each other, and my heart broke every time I had to say goodbye. I'd cry so long and hard inside that I could feel my insides starting to burst at times. Unless you walked a mile in my shoes or close to it, you'll never understand the pain and heartache of having your mom within your reach but never being able to touch her. Virgie and Ardy took that away from both of us and for that alone, I can't wish them any happiness on earth. However, if there is such a thing as reincarnation, I hope they find peace in their next life. I also hope they remember these deeds they've done as their last dying thoughts.

I theorize that when my biological mom found out Donny was molesting me, she simply had to do whatever was needed to get me out of that situation. She did what any good mother would have done. She did her best to protect her little girl, even though I thought she was wrong, I now know, she was right for trying to protect me and get me to safety. My mother suffered dearly over the loss of me and that is a grief I'll never get over.

What I know is, that I made it. I made it out from a lifestyle that would make your toes curl and put your curly hair straight. I made it, and I made something of myself. I am a good person. I love people, and I treat people right. I try my best to be honest, and I do not steal (I'm not stealing bologna sandwiches out of grocery stores, or clothes from Goodwill boxes anymore).

I am happy. I adore life and all that life offers such as the sounds of children giggling, the ocean, and a thunderstorm. I enjoy the commotions of dogs barking, bullfrogs at night, crickets chirping, and watching the bats fly around looking for their dinner.

I love the South and I appreciate the smell of, lilacs, rosemary, BBQs, and bonfires. I adore the mountainsides when the fall is turning the trees into a patchwork of art with such beauty and color. I appreciate walking on the sandy beaches at the ocean and listening to the waves ruffle against the shore, it's truly harmonious. These sounds, sights, and smells are life. A good. Simple. Solid life.

I refuse to dwell on any of the four horsemen of the apocalypse any longer. They have taken up too much power and time out of my life.

I have quit the game of Hillbilly Chess into which I was adopted. Now, I am my own Queen, and not only have I overcome all the ruthless pieces, but I have also hurled those uncouth members into the sea of **Kiss My Ass!**

I have moved on with a smile on my face and a glass of wine in my hand-Cheers-Bitches, you lose, and **I win!**

Now, watch me move on with my best life ever!

LETTERS
FOR PEGGY

Dear Peggy,

In response to your request for information from the time in our foster home.

As I recall, you came in late spring and left in late fall of 1974 thereabout. And, during this time, we tried to provide for you and get you involved in many activities that we thought you'd like and that were appropriate for a young child your age.

I remember getting you involved with our church and the youth groups. You appeared to enjoy being with and around the church people, and you especially liked the newspaper drive and pop-can drive to raise money for the Cedar Point trip with the youth group.

We wanted you to be around suitable people who might make an impact on your life and show you love and hope. We wanted you to be active and enjoy life, such as a young child should.

However, when we first got you, the Department of Social Services told us there were security issues and risks, and you were not to appear in public. This request made it a little harder to get you involved in the community and events out and about, but we managed. With this demand from the courts, you had to stay in the backyard and play so no one could drive by and see you. I know this was tough on a little ten-year-old girl.

We lived close to Emilio's Mexican Restaurant, and often I'd go down and bring home tacos for everyone, and you seemed to love the tacos. There was other food you enjoyed, but I recall you loving your newfound food, tacos.

Besides finding new foods and people who were kind to be around, we also wanted to give you a personal area, something that you would enjoy, such as your 'own' room. We allowed you to pick your wall color. You picked a darker purple, and Marylou convinced you to go a little (lot) lighter lavender, and you seemed to love it.

We let you personalize it and make it yours, and you sure did with trinkets and your rocks. You made it your own, and that was a good thing. You seemed happy, and that was our goal to make you feel safe and content while you were living with us. I think we did that.

We had a yellow lab, and you seemed to adore our family dog.

One last thing I recall, and it's been years, but I can still remember the disappointment when you had to leave our home. You were a very saddened little girl when you left and had to return to your family. We hoped and prayed everything would be good for you when you left.

It's nice to hear and see you are doing well today. Makes me feel good to know I had a part in the better part of your life and maybe, just maybe had a decent impact on you.

— Sincerely your Foster Dad, Jim Bax

Peg,

Having a friend that can hold so many memories is such a treasure. There have been so many fun, sad, and just darn crazy times, especially in the days when we all lived in the same apartment complex and worked at the club, which would be some of the crazier times.

I lived upstairs and you lived downstairs in the back and the guys and another girlfriend in the apartment building. Let's just say this was not a high-end apartment complex, we girls could discuss all our problems without leaving our apartment by just sitting in the bathroom. And let's not discuss what else we could hear when someone had "visitors" and decided to take a shower.

And as we moved to higher-end places (right across the street from each other) I always laugh when I tell the story about my daughter running away to your house.

Life was always a journey with us, and I would not ever change one thing. Love you and wish you all the best with your new book.

— Kelly

Hey little sister,

There is so much I want to say, but first, let me tell you how proud and happy I am that you are living a good life finally. Mom would be proud too.

I know you've been through hell and back living with Virgie and her bunch, and I wish there would have been something I could have done but, I was just a little kid too. Neither one of us had any control or knew how to make things better, we were the kids.

One thing I'll never forget is when I witnessed ██████ (Donny) molesting you while you were sleeping. I told, and the family found out I was going to testify, and that's when Uncle Buck pulled me aside. He told me, I was going to send my cousin to prison for life if I told. It was as if they knew but didn't care as long as the perpetrator was free to do it again. Well, they won because back in 1974 the courts did nothing.

There are so many memories, secrets, and lies hidden in this family.

I was little when the family took you from our house, so there are not many things that I can recall about the actual events leading up to that day but, what I can tell you is, that there were many nights I listened to our mother cry herself to sleep and pray to ask God to bring her baby back home to her family.

All kinds of different stories about what happened between your bio parents were told. It seemed that everyone had their version, telling it better than others to make themselves look good. I believe what our mother told. Her story was the only one that never faltered in the same tale. She claimed that ██████ (Ardy) had his way with her, plain and simple.

Two families went against our family in 1963. There were threats made about turning her into Social Services for being unfit, and having the rest of us kids taken, burning her, and all of us kids up, having us disappear. They threatened her regularly, and then when she finally broke, they took you from us.

We didn't have everything, but we had a loving, giving mother, each other, a roof over our heads, and food. Is there really any more a kid needs? That family was nothing but a bunch of lying conniving thieving assholes. The ones who broke my mother's heart and stole my baby sister and for these reasons alone, I've always hated them. They were a selfish group of uneducated backwoods assholes.

I'm glad you walked away. I'm happy your kids don't know them. We've endured (Mom, you, me, and our siblings) enough pain and hurt. It's time to stop and tell the story!

Love you, little sister, you are stronger than you know!

— *Your big brother, Glenn*

Peggy,

They say if you have cousins, you will always be surrounded by friends. That is true of my cousin and friend, Peggy. Since you were a few years older, it was cool to hang out with you, and whether you knew it or not... I was ecstatic anytime I got to spend the night with you.

I never knew you as anything but 'Cousin Peggy' until mom sat us down and explained that you were missing and the reason you may have run away. She told us as little as possible... I only knew I was worried for you and was grateful when you returned.

As time went on... and we grew our separate ways, when we reunited, we simply picked up where we left off. Each time we hang out... I learn something new about you and you still put me in awe.

I am so proud you finished the book and can't wait to read it. It's been a long time coming!!!

— *Sandy (My mothers family)*

FROM MARYLOU BAX'S FUNERAL PAMPHLET:

"The reason why people fail at their goals in life is because they lack the courage that it takes to believe in themselves… I have always believed in myself."

Marylou spent her entire adult life trying to get kids to believe in themselves.

———

Marylou and Jim Bax,

Thank you both so much for believing in me and showing me a normal home if even for a little while, it mattered, you mattered, more than you'll ever know. And thank you for introducing me to tacos not so much hominy though, it still looks like teeth and taste icky!

Always,

Your first foster daughter, Peggy Ann.

Both my foster parents have passed but I am honored to have been a part of their family and learn decent acts and examples from them. They were amazing folks, and I can't say enough about how well they treated and cared for me while in their household. I was one of the lucky ones in foster care.

TOLL-FREE CRISIS HOTLINE NUMBERS

Child Abuse	1-800-422-4453
Child Sexual Abuse	866-FOR-LIGHT 866-367-5444
Family Violence	800-799-SAFE 800-799-7233
Help for Parents	855-4APARENT 855-427-2736
Human Trafficking	888-373-7888
Mental Illness	800-950-NAMI 800-950-6264
Missing/Abducted Children	800-I-AM-LOST 800-426-5678
Rape/Incest	800-656-HOPE 800-656-4673
Substance Abuse	800-784-6776
Suicide Prevention	800-273-TALK 800-273-8255
Youth in Trouble/Runaways	800-RUNAWAY 800-786-2929

Retrieved from: www.childwelfare.gov/pubs/reslist/tollfree

Thank you for taking the time to read my story. If you know of any children or adults who are being abused, please don't hesitate to help them. No one deserves to live in abuse of any kind!

And, if you were abused, I hope you find the peace you so desperately need!

Remember, you owe it to yourself to heal and move past your past!

FIND ME HERE

Made in the USA
Monee, IL
24 October 2023

45059354R00201